D1250930

Remembering the Great Depression in the Rural South

UNIVERSITY PRESS OF FLORIDA

Florida A&M University, Tallahassee
Florida Atlantic University, Boca Raton
Florida Gulf Coast University, Ft. Myers
Florida International University, Miami
Florida State University, Tallahassee
University of Central Florida, Orlando
University of Florida, Gainesville
University of North Florida, Jacksonville
University of South Florida, Tampa
University of West Florida, Pensacola

REMEMBERING
THE GREAT DEPRESSION
IN THE RURAL SOUTH

Kenneth J. Bindas

University Press of Florida
Gainesville · Tallahassee · Tampa · Boca Raton
Pensacola · Orlando · Miami · Jacksonville · Ft. Myers

LIBRARY OF CONGRESS CATALOGING-IN-PUBLICATION DATA
Bindas, Kenneth J.
Remembering the Great Depression in the rural South / Kenneth J.
Bindas.
p. cm.
Includes bibliographical references and index.
ISBN-13: 978-0-8130-3048-7 (alk. paper)
1. Depressions—1929—Southern States—Anecdotes. 2. New Deal,
1933–1939—Southern States—Anecdotes. 3. Southern States—
Economic conditions—1918—Anecdotes. 4. Southern States—Rural
conditions—Anecdotes. 5. Southern States—Social life and customs—
20th century—Anecdotes. 6. Southern States—Bibliography—
Anecdotes. 7. Oral history. 8. Interviews—Southern States. I. Title.
F215.B58   2007
975'.042—dc22   2006028486

The University Press of Florida is the scholarly publishing agency for
the State University System of Florida, comprising Florida A&M
University, Florida Atlantic University, Florida Gulf Coast University,
Florida International University, Florida State University, University
of Central Florida, University of Florida, University of North Florida,
University of South Florida, and University of West Florida.

University Press of Florida
15 Northwest 15th Street
Gainesville, FL 32611-2079
http://www.upf.com

CONTENTS

ACKNOWLEDGMENTS

One of the joys of a project such as this is the many people who contributed to its completion. I thank Kent State University for allowing me to manipulate my four/four semester teaching schedule to provide time to write, as well as for granting me a semester's sabbatical. I also thank those colleagues at Kent-Trumbull who forgave me for not serving on as many committees as I should have, and I am grateful for their continued efforts to make the university a better place to work. Several scholars read parts or all of the manuscript and provided critical and meaningful comments. I thank them for their efforts. And also thanks to Jean-Anne Sutherland for introducing me to many aspects of the South. I give thanks for my children—Zachary, Colin, and Savannah—as their enthusiasm and love continue to be a driving force in my life's journey.

I especially want to thank all of the students who took the time to interview and then write papers based on their experiences. I also want to remind them of how much fun they had doing their interviews and how much they learned from their informants. In the student evaluations from the courses in which we did oral histories, again and again the students thanked me for letting them do the assignment, and nearly all said that they not only learned a lot about history from the assignment but also gained a new respect for their elders in the community. Many interviewed family members, and these oral testimonies became part of their family history, to be passed down to future generations.

It is to the people, whose many voices make up this book, that I give my most sincere and heartfelt thanks. Reading through their stories brought me to a closer understanding of the time period, and I will never forget the inherent lessons drawn from their testimony. They lived through difficult times, witnessed profound change, and emerged from the conflicts humbled, thankful, and open to the possibilities of humanity. Theirs are warm voices, reminding us again and again of the potential for positive change. Their struggles opened their hearts and allowed them to see the world in a different light, full of equality, charity, hope, and love. It is to their voices and ideals that I dedicate this book.

INTRODUCTION

THE PEOPLE REMEMBER

While Richard Sutherland and I were walking in a wooded area on the outskirts of Leesburg, Florida, several years ago, we stopped to watch something emerge from just below the sandy soil. It was rather large, and having grown up in northeastern Ohio, I was excited to see any animal in the wild. When it was fully out of the sand and began to move, I saw that it was a tortoise, but Richard told me that rural Floridians called them "gophers." I laughed at this regional difference, and over the next hour or so, he told me a variety of other stories about Florida and his childhood. Born to a large family working a small strawberry farm outside Plant City, Florida, in 1931, he relayed story after story about growing up in the South during the years before World War II. Concerning that gopher, he said his family called them "Hoover chickens," and it was a lucky day when he or his brothers caught one of these "chickens" for the family meal.

Looking back, what strikes me most about that conversation, aside from some of the humorous stories, is how vividly Richard recalled aspects of the Great Depression, even though he was but a child during the crisis. As I was going through the hundreds of oral histories that make up the font of this book, it occurred to me that most of the informants were telling the same tales as Richard, with slightly different twists. Their stories rang a bit more true, perhaps, as no one born after 1920 was considered for this volume, but what they said and how they phrased it was nearly identical. I asked myself, what does it mean that so many people seemed to recall the New Deal, Franklin D. Roosevelt, and the 1930s in a similar manner? Is it that the president and his policies actually touched that many people's lives during the 1930s and thus FDR (and his New Deal) deserves even more credit as a people's president? Or are their voices merely the result of active manipulation of public opinion and historical memory through the various state apparatuses? Or perhaps there is a third path: FDR and the policies of the New Deal resonated deeply within the American people, and as these people took jobs throughout the American states—mostly outside the culture industries—the generally accepted stories of the many became the generally accepted stories of nearly all.

If this third path is the genuine one, what was it about the Depression era that made the historical memory so clear, so uniform, so much a part of the collective experience? The Depression era transformed the United States, and in politics, economics, industry, art, dance, music, literature, social relations, radio, film, and identity, one witnessed the birth of a new America. This reformation did not come from the state down, nor did the people force it upon the government; rather, the multiplicity and complexity of the crisis allowed for a more active negotiation between the two. The solution to the Great Depression meant not just getting the economy rolling again or providing jobs for the people, but creating a more meaningful definition for America's modern democracy.

The rapid pace of industrialization and modernization had created a society out of sync with itself. Development and growth had taken place in fits and starts, and the resulting benefits were distributed unevenly from region to region. As the century progressed, the state and its people tried to mediate the newer ideals of capital with the traditional ideals of individualism. This modern dilemma helped expose and widen divisions (whether between regions, workers, companies, or government) and stressed competition over cooperation. Even as many called for a more planned and organized society, the overriding ideology continued to reinforce the frontier myth, supplemented by the reward of economic security. The cowboy and the social image that accompanied him were not simply fabrications but imagined realities—a sort of unified mythic history. Although the pioneer and the cowboy fought injustice and brought civilization to the wilderness, they did so for their own reasons and rewards. The same was true with the new modern ideology. Even as cities replaced farms as the informer of American mores, the pioneer ideal continued to identify the American spirit.

When the economy collapsed in the latter part of the 1920s and flattened out in the early 1930s, the initial response called upon individuals to take care of themselves, with private agencies seen as the last resort. As the crisis deepened, it remained incumbent on each individual to solve the larger economic problem; failure to do so resided within the individual rather than the state and the new modernist ideals. This personal responsibility helped to give birth to the idea of the Great Depression in the people's minds. Furthermore, the reality of the situation forced the people to challenge their ideologies and work to modify these structures in order to better address their needs and understanding of capital. This reformation of the American ideal is at the heart of this book, as it reflects the way in which those interviewed talked about this crucial time. John K. Davenport of northwestern

Georgia is emblematic of this type of reformation; he recalled those days at the urging of a young student in 1990 by saying, "Those were the good old days, but those good old days were pretty rough times."[1]

This volume is an attempt to understand how the American people came to view and understand this reformation of which they were so much a part. To get at this consciousness, I created a standardized list of open-ended questions, with plenty of room for follow-up and tangential conversation, and charged my U.S. modern history classes with the task of going out and interviewing someone who had lived through the era, with the stipulation that these interviewees be born before 1920. The first time I used this assignment, the students moaned, but in the course evaluations, many praised the oral history assignment as a valuable learning experience. Over four years (1989–93), we collected more than five hundred oral histories. The majority of those interviewed lived in central and western Georgia during the Depression era, but a considerable number of interviewees lived in eastern Alabama or southern Tennessee, with the remainder from a smattering of other states.[2]

My initial intent was not to produce a body of information for research purposes but to expose the students to the personal and individual aspect of history by allowing them to interview a family member or someone from the community about his or her lived experiences. Yet after listening to and reading through the oral histories, I began to consider what their voices were saying about the era, and I remembered my conversation with Richard Sutherland. What they and he chose to recall and not recall said something about 1930s America and the development of our shared historical memory. I wanted to know how the interviewees felt about the situation, the government, and themselves, so that I might gain a clearer understanding of their place in this difficult period. Of course, I hoped they would challenge existing paradigms and open up new avenues of research or understanding. After all, most of those interviewed were from the rural South, a region largely overlooked in Depression-era studies.[3]

What I discovered was the profundity of their voices, their stories, their lives; rather than altering these to fit my own agenda, I decided to let them tell the story. Their voices became like a chorus singing the song of how the American people continued to rely on the individualistic ethos even as they adopted and accepted the new ideology of social cooperation. I heard how they came to view FDR and the New Deal as an agent of positive change and empowered these federal programs to remake their lives in a way that benefited all the people. I was moved by how the people dealt with the internalization of guilt associated with not being able to participate in the economy or find credible work, and how they retained traditional folkways even as they adopted modern technology. I laughed as they told nostalgic Depression stories, designed to communicate the hardships they went through to those who had not suffered.

Remembering the Great Depression in the Rural South is a tapestry with all the different voices, like many different colors of thread, combined to provide a detailed and a personal history of the 1930s from a rural and southern perspective. These people look back at their youth from the late twentieth century and reflect on its meaning—how did those times identify their lives? What lessons did they learn, and how did these help define them and their experiences? The chapters are designed to see into their world by examining the issues that dominate their memories: getting a living, government, food and home life, consumption and fear, and of course, tales of privation. These reveal a consciousness—an understanding similar to that of those who have lived through combat—of people who endured, and their stories capture a historical moment and its meaning. Part of the aging process involves making some sense of both the individual and the collective past, and "the process of telling one's own life story" is instructive to finding this meaning. When there are dramatic historic or personal events in the recollection, there is "likely to be a more vivid memory of those events and times." Elizabeth Tonkin's excellent discussion concerning memory and the social representation of oral history reminds us that "our identities are both personal and social," and thus people try to either connect to the accepted representations or challenge that past. Their place within the context of the larger social structure is therefore part of the way in which they frame, or see, their past. This suggests that memories are far less individual and much more connected to the social relationships constructed during and after the historical epoch. Memories are social, and thus oral history interviews based on these memories should be viewed within the larger social construction of the people who made them.[4]

When constructing the interview questions, I did not ask specific questions about class, occupation, status, or race, relying instead on self-identification and descriptions of life that would illuminate their place, as they saw themselves. Any study of the twentieth-century American experience has at its foundation the intersection of race, class, and gender and how these operate within the confines of the dominant social and political ideology.[5] To suggest class identity via a checklist—poor, working class, middle class, and so on—invites a more complex discussion of the social definition of class, as these terms have varied meanings and definitions, particularly within the context of an oral history interview. It also raises the specter of empowering one category over another. Given the lack of clarity that often comes with this categorical approach, I chose instead to allow their recollections to be their definition of class and status. In their recall of the 1930s, nearly all placed themselves within the working-class or subsistence-farmer rubric, detailing stories of hard work for low wages while living in (by today's definition) substandard conditions. From their own descriptions and without having to accept an external definition, they overwhelmingly placed themselves within the hard-working, struggling-to-make-ends-meet category of social class in America. Oftentimes, these recollections are told as lessons and read as allegories of faith, hope, and the struggle of ordinary experience. The informants' narratives are refracted against sixty years of living and changes to their world, so what they remembered were those things that most mattered—for that is what they chose to recall. The questions were mere prompts, ideas designed to jog their memory without leading them into an answer. "You know it's hard to sit down and bring back, at seventy seven years old . . . memories," lamented Maurice Sponcler of Newnan, Georgia, to his interviewer. Because, he continued, "you just hit the high spots of the things that *really did make a difference.*"[6]

I also did not require students to ask the race of their informant, as I wanted to allow them (both the student and the informant) to define their own experience. Yet, as with class and gender, race plays a central role. Foundational to any study of the American South during this era is how race informed the ideology of the people. President Roosevelt and members of his administration tried in both rhetoric and policy to suggest inclusion rather than exclusion, and the general population, including those in this study, were keenly aware of this desire to break old patterns to help solve the Depression. Perhaps this is the reason why, when being interviewed, few mentioned racial issues or problems but instead spoke in terms of helping each other out and working with each other. Had the interviews concerned the 1950s or 1960s, no doubt the tone of the conversation would have been different, but the interviewees used their time to discuss the awareness that from the president on down there was an emerging ideology that suggested working together, getting along, and helping one another.

This consciousness is at the core of this book, for it identifies how the people saw their past, and this view informs our history. That the recall of the 1930s (in contrast to the following decades) is largely positive suggests that the people, both white and black, saw in the era a glimmer of hope for a better future. Thus, if they self-identified race, it suggests that race played a central role in how they saw their past and how they retold it to their interviewer. Conversely, if a student asked a question concerning race, it suggests that this student saw in the interview the need to understand better the role race played in her or his informant's life history. The issue of race in the South during the 1930s deserves a complex explanation; throughout this volume, I discuss how race was framed and what this meant with regard to the development of consciousness of the era. I do not, however, attempt to analyze race in a manner that places it at the center of the discussion, because few interviewees self-identified race (making it hard to draw conclusions), and to assume race for the purpose of analysis would suggest that I was trying to make their responses fit my agenda. Their responses are their own, and what and how they chose to recall was not directed by the interviewer—there was no agenda in the questions. Their recollections were not forced into a paradigm not of their choosing; *Remembering the Great Depression* is driven by what they felt most strongly about. "In retrospect," Ada Kane reflected to her interviewer, "you can only see the things that were taking place at the time. You lived your own life too and didn't know what was going to be history later on."[7]

Over the past thirty years, the scholarship concerning memory, language, and power in oral history research has opened up new avenues of understanding. Works by Paul Thompson, Ronald Grele, Michael Frisch, and a host of others have addressed methodological and theoretical questions to better define and validate the use of these voices in our collective historical understanding. Their scholarly investigations have helped others to better understand the importance of who is speaking, what is said, and what is significant about the manner in which people reconstruct the past. They ask scholars to consider the value of these memories not as objective documents held up against the historical record but as subjective ones designed to explain why people choose to reconstruct the past and what this suggests about the historical process. How the people see their past and their role in it is as important as what actually occurred.[8]

Oral history is a directed conversation designed to gain insight into a specific event or time period. In this dialogue, the desires of the interviewer for "evidence" are often in contention with the interviewee's need to tell his or her story—the "point of view." Samuel Schrager's research suggests that the stories people tell in the oral history interview reflect both their actual and their representative experiences: in other words, what they truly experienced and what *they*, as part of the larger society, lived through. When

Mae B. Biggart said, "I would have to get up at 5 o'clock in the morning just to make it to work on time—by the way, we could not afford a clock then, I had to rely on God every morning to wake me up," she was recalling not only her experiences in the 1930s but also her state of mind and, by extension, the larger consciousness of the Depression era.[9]

Oral histories are laced with symbolic and even imaginative information. Being subjective, they require unraveling, for it is in the construction of the explanation that we recognize the theoretical and ideological meanings behind what is being said or not said, how the answers (and questions) are constructed, and the role of language, gender, and class. By recognizing these issues within the oral testimony, we unwind the thread of consciousness by situating the social and ideological roles that society and memory play in the construction of the past. Oral histories help paint a more complete picture of the people's experience outside the traditional boundaries of history and help inform us, writes Barbara Allen, about the "larger structures of historical consciousness within the individual . . . experience."[10]

There are various ways to look at these historical voices. Region, class, race, and gender typically divide them. For example, of the interviews used in this book, more than half come from recollections of women, and both methodological and theoretical research suggest that their voices need to be heard in a unique way because of the rigid patriarchal structure of society then, and its continued institutional reinforcement. The women interviewed here were well aware of their roles and how this position informed what and how they recalled the era. When listening to women's voices, one has to be willing to hear both their real place and the situation in which society had placed them. In the first third of the twentieth century, women and girls in the United States had prescribed roles and languages within these situations. Girls observed more closely and used speech to establish and maintain relationships, while boys used speech to establish dominance and to assert position. This dichotomy of language and its social role was especially rigid in the rural areas of the American South, where the ideology of family, community, and religion also defined accepted languages for women and men.[11]

What this means is that we need to adjust the way in which we hear women's voices, as they are filtered through a variety of social and cultural ideologies. Several scholars have outlined how we can listen to women's words with a more open and directed ear. For example, women are more likely to use the personal pronouns *we* and *us* when discussing their past. They are also more likely to talk about family issues, relate stories about their

Mandy Handley, wife of tenant farmer. Walker County, Alabama. 1937. (Courtesy of Library of Congress.)

mothers, and talk about how hard their fathers worked to make the family strong. These phrases identify a woman's ambiguous place between society and self and open their narrative to hermeneutic scrutiny. Understanding the symbolic meanings of women's words (or those of workers, or people of color, or any other group struggling for legitimacy) allows the listener to better place where they saw themselves within the historical moment and the larger structure of the nation's history.[12]

However, too much focus on the symbolic can take our attention away from other factors that help define place in modern America. Other situations, such as race and class, are significant as part of the larger structure of listening to women's voices. Other factors also help identify consciousness, including region, family, religion, and the historical context of both the interview time period (in this case the Depression era) and when the interview took place. During the Depression, women faced unique and difficult problems that were accentuated by the economic crisis. Their roles as mothers and sisters were reinforced while the liberation some women had experienced in earlier eras was slowly erased. Women needed to find work, to support their families, and to take care of themselves all within the confines of a society that viewed them as threats to "breadwinners" and the family structure. How the women in this volume recall their experiences resonates against these theoretical and contextual underpinnings, and the reader will quickly discover how their voices differ from those of their male counterparts.[13]

This same type of concern for *hearing* the authentic voice is at play when considering the role of the narratives in this book. When I began writing, I had to consider how to present the interviewees' voices. Should I extract from the multitude a select few that exemplify the larger issues that concern the topic, or should I try to weave the many threads together to form one tapestry of Depression-era tales? In the end, I decided that it was important to hear (or read) as many voices as possible, so that the overwhelming chorus of voices could drown out those who suggest that this type of study reveals little about the historical moment or the construction of memory. But I also decided to use the oral histories to create a series of vignettes in the final chapters, where I tell more about how these individuals operated within the home and the larger allegories of their experiences. By using both techniques, I hope to reveal the story of how these people came both to participate in the historical moment and become simultaneously the object and the process of the historical experience.

Chapter 1 explores the effect the Depression had on the American South and how this affected the people's ability to get a living. What types of work did they do, and how did their labors help define their understanding of the era? What larger lessons did they take from their hard labor and the misfortunes of the era? The next chapter looks at the role and image of President Roosevelt and the many New Deal programs. How did the people view these programs even if they were not directly affected by the federal attempts to help their neighbors? What was Roosevelt's role in their understanding of the era, and how does that relationship shape their memory of the era? Chapter 3 explores the issue of consumption in an era of declining resources and expectations. How did the people negotiate the complex relationship between the expectation of being a consumer and the reality of not being able to consume? How did this ambiguity affect their understanding of the era and themselves? Chapter 4 focuses on the daily experiences of the people by looking at how they cooked, cleaned, and went about their daily lives. How did the larger social and political crisis affect their daily existence? And how do their recollections about these (often mundane) activities better complete our understanding of the era? The fifth chapter recounts some of the tales that came to be associated with the Depression era. Sometimes these privation tales suggest a nostalgic recall of the decade, but more often than not, they reflect the general despair that permeated both the Depression and the people's consciousness. The final section is a brief postscript that tries to place into context the stories and their meaning.

Interspersed throughout the text are black-and-white photographs taken by photographers associated with specific projects, primarily those of the Farm Security Administration (FSA). These images are designed to provide some visual identity to the stories, and because of their close association with the New Deal and the Depression era, they help frame the context of the informants' collective memories. Within the larger social and cultural framework of the era, artists, composers, painters, actors, documentary filmmakers, and photographers navigated between politics and art in an attempt to make what they created relevant, meaningful, and definitive of those who came to be called the "common man," or citizen. Within the FSA, this meant that photographers captured the faces and situations of those forgotten citizens whose continued suffering demanded increased government assistance. Though most of the FSA photos detail the process of planting and harvesting, the documentary photographers also trained their cameras on individuals and scenes that reinforced the political agenda of the New

Deal and, to a larger extent, more radical social politics identified with the Popular Front. These photos were supposed to influence consciousness, to promote activism, and to help bring about reform. As such, and perhaps because of the stark presentation of the black-and-white scenes, many of the images created became synonymous with the Depression. In this way, the collective memory of the era was influenced by both the tone and the vision of the photographs, which helped frame what the informants in this study saw as part of their lived experiences. The South was one of the primary areas targeted by the FSA, and the images reproduced here play upon the dominant interpretation of the region by the North and reinforce the notion that without significant aid, the region would continue to be mired in poverty, ignorance, and racism, and if the rest of the country allowed this to continue, these ongoing problems would slow the larger recovery. Designed to evoke sympathy, outrage, fear, or pity, the photographs became linked to the southern vision of the Depression era.[14]

"I suppose the thing that I remember best is my struggle," Anna Nilsson told her interviewer. She then detailed how her family continued to entertain themselves, creating games and prizes from items around the house, but added that they never forgot they were part of something bigger, more complex. *Remembering the Great Depression* gives us a firsthand look at how the people saw themselves and the United States during this reformation and how the era, in its own way, helped to prepare them for the next major challenge: World War II. The combination of these two cataclysmic events defines the American experience after 1945. The people wanted to make sure that future generations would never have to relive the struggles they had gone through. This desire manifested itself in different ways for different people. The struggles of those who lived through the Depression era and whose voices are present in this volume are those of a new America, and documenting their collective experience helps us to understand better the contours of modern U.S. history.[15]

1

"IT WAS JUST HARD TIMES"

Getting a Living

When A. B. Baughtman described life in the 1930s to his young interviewer, the lifelong resident of Lowell, Georgia, detailed the good times and the bad. His family was close, he recalled, and people made do with what they had. "It was just hard times, that was all," he said, pausing to add, "Just have to fight for a living back then." Baughtman's recollection is not unusual in the over five hundred interviews that are part of this volume. Descriptions of how they were able to get a living were often paired with stories of family togetherness and a sense of unity that seemed out of place in their world of the 1990s. Perhaps this reflects the age of the interviewers and the loneliness that often besets the elderly, but in their recollections of the struggles they faced to make a living, they impart how the reformation of the United States during the Depression era affected them and transformed their world. There is surely nostalgia in the way they recall their farm and work life; although these early days may have seemed simpler and less hectic than their later lives proved to be, getting work in the American South—whether in the factory or textile mill or as a sharecropper or tenant farmer—was difficult, particularly as the economy was rooted in a cycle of poverty, ignorance, and subservience. As a young African American woman in Atlanta during the Depression era, Dorothy Hill began working in earnest at age fourteen doing housecleaning. It was hard work, and the competition to keep the job was keen. But she told her interviewer that those days were "the best hard times that you can have" because they made her "more appreciative" of all the things that came later. The reformation of the 1930s begins with an understanding that getting a living was difficult and that the contest for work involved a variety of factors, from agricultural transitions to the issues of gender and race.[1]

That the South lagged behind the rest of the United States in terms of income, education, health care, and myriad other issues was not lost to those of the era. As the 1930s dawned, many of the region's 37.8 million people (out of 122.7 million) were among the least educated, most underpaid, and most easily forgotten of America's underclass. In virtually every category, southern states ranked near or at the bottom. While the rest of the nation's estimated per capita wealth hovered near the $3,000 mark, the South's average of $1,736 was the lowest of all the regions, with Alabama's $1,284 at the bottom of the forty-eight states. Per capita annual personal income also ranked last, as all those in the Southeast averaged only $365, compared to the next lowest (in the American Southwest) at $564. This lack of wealth and specie had social effects, particularly regarding education and health care. The southern states were all ranked at the bottom in terms of illiteracy, going from Kentucky's low of 6.6 percent of the total state population being illiterate to South Carolina's high of 14.9 percent. The problem was that there were scant resources for the region's nearly 4.2 million school-age children. With farm and industrial wages well below those of other regions, the taxes necessary for education simply were not available. The southern states also ranked last in the number of physicians and hospital beds available. Malaria, syphilis, and pellagra plagued the southerner and pointed directly to a lack of proper diet, education, and health care. In virtually every social statistic, residents of the South lagged significantly behind the remainder of the citizens of the United States.[2]

Directly connected to this social crisis was the situation of the southern worker. Whether factory worker or farmer, the southern worker earned less than half the wages of any other American worker and constantly faced under- or unemployment, all before the economic downturn of the early 1930s. Being poor and working hard seemed to be the way for everyone. Time and time again, people like Mary Thaxton talked about their hard labor in a way that indicates they knew there was no other option: "we worked for everything we had . . . we were paid fifty cents for every one thousand pounds" of cotton picked. She then added in exaggeration, "that was considered good money back then!" Grover Hardin and his father dug ditches in and around Alexander City for "fifty cents a day" and were thankful for the money they made that year—"$106 apiece." Most placed little value on the fact that they were poor. "If you're poor you're poor and there's nothing else to it and you don't know any better," Vera Pulliam told her interviewer. All they knew was that to survive, everyone worked. Thomas Cairns had to quit high school in his sophomore year to help the family make ends meet, and he considered himself "lucky enough to get a job to help [the family] out." Irene Bolding told her interviewer that her house had no running water and only two bedrooms for the large family. "We were poor people," she said,

Hoeing. Alabama negro tenant farmer and part of his family. Eutaw, Alabama. (Courtesy Library of Congress.)

and even the "children had to go out and chop cotton and pick berries and . . . anything [they] could do."[3]

That they were poor and had to work hard for everything they had became a source of pride. "Everybody had to work [because] we had so much work to do," Mamie Camp told her interviewer. But this brought the family closer together. Howard Spain's family all slept together in one room—"mother and daddy in one bed" and the kids in the other. The only other room in the house was a small kitchen. They were happy and worked all morning before walking to school, returning later to work in the fields before sundown. Bessie Pendergrass's house was similar to the Spains's, and she described the gaps between the wood slats in the kitchen as a way to keep the chickens fed: "The kids would [drop] crumbs down there . . . [and] the chickens would eat the crumbs." One hears or reads repeatedly in oral histories that the family learned to do without or did not have enough money for this or that, but that this was the way it always was and there was some form of nobility behind it—that they were at least self-reliant and thus, by their definition, American.[4]

At the center of this culture was the family. As Wayne Flynt argues in *Poor but Proud,* poverty and the lack of education made the poor whites of Alabama—and throughout the region—powerless in the modern sense, so they turned to traditional remedies for their particular problems. The lack of warm homes meant that quilting bees were an important function; the lack of money for candy or gifts meant taffy pulls or handmade toys. Audrey Willingham told her interviewer that "all the ladies did their own sewing and making their own clothes." They then took the scraps and made family quilts. "We had to make our own quilts to have warm cover," she said. What they lacked they made, which reinforced their traditional way of being (discussed in greater detail in chapter 4).[5]

Tied to this traditional way of being was the region's reliance on tenant farming and low wages. By the 1930s, over two-thirds of the South's population lived in rural areas. Of these, over 42 percent worked on farms as hired hands, tenants, or sharecroppers. More than half of the region's farmers were tenants; of these 1.8 million tenant farmers, 66 percent were white and 44 percent black. In some states, such as Mississippi, the rate of tenancy/sharecropping ran as high as 70 percent of all those who farmed. Tenancy and sharecropping meant signing a contract with the landlord (only one-tenth of all land was owned by corporate interests) outlining work performed and "pay" defined. Mattie Walthall told of being freshly married during "very hard times to live." She and her husband worked the cotton fields for "half and half"; at the end of the year, the landlord took half the crop. Some worked as cash tenants, with the farmer paying the landlord rent at the end of the season for the use of the land. Others were share tenants—at the end of the year, to pay their debt, they shared some of the resources (one-third of the grain or livestock and one-fourth of the cotton or other commodity) they created. The most pervasive form of tenancy, however, was common sharecropping. In this system, the owner supplied the tenant with everything that would be needed, from home to seed. "We worked for the man who owned everything," Guy Knight recalled, and when the crop came in the fall, the landlord would take his share plus expenses. This left Knight's young family with enough to "buy us a pair of shoes and a pair of overalls and a shirt." Cropping was common for both black (77 percent) and white (45 percent) farmers. Exacerbating this situation were the high prices and credit interest charged by the landlord for the items utilized by the tenant or sharecropper. All the things necessary for survival until the crop came in were purchased on credit, and when the sale of the crop was finalized, the cropper then had to pay his or her debt to the landlord for these commodities. In Alabama in 1933, this meant that 40 percent of the tenants carried their landlord's debt for more than a year. For Martha Scott, when the landlord came to claim his half, she understood it meant that he "got it all . . . because everything we got [during the year] we got through the landlord." Each year the tenant fell further and further behind, and with the decline in cotton and other commodity prices in the 1920s and '30s, the possibility to break even or get ahead was nearly impossible.[6]

After the crash, many of these contract farmers lost their places and were forced into day labor positions, in which they were paid by what they picked and had few options. George Potts was lucky enough to win a scholarship to Mercer College, but when he returned home to Roscoe, Georgia, "they was a big mule waiting for me [and] I plowed just like . . . everybody else." Max Smith picked cotton for "fifty cents a hundred" pounds and was "glad to get that." That was a sight better than what Opal Hunter got in Carroll County, Georgia. She recalled being paid only "thirty cents a hundred," and no matter how hard she worked, she was never able to earn more than "sixty or seventy cents a day." Henry Clark recalled the day in 1932 when a man driving a truck came into his small northwestern Alabama town and offered work picking cotton on a farm in Missouri. About twenty of the local teenagers agreed and then drove through the night to get to the man's farm. They made good money—"a dollar a hundred pounds"—and saw the experience as an adventure. Others were less excited about the prospect of having to labor so hard for so little. George Weaver minced no words when describing cotton picking—"back-breaking." He told his interviewer that he would pick all day long for less than a "dollar a day," describing his life then as "tough."[7]

Many of those interviewed, like Benny McKissick of rural Compton, Georgia, recalled that they "had plenty to eat," but the 1938 *Report on Economic Conditions of the South* paints a different picture. Less than one-fifth of what they grew was edible, as six out of every ten acres was planted in cotton, with the rest in livestock grains. Perhaps it was closer to how Louise Smith described the time: "we always had plenty to eat *of what it was.*" According to Cornelia Presley, what they ate was "cornbread and syrup for breakfast" and "pancakes made out of cornbread" for lunch. She was happy to get even that. Joyce Ison recalled that on her family's tenant farm they grew cotton for money, but that all the "corn was raised to feed the stock, the mules, the horses, the hogs, and to make meal for cornbread." The region that had the largest rural population in the country produced the fewest consumable food crops—from livestock to potatoes. This meant that the majority of those who farmed in the region did not own their land, nor did they control what they grew.[8]

For more traditional workers—those who labored in factories or mills—the picture was not much different. The first third of the twentieth century saw a number of new industries established in the region, most significantly the textile industry. Once the specialty of the New England area, textile companies moved to the Southeast to take advantage of lower energy and labor costs. By 1933, the South was home to nearly two-thirds of all those working in the industry. Located mainly in small towns, these facilities followed the same general pattern as the tenant farms, in which the balance of wages and expenses kept the worker poor and without power. Workers earned less than half the amount paid to their counterparts in other regions of the country, worked more hours per week, and suffered from the highest rate of child labor. Of all those between the ages of ten and fifteen who were employed in the country in 1930, over three-quarters lived in the South—108 out of every 1,000. The workers of the land and of the factory thus found themselves in the same position: caught in a cycle of debt, poverty, and undernutrition, a system of dependency that guaranteed that those who had power and money retained them and that the social system, built on the segregation of the races, remained intact.[9]

The social crises described above were endemic throughout the South, including the states of Georgia, Alabama, and Tennessee, where most of the people interviewed for this book lived. When the Depression became a national phenomenon, an already dire situation in the South became worse, although many agreed with either June Adams, who told her interviewer that "the Depression hit our house long before '29," or Joyce McClellan, who observed, "We didn't know what we were—we were poor like everybody else but we really didn't know it." Cotton prices collapsed, and profits were slashed from $1.5 billion in 1929 to only $45 million three years later. As Pearl Nix recalled, "cotton dropped from twenty cents a pound to less than five cents a pound," and her family could no longer afford to farm. Many of the tenants and sharecroppers found themselves without a contract or land to sow. As Fisk University's Charles S. Johnson said in 1933, "the general depression reached the south when it was already prostrate and sadly crippled by an outworn tenant system." Many rural folk were like Jennie Kilburn's family, who were forced from their Alabama tenant farm and had to move in with relatives in Georgia. "I don't know what we would have done if it

White sharecropper family, formerly mill workers. (Courtesy Library of Congress.)

had not been for them," she said. Some repaired to the cities, where the situation was just as bad. Most southern cities saw unemployment rates near or beyond the thirtieth percentile, and as statistics often do, these numbers hid the thousands who lived beyond the edge of examination. Just married in 1931, Catherine Hoyt Bohne found that she and her spouse "had to live with [her] husband's mother for a good while," as there was no work to be had in Birmingham, Alabama, at the time.[10]

As the Depression worsened, finding and holding a job became increasingly difficult. Many of the respondents recalled situations in which they worked for free to latch onto a permanent job. When Clarence Bowman went to work for the Sewell Manufacturing plant, he and other trainees had to "train on our own time [to learn how] to operate a power machine." They used rags and other waste cloth to practice before working for pay, which was "very little . . . [only] two dollars" a day. After graduating from secretarial school in Mobile, Alabama, Beulah Johnson returned to Griffin, Georgia, to find that there were no available positions. To get her foot in the door, she worked for a local judge for a full year—"no pay, just to get experience." Allan Furline's story exemplifies the lengths to which many young people were willing to go to get a job. He told his interviewer how proud he was when he got a job making fifty cents a day and then paused and said, "Let me tell you how I got the job." He heard that they were building a road through the Athens, Alabama, area and went to the foreman and asked for work. Denied, he simply picked up a pickax and started working. "When the boss returned he told me I had to leave [and] he didn't have any money to pay me. He cursed me and told me I'd better get out of there." With nowhere to go, Furline kept working and returned the next day before anyone else to make sure he got a tool. The boss cursed him and demanded that he leave, but to no avail. He continued this for the entire week, and on Saturday the foreman said he would get paid for the week if he did not come back on Monday. First thing in the morning on that Monday, Furline was there and was hired. It lasted only a few weeks, but it was a job.[11]

Finding and holding a job were hard, and the pay was low. "There wasn't no work," Guy Knight told his interviewer. The only money being brought into his family's home was from his sister, who did piecework for a local cobbler for three dollars, and "that was big pay!" Often people would hear about a job and have to move quickly before someone else took it. George Wright was working with the Civilian Conservation Corps (CCC) in the late 1930s when an uncle said he was ready to give up his Georgia route supplying Orange Crush soft drinks and return to working in the plant. Wright went to his commanding officer and asked to be let go immediately. His uncle drove him to the plant in Florence, South Carolina, where "they put [George] up in an old cot upstairs over the plant to sleep on" while they processed his papers and loaded his truck. He made nine dollars a week and drove throughout rural Georgia filling orders. Gene Autry remembered that in Atlanta, one "couldn't buy a job anywhere," so when he was offered the chance to work for ten cents an hour hauling plaster up to the plasterers, he jumped at the chance. But after "four or five trips up" the three flights of stairs, he could do no more. The plasterer, afraid that this might mean he would lose his job, carried the plaster up himself and kept working until Autry regained his strength. When Sam Davis's father died in 1933, he left a family of seven. As one of the oldest, Sam tried to find work "to pay [his] father's funeral expenses." But in rural North Carolina, "it was extremely hard to find a job." The best he could do was working on a road crew for twenty-five cents an hour, ten hours a day. Having few other options, Raymond Giles began cutting hair for neighbors for "fifteen cents a head" or "whatever they had." Living in rural Douglas City, Georgia, he had "no other way to make no money." As a deputy in the sheriff's office in Douglas County, Mac Abercrombie told his interviewer that they "had a lot of trouble with people making bootleg whiskey." He felt sorry for them, as they turned to bootlegging because "they couldn't get a job." Frank Howland bounced around from one temporary construction job to another in the Etowah, Georgia, area all through the early 1930s. Once, he was dispatched with some others to a job in Copperhill, Tennessee. They stayed only a short time because the locals "came down [to the site] with shotguns ... to run us out." They left shortly thereafter, but Howland added, "I [didn't] blame them, the work belonged to them."[12]

The solidarity expressed by Howland exemplifies the common bond shared by many of those who struggled for a living during the Depression era. The respondents repeatedly recalled these hard days in a way that suggests they felt as though they were all caught in the same situation—there simply were not enough jobs to go around, and even if one had a job, the pay was so low that it barely mattered. Brewer Hoyt Douglas was one of the lucky ones in Oklahoma City, Oklahoma, for he had a semiregular job at a foundry near the outskirts of town. With the foundry situated near the railroad tracks, on his lunch break and at the end of his shift he watched as people who "didn't have no home or nothing else" wandered around the rail yard in hopes of finding some scraps to eat or sell. Douglas would give them a quarter or something so they could eat, not out of pity but recognizing that they were in a "rough spot" that could just as easily have been his. "Every place you went," Gene Autry told his interviewer, "nobody had anything to do; nobody had anything to eat." Americans understood that the hard times were real; they also understood that, as Martha Scott of Newton County, Georgia, said, "everybody had to go to work or they would starve."[13]

For some, like Scott, this meant working in a textile mill in the company town. Maurice Sponcler's stepfather was president of Arnco and Arnall Mills outside Sargent, Georgia, during the Depression era. After Sponcler graduated from Georgia Tech, he returned home to work and in his interview provided an excellent view into the mill and the village where the workers lived. The village was made up of 186 houses rented at a weekly rate of twenty-five cents. There were also 50 or so sharecroppers' houses surrounding the mill, with these farmers growing cotton on about half of the 2,100 acres that surrounded the mill. The houses consisted of four rooms, having no indoor plumbing but with an outside spigot for fresh water. The houses had electricity via long cords hanging from the ceilings. "They were rustic," but Sponcler remembered that the residents "all seemed to manage pretty well." The workers toiled from six to six, with an hour for lunch, and five hours on Saturday, for six dollars a day. There was even a company school for the children through grade seven, after which they "would come to work at the mills." Only a few "would [go] into Newnan to the high school." Sponcler recalled that several families had all of their children in the mill, and the father would draw the paycheck for all of them and then "disperse it out."[14]

Once rent, food, electricity, and other charges were deducted, there was little money to distribute. Annie Young worked at the Arnall mill and recalled earning about eight dollars a week, although she rarely got that much after rent and food were deducted. Jessie Pearce's husband worked at the mill while she stayed home with the children. His "seven or eight dollars a week" took care of the family, but as with Young's income, after rent, food, and the water bill, there was rarely anything left over. Ethel Shockley remembered the Sargent mills' rent to be two dollars a month, and when she got her "pay slips . . . [she] wouldn't have much left [because] everything was included." The situation at the Sargent mills was indicative of the type of textile labor that many in the South experienced. These mills dotted the rural landscape and became magnets for displaced farmers and tenants seeking work. When Katherine Melton's father had to leave farming, he took the family to the mill village at Lindale, Georgia, where he and the children old enough went to work. Several children were too young to work and both parents needed to work, so they had to find someone to care for their children. When her parents were working in the mill outside Tallapoosa, Georgia, Claudia Ward and her two younger brothers would often have "to be boarded out during the week" because their parents sometimes worked the night shift and had to sleep during the day. In 1938, Joe Johnson of LaGrange, Georgia, got married to a woman he worked with at the local textile mill. He told his interviewer, "we was making approximately twelve dollars apiece each week," which was better than earlier in the decade. But, he added, "that's what we had to begin our life on . . . and we had to establish a home and start raising a family."[15]

Women had to work so that the family could make ends meet; at least, that is how most of those interviewed remember their employment. As Julia Blackwelder has argued regarding women in San Antonio, Texas, during the Depression era, many women worked to pool their resources within the family in order to survive. While on the surface this approach seems sensible, it suggests that women framed their work experiences as nonessential, necessary only as the emergency warranted, while their primary tasks remained within the household: cooking, cleaning, raising the children, and keeping an orderly house were the paramount goals, and work outside the home took them out of this pattern. "My mother had never worked until the Depression," recalled Clifford Oxford. But the family's need forced her to try "every way she could to help earn some money" for the family. Note how Oxford frames his mother's employment as need rather than desire for a situation outside of the home and stating that previous to that, she "never worked."[16]

Women interviewed as part of this project discussed their work outside the home much within the context of daughter, wife, or mother helping out during hard times, even if that meant, as it did for Bessie Pendergrass, sewing for the "public for about forty years." Few women discussed their need to work as part of an evolution toward a career or earning money for themselves. Instead, most of those interviewed framed their experiences within the context of the family and their role in it. Unlike men, they never saw their work outside the home as a substitute for the work inside the home but rather as an extra burden added to what they already had to accomplish. Theirs was the start of the "second shift," as defined by sociologist Arlie Hochschild. After a day or night of labor, a woman returned home to continue the tasks assigned for her in the household, even if the man was not employed. Rarely did gender roles shift and the man accept more household responsibility to accommodate his wife's employment; instead, since women's employment was framed as supplemental income, their household chores continued. For the women in this study, it was almost a given in their responses that their work outside the home would not detract from their *real* work in the home. For farm women like Pearl Johnson, this meant "working hard [in the fields] and having babies." Olga Ragsdale worked with her husband at Gulf Oil in Atlanta during the era as a filing clerk. When they came home at night, she would "cook supper and do [her] house chores and go to bed and get up early the next day." Her husband, JR, chimed in at this point with "during that time men didn't do housework." When asked if she worked during the 1930s, Lizzie Johnson said she "worked at home." Then she added, "even when I worked at Sewell's (a textile plant sometimes six days a week) I'd help [by] baking cakes and things for Sunday dinner."[17]

But women did work for wages during the 1930s, and their need for employment was not just part of the emergency. As numerous scholars have pointed out, women had been working all along and not just in the home.

Nearly 25 percent of women, historian Susan Ware reminds us, "worked outside their homes for wages during" the Depression era. In fact, during the era, the total number of women employed increased despite social and government pressure for women, particularly married women, to exit the workforce to make room for male breadwinners. Some, like Atlanta's Ruby Henry, were forced into work because their husbands were no longer able to care for them. After their first child was seventeen months old, Ruby went to work because her husband "didn't make enough to support us." Later, his botched appendectomy forced him to lose his job, and she was lucky enough to get hired on at the Chevrolet plant in Doraville, Georgia. He would drive her to work with her young son, who "would always scream for me when I would leave him" to go into the factory. Her having to work tore at her husband, who begged her to quit, but with "no money coming in and no other way," she had to continue working until she became pregnant with their second child. Many were in positions similar to Ruby's, not really wanting to work outside their homes but doing what had to be done with little complaint even as they continued to maintain their multiple roles as wife, mother, and homemaker. Bessie Birdsong's husband, Lester, "wanted [her] to work . . . because he didn't make enough to provide for everything [they needed]." She paused, then added, "but, he always wanted me to be a housewife. And I was." Maggie Jones's husband died in the mid-1930s, and she was forced to invent work by gathering up wild shrubs and using them for landscaping local churches and schools in the small town of Heflin, Alabama. "Well, it was a hard time," she recalled, "but everybody had a hard time." Lillian Chambers remembered that her "mother worked and a lot of people didn't" in Rome, Georgia. She felt sorry, she recalled, not for her mother but for the many mothers who could not get work, because it meant they had a lot less than her family, who "had nothing." Olga Lamp's mother did not work, but she had "one friend whose mother worked." It "amazed her to think that her mother had to go out every day to a job and then come home to take care of the house."[18]

Elaine Tyler May's pathbreaking study on the role and image of women and families from the Depression era through the cold war outlines the contradictory long-term pattern established during the 1930s. Women and families were reminded on a daily basis that the crisis demanded individual sacrifices and that everyone had to do his or her part. Yet within this crisis, women were expected to shoulder a larger part of the burden, as the man earned the "family wage" while the woman supplemented the income and maintained the household. During the Depression, and then the world war and the struggle against communism afterward, American women became convinced that it was their patriotic duty to accept this duality.[19]

For some of the interviewed women who were teenagers during the crisis, this gender definition within the family did not go unnoticed. They took the lessons within their families as keys to their own lives, where they sacrificed for the good of the family. When Lois Scroggins's father died in the early 1930s, her mother moved the family of girls from rural Alabama to Villa Rica, Georgia, because the older girls could get work in the hosiery mill. Lois had to wait until she was fourteen before she could get in at the mill, and her weekly paychecks were given directly to her mother, who also took in boarders to make ends meet. Mary Carroll worked twelve hours a night, five and six days a week, for nine dollars throughout her teen years and even after she got married. Her checks went either into the family pot or to her husband to make ends meet. When Lillian Chambers turned fourteen, her mother took her out of school to get hired on at the hosiery mill looping socks. "I had to work," she told her interviewer, and she never considered either her education or job choice her own. Mae Biggart moved to Chicago after she graduated high school and was "lucky" to get hired by Montgomery Ward for $18.75 a week. She "would send all but two dollars of [her] pay" back home to her mother and sister. Lucille Campbell was fortunate enough to get a job with Sears Roebuck in Atlanta in 1929 and kept it through the Depression. She made ten dollars a week, which she gave to her parents. When asked why she never married or moved out on her own, she replied that she and her two sisters "had to help our parents" and could not get married because they would not let her go. Rose Conerly told her interviewer that she dated "a long time" because if she would have gotten married, she would "have to quit" her job at the hospital. Her thirty-five-dollar-a-month paycheck went directly into the family's budget without argument. Mildred Friedman lived at home and waited until she was thirty to marry, because if a woman "got married she was fired from her job." Hers was not a unique situation, as May and Scharf outline, for many women held off marriage and childbirth because of the economic crisis and to help their families. When Bessie Fowler became enamored with one of the men she worked with at the Shannon textile mill, she was warned by her mother not to get involved because, at sixteen, she made an income that was essential to the family budget. Eventually she ran off with a twenty-one-year-old yarn boy, much to her mother's disappointment.[20]

On the farm, the gender division of labor was often not as defined. Women worked on the farm as long and as hard as the men. Certainly the second shift was present here as well, as the primary tasks of taking care of the children, cooking the meals, and keeping the house were rarely shared. But many of the interviewed women who lived on farms during the 1930s understood that they had to do much of the same labor as their husbands or fathers and were expected to generate some income. Melissa Walker's study on upcountry southern women outlines this shared responsibility on the farm and suggests that many found the experience empowering. The added responsibilities that their husbands or fathers may not have permitted under other circumstances allowed many of the women to experience a sense of liberation and power, even as it conflicted with the dominant view society had of women and their roles. "We all worked in the field," recalled Thelma Hughes of her Depression experience. She and her husband would take all the kids out to the tobacco fields and gather up the crop. She also helped cure, bundle, and sell the tobacco as well as maintain the family garden near the house. Fulton County's Roxie Etheridge told her interviewer of the time when her husband could not afford to hire a hand to help with cutting and bundling the farm's oat crop. She told him, "I ain't never tied them but if you show me, I guarantee I'll keep up with ya." By the end of the day, they had "laid 100 bushels of oats." Geneva Stewart supplemented the family's income by selling "butter, . . . eggs," whatever she could, to help buy foodstuffs such as sugar and coffee. When Lucy Gable's interviewer asked her if her mother "sat at home with the children" while her husband worked the fields outside Cobb City, Georgia, she gasped and replied, "she worked in the field and worked just like he did [and] she helped to raise vegetables and all the produce." The interviewer was impressed, to which Lucy added, "yes, she stayed at home, she sure did."[21]

Laura Hapke, in her study on the image of working women during the Depression era, suggests a gulf between the actual and the fictional. That more women were actually working—up from 24.3 percent of all workers in 1930 to 25.1 by 1940, according to Alice Kessler-Harris—made little impact in the fictionalized life of America's women. Hapke points out that the overwhelming image of the woman in fiction was that of helpmate, pitching in when needed but still tied to the traditional home life. In this study, many women also accepted this as their identity, even as they worked (like Lucy's mother above) as hard as the men. Lisa Kolb responded to her interviewer's question about whether her mom worked with a resounding "no." Then she went on to describe how the father-in-law took ill and moved in with the family and her mom took care of the bedridden man for the next seven years. But, said Kolb, "she never worked." Some of the women interviewed

Sharecropper family near Hazlehurst, Georgia. (Courtesy Library of Congress.)

agreed with Vera Pulliam's response to the question of their working: "there weren't enough jobs for men. We knew they're not going to have enough for the women." Certainly, there was discrimination against women working in the Depression, as it was believed that only the breadwinners, presumably men, should have jobs. Some held that the unemployment problem could be easily handled if all the women working were fired and replaced with men. Government programs, particularly during the first New Deal (1933–1935), discriminated against women in general and married women in particular. Schools, railroads, and many other businesses made it hard for women to get work. Atlanta's Alma McKinzey told her interviewer that "wives that had husbands working weren't allowed to work. People just didn't hire women, they wouldn't hire them." In fact, by 1939, twenty-six state legislatures were still considering bills that would bar women from state employment.[22]

But women did work. Irene Bolding of White, Georgia, trained without pay for several days before being added on as an operator for the phone company at twenty-five cents an hour. "When I got on as a full time operator I made nine dollars a week for forty hours," she said proudly. Merrill Horton remembered that the few options available for working women were "housekeeping and school teaching." These were jobs, she said, that men were not interested in doing, so women were allowed to take them; men refused these jobs because they paid low wages and the work was extremely difficult. Henry Green managed a store that employed women as clerks. When the store closed at six, the women had to stay behind and "pricemark" the merchandise for another "hour or two hours" without pay. "That was the way it was," he said. Afton Fletcher was nineteen when she took her first teaching job in rural Texas. After a year there, she moved to a larger consolidated school and began to go to college in the summers. Her first job was in a one-room schoolhouse with eight students. They would supply the wood for fuel and provide her with foodstuffs. She lived in the school. When she finally got her teacher's certificate, she earned eighty dollars a month.[23]

The difficulty that (primarily white) women had in getting and keeping work was magnified by the social and cultural mores of the region and the era. The same held true for the region's large African American population, which in 1930 accounted for just over 30 percent of the total population. This meant that over 7.7 million African Americans lived in the Southeast and 64 percent of these lived in rural areas. In states such as Georgia and Alabama, African Americans accounted for over 36 percent of their state's population. Yet these same people were locked into a system that made getting and maintaining a living an extremely difficult task. Mirroring that of the rest of the nation, the unemployment rate for blacks in the South's urban areas, such as Atlanta and Birmingham, often ran two to three times that of the white unemployed. Textile mills, mainly located in small towns, rarely hired black women before the crash, and during the Depression era, these women found little mill employment. In the countryside, the transformation away from tenancy and into hired labor meant that black farmers worked harder for even less. Black women not only were expected to work in the fields, care for the children, and raise much of the family's food, but some tenant contracts also required them to work as domestics for the white property owner. "Over half of the Negro tenants are croppers," reported the Johnson, Embree, and Alexander study of the South published in 1935, "that is, in the lowest category of poverty and dependence." This meant that for many of the region's people of color, this study agreed with Clifton Grandison's recollection—"black people didn't have anything to lose," so the Great Depression "hurt the white man more than it did the black man."[24]

The election of Franklin Delano Roosevelt in 1932 signaled a change for the nation's black population. For the first time since Emancipation, African Americans voted Democratic, a trend that would transform and cause divisions within the party. However, the promise of change came slowly to the nation's blacks, as the legislation of the first New Deal made little headway. But with the start of the second New Deal in 1935 and the growing influence of Harry Hopkins, FDR's policies began to challenge at least nominally the nation's racial policies and ensured that programs such as the Works Progress Administration, National Youth Administration, and Tennessee Valley Authority made active attempts at wage parity. The New Deal after 1935 worked to transform the country into a more inclusive and open society. This reformation was not lost on either those who supported or those who opposed this transformation (see the next chapter for how the people viewed the change): the people understood that change was indeed taking place.[25]

In the context of the oral histories collected for this book, race plays an interesting role. Since race was not included among the questions the students were to ask, in the interviews the informants self-identified either by labeling themselves as white or black, or by using terms such as *us* and *them* when referring to racial situations. The tumultuous history of civil rights in the United States after the Depression era, to which the people interviewed were inextricably linked, suggests that their understanding and conception of race underwent some alteration. This is not unusual in oral history, as Luisa Passerini's study on Italian fascism suggests. In Passerini's interviews, she found that because of the negative view of fascism held in later decades, informants' discussions of their experiences under fascism fell into two broad categories: those who told their stories without any mention of fascism and those who recalled how it had affected their lives. Both groups had gone through the same period, but they chose different ways to recall this shared past.[26]

The same holds true for this interview set. When the standard questions about race relations were asked, there were clear divisions, along racial lines, over how the informants responded. Whites who chose to self-identify spoke of race in terms of three themes: everyone was in the same boat, segregation was normal, and blacks were good/bad workers. The responses of blacks who chose to self-identify also divided into three themes: their hard work/low pay, fear of violence, and an awareness of the totality of power whites held.

"They were poor just like we were," Isabel Hester told her interviewer about the black farmers in Carroll County, Georgia, during the early 1930s. "They would come and chop cotton, hoe cotton, pick cotton just for something to eat." In her response, one sees the dichotomy of this framing of race relations. The blacks were poor like Hester, yet they "were real good help" on her family's farm picking cotton for food. Not having their own farm or food suggests that they were not in the same boat, and given the power division between the races, their social and cultural position would have been nowhere near the same, either. But the reality of separation and division between these two poor groups in the South was difficult for Hester to conjure up, given the changes in times. So she, like Hub Waters of Swords, Georgia, framed the context of the separation by stating that they "never had any trouble" or talking about how they "worked and farmed together to help each other out." Yet, Waters continued, "we did not associate. We didn't go to their house and they didn't come to ours." The ability to get along was framed within separation: to whites, as long as each group worked and stayed in their place, there would be no trouble. "You didn't see any black people in a community like you do today," Maybell Loftin told her interviewer. "They got along but they just didn't associate with each other." Separation allowed the two races to get along during the Depression years, unlike the modern era, when the civil rights movement forced integration and then created racial conflict. "Whites and colored people lived in their own separate communities," Maybell said, and "the whites went their way and the blacks went theirs."[27]

The separation they experienced was deemed normal, and the change that came afterward forced a reframing of race. Segregation was not considered a bad thing, as it maintained the social order. In this way, their responses outline the normalcy of the situation. When Ruth Smith recalled the Depression in Villa Rica, Georgia, she talked about her father working at the grocery store for a dollar a day to supplement his farm income. They were poor, and getting a living was tough. Yet they had black tenant farmers on their land who "were not sharecroppers," Ruth said, because her father "got all the crops." The several black families on the land would pick, seed, and gin the cotton and be paid by weight. Another black woman lived in the house with the family, sleeping "on a cot in the kitchen"; she prepared meals and took care of the children. They paid her a "dollar a week," and Smith added, "of course we fed her too!" Geneva Ariail told her interviewer that she had trouble remembering "ever seeing a black person" while growing up in Commerce, Georgia. Her grandfather, however, had several black tenants who worked the fields, and she said he made sure "they were fed and clothed." Florence Murphy outlined to her interviewer the segregated situation in the Toccoa, Georgia, area in the latter part of the 1930s: "They would never sit with you or would come in your front door and they would never eat with you. They did all the housework and the cooking and all but they would never come in." She and her husband owned land and had tenants who lived in "little tenant houses" with no screens on the door or windows. "I don't know how they even ate," she said, "because we had nothing."[28]

"It (the color [of] one's skin) didn't matter back in them days," Woodrow Maffet told his young interviewer; "they stayed in their place, we stayed in ours." But the interviewer was not satisfied and asked if there was any sense of superiority or economic dominance, to which Maffet unequivocally replied "no" and added that "the colored didn't try to go in with the whites . . . they stayed in their place and they knew where they could go." Some were able to get jobs with more prominent citizens of Monroe, Georgia, to cook, clean, and take care of the houses. "We was all poor" and got along "back in those days," said Maffet. What would happen, though, if someone crossed the line and went where they shouldn't have, probed the interviewer? "They got stopped," Maffet said, but he quickly changed the subject when asked how. Billy Patrick, also from Monroe and interviewed by the same student, shed more light on the situation, comparing the blacks' situation to slavery: "They had to depend on the white man because they didn't have anything." To survive, they had to work on the land for whatever wages were available and "accepted it because they had to." Growing up on the rural outskirts of Carrollton, Georgia, Ralph McCain told his interviewer of the numerous occasions on which he would fish or run in the woods with several older black men who lived on or near his family's farm. He also related a story about how, when they would walk to town together, the black children were reminded of their place—"they knew they were supposed to walk a good little ways back behind us so it wouldn't appear that they were with us." McCain did not quite understand why this was, but he was told by whites and blacks back home that that was simply how things were. What would happen if they crossed the line? Although few of the informants tackled this question (in fact, few of the interviewers ventured to ask), Cornelia Presley told her interviewer that breaking the social norms was met with harsh treatment. The punishment that black farmhands received for "stealing" involved taking "them out to the barn and whip[ping] them." This was not done to whites, "just done to the blacks," she added.[29]

While white residents rarely remember the more negative realities of the segregation and racism institutionalized throughout the South, those inter-viewed who self-identified as black painted a starker portrait of the era's race relations. They talked of hard work for unfairly low wages, working in the most mundane jobs, and violence—both physical and emotional—inflicted upon their persons. What comes through most loudly in their recollections is how aware they were of the discrimination they faced. In their language, there is little hint that they accepted the way things were or were unaware that other options exited. They repeatedly described their place, cognizant of society's unfairness. They not only pointed out the dichotomy that existed in the South at the time but also, in their descriptions, recognized the long-term impact of a system that held them as inferior and prevented their full incorporation into American society.

William Gordon of Bullard City, Georgia, leaned back in his chair and responded to the question about the mood of the country in the 1930s by saying, "man and woman could barely live, they had to work for the white folk." He told of how his "mother would work in the white folk's house and bring home the food they had left over" to feed her family. That African Americans worked as domestics in the South, and the North for that mat-ter, is not the point. Rather, the tone and the language used by those who self-identified as black and discussed working in this environment reveal an understanding that theirs was the lowest rung on the ladder and that this was part of a larger system of oppression. Getting work meant working for the white folks doing what they no longer wanted to do or could barely pay a local black resident to do. Georgia Mae Calloway would have to wake up extra early to wash the dishes in the house where her mother labored as a domestic. Then she would go to school and return afterward to wash again and on the weekends. The one dollar she received each week went to her mother without regret, "because it took that dollar to help her pay" the rent. Calloway's mother worked until three, went home to take care of her chil-dren, and then returned to her job to cook supper. In the late evenings, she also worked part-time at the hospital where her doctor/employer worked. Calloway's father could not find work except the occasional field labor. And the work was hard. Lillian Arnold told her interviewer that she grew up in an extended family that included both of her grandparents, who had been slaves and knew how to work hard. Yet getting a living in the 1930s was difficult for her family of tenant farmers. Getting paid seventy-five cents to a dollar for 100 pounds of cotton picked, they struggled to get a hundred pounds. "If it was dry it wouldn't weigh much [so] you'd get out early before the dew" would dry off "so the cotton would be heavy when

[they] weigh[ed] it." Everyone in the family worked in the fields, as there were no other jobs to be had. Addie Baynard explained to her interviewer that only fieldwork was available because "we didn't get the education we would have liked to have." The lack of education meant blacks worked in the fields while "all the white folks had the factory jobs," added her friend Ossie Barlow. During the 1930s around Fayette City, Georgia, both recalled the limited choices of both their gender and their race. Ossie told their female interviewer that back then, "black girls your age couldn't go into no bank"; Addie chimed in, "no matter how [much] education you had you couldn't get no good job."[30]

The lack of education only reinforced the system. For those who tried to challenge the status quo, more overt forms of repression were available. "The white people told you what to do and you done that," Georgia Mae Calloway told her interviewer. "If you didn't," she continued, "you got beat up." The cities were no different, according to Dorothy Hill's recollection. She remembered blacks being forced to take the most menial jobs and being restricted as to where they were allowed to live and travel. When she had to venture into areas normally off-limits, such as the Five Points district in Atlanta, she suffered taunts and "white children throw[ing] rocks" at her without retribution. To get to her job, she had to ride the streetcar through the area and regularly had to give up her seat to entering white patrons as a matter of course—"wasn't nothing you could do about it, you couldn't say nothing." The feeling of powerlessness, combined with a real sense of injustice, permeates many of the recollections. Growing up outside Opekia, Georgia, Ella Gibson would walk the country roads to school after she finished her chores. Some days, when the school bus filled with white children would pass her on the red dust road, the driver, whose name she recalled as G. W. King, would stop and let some of the white kids out to "jump on us." The schoolchildren "would be chucking they rocks and we would be chucking ours" until they got back on the bus and drove off. But she never backed down, and she recalled that sometimes "we would beat them up."[31]

Her reluctance to back down even as she understood the danger of her action suggests within the context of the interview an understanding of the unfairness that permeated her world. Rather than the tacit acceptance that white respondents recalled regarding race relations, many of those who self-identified as African American recalled understanding that the system prevented their full acceptance. "I was not able to go to school," William Gordon told his interviewer, "because in them days the white man wanted you to go to the fields and work." The system, he suggested, made it im-

Alabama tenant farmer and children. (Courtesy Library of Congress.)

possible for a black teenager to stay in school. Besides, what other type of employment awaited his graduation in Bullard City, Georgia? The system was no different in Milledgeville, Georgia, where Geneva Mack lived. After her graduation from high school, the only job she could find was working as a timekeeper at a local college for boys (Georgia College) where other blacks from her community worked as painters and landscapers. Her impression of work and society was fairly simple, and there was no "confusion" about one's place because "white people in small towns and big towns have always felt superior to the black folks." No matter your occupation or education level, "you was Aunt Jane [or] Uncle Tom [or] Uncle John." Given this, there were "no problems," because the blacks had no power to create them. Viola Elder echoed this powerlessness when talking about life in Carrollton, Georgia, during the same era: "They didn't even 'low [blacks] to stand on the street corners [before] they run 'em off." Then she added, "I'm sure they didn't do that in the white section." Beula Youngblood grew up in a tenant household in Georgia and grew to envy the white family that her family labored for. The owner's youngest daughter was the same age as Beula and had the same name, which created many problems. She recalled, "I quit answering to my name" so as to stop the taunting she took from the white Beula, but she understood how things worked. "She had more than I had," said Beula Youngblood, and the Youngblood family did all the white family's labor—in the fields and in the household. "I knew something was wrong," she said, adding, "we went to church, God bless the church." The church had traditionally served as a safe haven for activism and free speech, particularly in the countryside. Beula's father understood this and kept his mouth shut elsewhere, because "if they talked out like . . . the young do now, somebody was gone get hung [or] drowned in the river."[32]

The difference in how the two groups recall the racial experiences of the era helps us to understand better how the framing of race has changed since then. Ronald Grele's groundbreaking work on oral history, *Envelopes of Sound*, helps to place this situation within a theoretical context. He suggests that during an interview there is "active participation" between the interviewer and the informant through the phrasing of questions, gestures, body movements, and even the choice of clothing. These cues often serve to direct the flow of what he labeled the "conversational narrative." Interviewer and interviewee share cultural symbols and language, and these relationships help maintain the interaction during the interview. For the white informants discussing race with their white interviewer, although the two may be unified racially and (generally speaking) culturally, a real separation existed concerning experience. Most of the young people who did the interviews grew up in the post–civil rights era, during which time racially disparaging comments have come to be considered incorrect, mean, and racist. For the informants to discuss race openly with their conversational cohorts thus might have revealed their less flattering sides. Instead, they framed the racial situation with words and phrases that suggest segregation and even violence without allowing the totality of the racism that existed to come through. Phrases such as "that's the way things were" and "everyone got along and stayed in their place" suggest the division between the lived experience and the recalled experience. While on the surface these phrases were true of the situation, they reveal little of the reality that had to be observable to the informants. But given the nature of how race and segregation had come to be framed by the 1990s, the informants' ability to talk in more frank terms was impossible. Had the interviews taken place in another era, the responses would have revealed more of the ingrained racism present but would also have been mitigated by the historical situation. Similarly, when the black informants discussed their situations, they did so within a new framing of race that allowed them to be more critical of their past. Their interviews were imbued with the same consciousness as those of whites, yet the position was reversed. In this situation, the modern framing of race allowed for them to discuss more openly their feelings about the situation and how the racism affected their daily lives. Society had created an open space for their conversational narrative that had been closed for many years. Had the interviews taken place in earlier years, certainly the stories would have been framed differently. But in the 1990s, their stories were jeremiads documenting the struggle of the oppressed. Interestingly, discussions concerning gender reveal little of this dethronement/empowerment dichotomy. This abstraction of the interview relationship is significant, according to Grele, because it reveals not only the historical recollection but also the "larger community and its history" as each informant and interviewer views it. The interviews expose "hidden levels of discourse" that open up new understandings as to how both groups view their history and their place within it.[33]

For blacks in the South, getting a living was difficult, and the recollections were informed by the institutionalized racism under which both races labored. In the larger view, many of the white informants were able to see that the decade of the 1930s was the beginning of the era of change regarding this racial situation, even if that understanding came later rather than as part of the era. One can see this pattern in many of the interviews in which white informants talk about FDR and the New Deal programs. Many echoed Clifford Oxford's eloquent understanding of the power of FDR, saying that "Roosevelt encouraged blacks by giving them an opening to government jobs and encouraging the states to give them the right to vote." This inevitably led to the demise of the all-white primary in Georgia, he told his young interviewer, and "started the revolution [that] was slow in coming" but powerful. African American recollections of the racial situation also portray the period as one of reformation, during which the daily struggles to survive inevitably opened up new opportunities. One of most moving testaments to this reformation came from Ella Gibson, who was raised in rural Lee City, Georgia. After she described getting up before dawn to begin farmwork and the back-breaking labor she endured as a child, the interviewer asked her almost incredulously, "Well, what about school?" Gibson took a moment and then said, "Well now y'all blessed, y'all really blessed. But you know what it is y'all livin' on—people's prayers from back then up until now. They prayed for this day. But it's in y'all's time. Now you know it makes me happy to see children try and make something out of themselves, going to school, learning something I didn't have."[34]

Getting a living was difficult in the American South during the 1930s. People accustomed to working their own land found themselves trying to scrape together whatever work they could find. For many whites in rural Georgia, this meant going to the textile mills that dotted the landscape. For others, such as many of those in rural Alabama or Tennessee, it meant trying to piece together enough pick-up work and create alternative strategies for survival. Women, both black and white, faced a social system that devalued their labor while demanding their contributions. They did whatever they could to try to help the family, including selling their surplus farm commodities and taking jobs outside the home. For the region's black population, getting a living became even more precarious, as tenant contracts either were abandoned or became so restrictive as to make mere survival nearly impossible. There were few employment options, and migration out of the region—which had seen over 1.5 million people leave the South between 1910 and 1930—had slowed because of the economic crisis. This put added pressure on many African American women, as they not only had to continue their mixed roles as farm laborers, mothers, and wives but also increasingly found they needed to supplement the family's meager income by taking on domestic employment.

The people recalled that getting a living during the era was tough, to say the least. There were but a handful who talked about their employment in a way that suggested job satisfaction or that the expected job came through. Most were thankful for whatever job they were able to get to make ends meet; only rarely did they discuss career aspirations. Their stories are ones of survival, in which work was expected to begin at an early age and was labor intensive. The idea that shines most brightly through these stories, and perhaps allowed the interviewees to recall the times with some fondness, is unity. While they all discussed the difficulties of getting and keeping work, and the hard labor that was part of their day-to-day existence, they tended to frame these experiences by suggesting that everyone was in the same boat. Again and again one hears in their discussions of their work lives a solidarity that suggests working class. White or black, male or female, they defined themselves as people working in the fields and factories for wages not under their control in an unstable marketplace. Their perception of this work reality perhaps helps to explain why they came to view FDR and the New Deal in a positive light, as these programs sought to bring stability and control to southern working people's lives.

"I THOUGHT HE WAS GOD'S HALF-BROTHER"

The People's View of Roosevelt and the Federal Programs

Bessie Fowler called Franklin D. Roosevelt "God's half-brother" because she believed that without FDR and the New Deal, the country would not have survived the Great Depression. Hers was not a unique description, for given the precarious nature of the economy and society, many people placed tremendous hope in the newly elected president. Herbert Hoover had failed to help the people, James Shope of Ranger, Georgia, recalled, and if he had gotten reelected in 1932, "everybody in the south would have starved to death." When FDR and the Democrats were swept into the White House in 1932, Delmas Easterwood remembered, "everybody was real excited." The small Alabama town where he lived celebrated with a parade, speakers, and even a free picture show. "We were glad to hear President Roosevelt was elected," Irene Bolding recalled of the 1932 election, "because he had ideas and things" that could help the nation's people. Roosevelt was seen as sort of a native son, given his residence and commitment to Warm Springs, Georgia, and with John Garner of Texas as the vice president, the South appeared to have captured the White House.[1]

In his inaugural address, FDR did much to suggest hope, at least in part because of his commitment to do something. He told the people that together they were going to build "great public projects for the benefit of the public" and that the days of money for money's sake had passed: "these dark days will be worth all they cost us if they teach us that our true destiny is not to be ministered to but to minister to ourselves and our fellow man." This rhetoric was not lost on the young Citadel cadet William Perreyclear, who remembered that the speech encouraged him to work harder and "just believe in [him]self and go to work." The programs of this New Deal, while not specific, indicated a federal government willing to shoulder some of the responsibility and help the people, a message not lost to those in the rural areas of the South. Norma Brumback did not remember much about the specifics but did remember feeling, as a young married woman, that the New Deal had "an encouraging ring" to it. For Brewer Hoyt Douglas, FDR's election was tied to his honesty. "He didn't lie to [us] about it," Douglas recalled, but told the people "let's try it, let's try it, you know. That's what made it work." "President Roosevelt started us on our way," Alabama's Lela Knight recalled, "and with the hard work and determination of us all we made it." To M. Oxford, FDR's ability to overcome his physical limitations pointed toward a hopeful future: "the fact that he could overcome this tremendous handicap (polio) gave him a spirit that could not be defeated. He transmitted that enthusiasm and hope . . . to the great majority of people."[2]

Hope was identified with FDR's election in the minds of the people. Few presidents had come into office with such a clear groundswell of support as did FDR. Despite being unable to articulate exactly what his programs were or would do, he served as a knightlike symbol for many looking for hope in desperate times. When he came into office, "people began to feel like better times were coming," said Joe Johnson of western Georgia. While unable to cite exactly why, most interviewees agreed with Urban Farnsworth when he said that FDR "was the one who gave everyone courage and hope in those days . . . [because] at last [somebody] was doing something . . . to get us back on our feet so that we could go ahead." Geraldine Beck claimed Roosevelt "restored confidence in the American government," while Frances Clements believed the president had "lifted the spirits, you know, of the people."[3]

The social and economic situation in the American South was desperate, and FDR knew he had to deliver more than just hope to the region. In the rural areas of Georgia, Alabama, and Tennessee, as across the entire South, the economic collapse had flattened both farm and factory. Cotton sales fell to $45 million in 1932, down from the 1929 high of $1.5 billion, with similar drops in other cash crops such as peanuts and tobacco. As a result, many of the over eight million tenant farmers and sharecroppers were thrown out of work, competing with the small-town factory unemployed. Those who were able to hold onto their agricultural jobs continued to labor with little likelihood of profit at the end of the season. The southern tenant economy was already weak before the crash, and the economic downturn only served to make a bad situation worse. In the small towns and urban areas in the region, the situation was no better, as the rates of unemployment often exceeded 30 percent. By 1933 this meant that over one-eighth of all the families in the cotton-growing region received relief from the newly created Federal Emergency Relief Administration (FERA).[4]

The situation was compounded by the social and political situation born and bred in the plantation culture of the rural South. For the federal government to get involved, the complex relationship between landowner and tenant farmer or sharecropper had to be navigated. This meant challenging the traditional southern power structure, which relied on the ethos of self-reliance and a tightly controlled labor pool. The paternalism of the owners and politicians had to be broken down, and as the Depression deepened, loyalties moved from the local ruling classes to Washington. Whereas in the past, the people might have looked to the landowner, factory owner, or local politician to provide relief, the overwhelming depth of the situation in the 1930s encouraged them to look to the federal government for assistance. In Georgia, for example, the county unit system had been designed to make sure that local power remained in the hands of those who had traditionally held power—landowners. This meant that when and if the federal government established a program, it would have to work through each of the 159 counties in the state. Most of these counties were controlled by a powerful ruling class that saw as its responsibility the well-being of its people. Since the poor and dispossessed had little political power, they were often ignored and marginalized, to be dealt with only if their numbers grew too large or their actions menacing. The desperation brought about by the crash, however, challenged this relationship and altered the caste/class system, transferring loyalty from the local to the federal level and weakening both the political and the social power that the aristocracy of the South had once enjoyed.[5]

FDR and his advisors were aware of this situation and therefore understood how important it was to get their message to the people. For a variety of reasons, they turned to the relatively new medium of radio to meet their need. They hoped that the people would respond as western Georgia's Henri Herron and his family had, putting aside everything when the president's voice came over the radio, for they "always stopped and listened." His kind voice projected a "feeling that everything would be alright," remembered Wyolene Warren, and the type of trust and hope that came forth on the radio was central to FDR's use of the medium. He had to convey to the people his empathy. With many southerners, he was successful. Those in Viola Elder's African American neighborhood in Carrollton, Georgia, rushed "to get around somebody" with a radio so as not to miss anything the president might say. She said she used to imagine him "sitting down by the fire talking" to the people, as if they were right in his living room. When Roosevelt's voice came over the radio in Warren Brockway's house, "people glued their ears to the radio and listened" to what the president had to say.[6]

FDR worked hard to personalize his message and reach out to the people; the radio was the perfect medium for that message. Many of those interviewed as part of this study vividly recalled Roosevelt's use of the radio because it made them feel connected to the president. For many, hearing the president's voice over the radio encouraged them to feel as though FDR were one of the family. "When things would get rough," Martha Bailey recalled, "he would sit down and talk to you like a daddy and tell his children 'just stick with me, things are going to get better.'" This testifies to Roosevelt's ability to reach the people. They *heard* him, and that made them "feel secure . . . like your father sitting down and giving you good advice," recalled Joseph Foster. For Anne Pierce, it was Roosevelt's ability to "comfort her" that made her view him as a "father figure." Wayne J. Flynt argues in *Poor but Proud* that poor whites and blacks in rural Alabama relied less on the written word and more on oral tradition. Whether in folktale or song, much of their cultural tradition was rooted in this less formal system. Perhaps this helps to explain why the radio played a primary role in their understanding of the political situation of the 1930s and their unbending support of FDR and his policies. Not bound by newspaper assessments (which FDR's administration had determined by 1935 were not supportive), many in the rural South trusted the word of a person more than what might be written. High illiteracy rates and the lack of distribution networks for newspapers in the rural countryside meant that for many, the radio became the connection to the outside world. FDR's word came to be trusted.[7]

Roosevelt understood the potential impact of radio, believing that it could "restore direct contact between the masses and their chosen leaders." The radio and communication industry had grown phenomenally since its advent in the early 1920s. Network hookups linked local stations together by the early 1930s—CBS's seventy-nine network affiliates and NBC's Red and Blue networks, numbering sixty-one each, meant that by the time of the New Deal, radio's audience went beyond 41.4 million listeners daily. In the mid-1930s, over 24.5 million people owned at least one radio and were tuning in for an average of five hours a day. Featuring a wide variety of programming, from comedy and drama to musical broadcasts, sports, and politics, the radio emerged as an important entertainment medium during the 1930s. With the network hookups, it created a more unified cultural ideology. All in all, in the midst of the crisis, radio helped to build a national consensus of hope during the 1930s.[8]

With this vast audience in mind, and coupled with FDR's belief that print media opposed his efforts, by 1934 radio had become the central medium for the dissemination of the New Deal's message. Both major networks supplied FDR with hundreds of hours of free broadcast time—NBC provided over 250 hours between September 1933 and September 1934 alone. Press secretary Stephen Early screened and coordinated airtime to tout particular New Deal programs. In 1938, for example, the Works Progress Administration's Federal Music Project produced more than 2,831 radio broadcasts in a variety of markets and used the NBC network to broadcast the premier of an American opera called *Gettysburg* in July of that year. The network's desire to provide this airtime came from both their support of FDR and his influence in the passing of the 1934 Communications Act, which gave the Federal Communications Commission tremendous latitude. Not supporting the administration's requests for airtime might create problems with additional licensure, so the broadcaster's best interest was to give the government as much time as necessary.[9]

Of all the broadcasts sponsored by the administration, FDR himself best utilized the radio. Through a series of presentations beginning with the banking crisis speech on March 12, 1933, the president initiated a regular series of informal talks to the American people called the Fireside Chats, a term coined by CBS's Harry Butcher after the May 7, 1933, speech. Their success as a "revolutionary new medium of person-to-person communications" encouraged FDR to utilize the chat format over the next decade as a way to reach directly into American homes and to stay in touch with the people. He broadcast seven domestic policy chats during the 1930s and, beginning in September 1939, eighteen chats concerning America's response to growing tensions and (later) World War II.[10]

The Fireside Chats became near folklore to those who were interviewed for this project. They recalled with special fondness their time gathered around the radio listening to the Fireside Chats. Paul Morgan's whole family would sit "around the radio" and listen "every time he had one—hell, didn't anyone miss it." For Maria Jett's family, the chats were like a special occasion. The "family would finish dinner and literally sit by the fire and . . . listen to what Roosevelt had to say." Several people remembered that folks in their families looked on these chats as special events. Ed Isakson remembered that when FDR spoke, "people always glued themselves to the small radio that they had to listen." For Elenora Hunt and her family, the chats were "something that everybody always looked forward to" and would be "gathered around the radio." One interviewer, upon hearing how the family would gather around the radio, suggested that the scene sounded like something out of the television program *The Waltons*, to which informant Geneva Davenport replied, "that's right, just like that." For Dorothy Bartley, however, Roosevelt and his chats were less interesting than Rudy Vallee. She preferred going to her girlfriend's house to listen to the bandleader's program and "didn't pay a lot of attention" to FDR or his radio speeches.[11]

Others remembered the Fireside Chats as a time when the people in the community came together. Bertha Hicks recalled that when it was announced that FDR was going to broadcast one of his chats, "people that had radios would let everyone know when" he was scheduled to speak and then they "would all go and listen very carefully to what he had to say." Irene Bolding remembered it much the same way—"people would go around saying come over to hear Roosevelt." For James Thompson, a young worker at the Callaway Rug Mills in LaGrange, Georgia, the chats meant that "everybody who could, g[o]t to where somebody in the neighborhood had a radio [and] would gather and listen at his speech." The Fireside Chats were something "that people kind of looked forward to," remembered Laura Lambert. Her family was one of the first in her Carrollton, Georgia, neighborhood to own a radio, and when the chats came on, her father "would turn it up kind of loud because there were people on the street trying to hear it." William D. Smith, remembering his days in Rome, Georgia, observed, "You would just go listen 'cause you didn't have to be invited to things like that. You just went to their house and wanted to hear Roosevelt." FDR's Fireside Chats offered an opportunity for many of these folks to come together, just as Roosevelt had hoped. People who had radios, recalled Charles Ricks, would invite their neighbors and "gather around so they could listen to what President Roosevelt had to say." They did this, Ricks believed, because he offered them a "ray of hope . . . [an] inspiration, and something to soothe the anguish, hardship, and heartaches of the people." In black communities, the radio played an additional role, as it connected them to the president and also allowed them nonsegregated public space. For many in the rural areas and small towns in the South, this was the first unfiltered information they were privileged to, and it created a sense of hope and optimism. It helped to alleviate the alienation and isolation of those outside the urban areas and empowered them with knowledge about state and national events.[12]

The decision to utilize the radio and the Fireside Chats seemed like perfect timing. Given the severity of the crisis, there was a tremendous need for someone in power to soothe and calm people's insecurities, very real in the Depression era. For the message to get through, this person had to convey trust. Roosevelt made people such as Joe Johnson feel as if "he had come into our living room and sat down and was just talking to us personally." Another factor that made the timing of the chats significant was the relative newness of the medium. Although radio had been broadcasting for several years, the decade of the 1930s was its golden age, and its impact had yet to be critically understood. Radio was new and as such transformed the dynamics of the preradio traditional home. As it became an acceptable part of the household, it became—in a modernist way—part of the family. "Roosevelt's voice was soft, friendly, and very comforting," remembered Norma Brumback, "like he was talking right to you."[13]

The radio altered the relationship that southerners had to their government, at least concerning Roosevelt. The people, who most likely had rarely heard any president before FDR speak, heard in their leader someone like them—human and in need of help. FDR used the chats to appeal to the people for support, and this encouraged them to trust him, to let him into their homes. He would begin the broadcast, remembered Sherman Shockley, by saying, "friends, and you are my friends" (although the texts of the chats do not reveal this); the words made Shockley feel "comfortable," as if FDR were sitting right in the room. Jennie Kilburn also put the president right in her living room when recalling the chats, still seeing him "in [her] mind sitting there talking [with] the sweetest looking and compassionate face." Since it was radio, FDR understood the power of imagination and suggested to the people that he was sitting in front of the fire, in his home, talking directly to the family. "Oh yeah," Brewer Hoyt Douglas said when recalling the chats, "he sat down in his living room there at home and talked." Never before had a president become so intertwined with the experiences, even if imagined, of the people. While many recalled that he spoke about his programs and what he wanted to do, very few could relate specific topics that he covered. Perhaps this is because they chose to remember the comfort and hope he projected. "I don't remember any of his words," Joe Johnson said in his interview, "but it was like a friend instead of a President talking to you."[14]

Central to this relationship and the memory of hope was trust. The people believed that FDR was on their side, that he was genuine or, as Verna Bland recalled, "his own man." She and others trusted Roosevelt because "his ideas were his own and he didn't have people writing a lot of stuff for him to . . . say." The familiarity of being accepted into the family meant that people could understand and empathize with his message. George Pope said that listening to Roosevelt and the chats made him feel as if the president was like him and was "not the type of person that would talk over the workingman's head." Many accepted the appeal Roosevelt made for unity and truly believed that their involvement in solving the crisis was just as significant as the government's activities. Mildred Curtis believed that this public support came from the people "listening to his speeches" on the radio, as she and others understood that the recovery of America was a partnership. "I remember his saying the country cannot do [it] without you," said Antonio Maniaci, and this appeal suggested that everyone, even the president, was in the same situation.[15]

The sound of the president's voice coming into people's homes had a soothing and comforting effect. "He had a golden voice," remembered William D. Smith of Rome, Georgia, and "had a way of imparting hope [that was] contagious." This atmosphere projected "confidence and faith and belief in our country," according to William Perreyclear. The trust that Roosevelt developed with listeners was not automatic, however. Maurice Sponcler understood the need for change during the era and remembered the chats as FDR's way of selling the idea to the people who might not understand the nature of the reforms. To Sponcler, the president "established a tremendous amount of confidence in the American people." Faced with economic problems that for many Americans seemed too complex to understand, Roosevelt tried to "make the people see that this wasn't the end of the world, that we had something to look forward to," remembered R. D. Simpson. To E. B. Cane, the president's use of the radio helped the people "anticipate better times [and made] everybody feel that good times were comin' pretty soon." Genevieve Meredith's reception of the chats had little to do with what he actually said, as she was "a little more interested in boys than the New Deal." But Roosevelt did describe things in a way that made her "feel so secure that [she] just didn't worry too much about what was really going on." She and others had faith in their president, and the Fireside Chats and the personal nature of the broadcast helped engender this type of trust and support.[16]

Roosevelt's use of the radio contributed to the public's perception of their president. FDR's voice came into the homes of millions worried about their futures and brought them a ray of hope and a conviction that their government was working toward a solution. "All you could hear was his voice," recalled Ernest Porter about FDR and the radio, "and he was able to project his ideas and his ideals through his voice." Mary Slack understood that FDR was the "first political leader that ever had any immediate contact with the public," and this encouraged the people to want to listen and hear about "what was going on." He was such a "great speaker," Sadie Wright remembered, that people believed his efforts would save the country. "I don't know what would have happen[ed] to our country" without him, she continued. Lucille Campbell likened his radio appeal to that of Will Rogers, as both men "laid the cards on the table." The people came to have such faith and trust in FDR that when he came on the radio, remembered Travis Dorrough of Leeds, Alabama, "Everybody came to a sudden halt and they were thrilled to hear [his] heart-to-heart talk with the people of the nation." Thomas Lipford of Franklin, Georgia, stated that "Republican people wouldn't even listen because he was so convincing" that he would convert them. "If he got on the radio for one of his Fireside Chats and said 'my countrymen, at three o'clock this afternoon it will rain pennies from heaven,'" Paul Maddox told his interviewer, "there would be twenty-five million people got out with pans to catch it."[17]

FDR and the radio worked well together. The people listened and gave him their support, because "every time the radio was on," remembered Jennie Kilburn, "the news was [about] Roosevelt" and the things he was trying to accomplish. Merrill Cheatham, finishing her schooling at the University of Missouri at the time, remembered that when FDR's voice came over the radio, it "inspired people to trust him and depend on him. He sounded strong and sounded in control of things. He came across as a person who truly loved his people." This ability to convey trust and hope was transferred to *his* people. In the early part of the 1930s, recalled William D. Smith, the situation around Rome, Georgia, was in shambles. He voted for FDR in 1932 because Roosevelt "offered the country hope and hope is a very important thing for people to have." Ordinary citizens such as Katherine Melton recognized in FDR someone who "was trying to help everybody," or as A. Young Lester said, he "gave us hope for the future, and people began to look up a little bit—better things to come." Without actually doing anything, Roosevelt was able to suggest activism and a better future because, according Ruth Rhymer of Canton, Georgia, "he worked with the people and for the people."[18]

When Doc Harris began to get painting work in the area of Tyus, Georgia, it made him feel "proud," and he credited FDR with helping to provide a "better life." Many people marked the election of Roosevelt as the beginning of putting "people to work," according to Marguritte Lilly.

"When Roosevelt came along everything changed," John Redden remembered. Leonard Crenshaw concurred, after painting a dire picture of the Hoover years; after the election of Roosevelt, Crenshaw observed, "folks [got] work," and soon factories reopened, new jobs opened up, and people's attitudes began to improve. FDR, to these people, seemed committed to, as Sadie Wright said, "helping the people to live better."[19]

Roosevelt knew that he had to back up this trust with specific programs aiding the people, all the while balancing them with other acts designed to benefit businesses and banks. The first hundred days' legislation cut a wide swath and convinced many that the president was actually going to do the things he had alluded to on the radio. The legislative activism—whether the bank holiday and subsequent changes in banking law, the creation of FERA and the Civilian Conservation Corps (CCC), or the myriad other significant programs created—was not lost on the people. "I think he did more for the people than anybody [else] ever did," said Edna Mann, especially "the poor people." Harry B. Johnson of Atlanta believed that FDR was "for the little man" and helped to create opportunities so "that the little man could survive." He felt "proud" to have Roosevelt as president. Others agreed, crediting the president with all sort of marvels. For Mary McClain, FDR was the "one who put the electricity through to have electric lights and phones . . . [and] mattresses." Up in the northern Georgia mountains, Ruby Painter recalled how FDR created a "work team of poor people," which relieved the locals from having to feed the vagrants who appeared at her family's door. Ruby Barlow recalled what local whites in Fayette City told her when Roosevelt died in 1945: "Y'all's president is dead." But to her it was a mistake to suggest that he had only helped black people, as there were "just as many po' white folks as it is po' black folks" who benefited from his programs. Even B. D. Stephens, who said he did not like or vote for FDR, could not help but admit that the president "done more for poor folks than anybody that I know of."[20]

The New Deal focused much time and money on providing relief and pointing to a more hopeful future for the South. With the creation of the Federal Emergency Relief Administration (FERA) in May 1933, relief streamed into the South. At the end of the year, nearly one in eight southerners was listed on FERA's rolls. In Georgia, Governor Eugene Talmadge tried to prevent the monies from coming into the state, regarding the relief funds as a challenge to his authority and coddling the poor. In response, Washington federalized the state relief agencies in 1935 and worked to distribute the monies. New Deal dollars began to come into Georgia in earnest the next year when pro-New Deal Ed Rivers was elected governor. Alabama and Tennessee both experienced immediate relief, as their congressional and state representatives more than welcomed the federal assistance. But FDR gave more than relief; his New Deal also brought jobs, which infused the South with cash and hope, two things in short supply. The Public Works Administration (PWA), a part of the National Industrial Recovery Act (NIRA), spent over $200 million in the South just constructing school buildings. The Rural Electrification Administration (REA), created in 1935, provided low-interest loans to rural communities for the purpose of encouraging electrification through cooperative investment. By 1939, over four hundred of these people-controlled electrical agencies had formed in the South, bringing electricity to more than 250,000 people. By the end of the war, in 1945, the South's percentage of electrical hookups had increased from less than 10 percent in 1930 to nearly 70 percent. Other programs such as NIRA, the Civil Works Administration (CWA), and the Tennessee Valley Authority (TVA) had tremendous impact in the region. From January 1933 to July 1939, the New Deal funneled nearly $2 billion into the southern states via FERA, CWA, and the Works Progress Administration (WPA).[21]

The funding transformed the South, not only through the infusion of capital and the encouragement of a consumer economy but also because the New Deal challenged and began to dismantle the backward economic and social system of the region. When in 1938 the president endorsed the Clark Foreman–directed *Report on the Economic Conditions of the South*, he in effect declared war on the traditional southern way of life. The report outlined a region that was backward in virtually every category except potential. What prevented the flowering of the region was not so subtly blamed on the aristocrats and landowners, who had used a variety of means to keep the people poor, undereducated, and dependent. The New Deal and the federal government, the report indicated, had to eliminate these barriers to growth and pointed to a brighter and more inclusive future. Unfortunately for FDR and his supporters in the region, his antagonists rallied and weakened the New Deal coalition in the latter part of the 1930s.[22]

Even as his programs challenged some southern Democrats and perhaps weakened his overall position, Roosevelt held firm to fulfill his promise to bring a New Deal to the region. Most of those interviewed supported the president and more specifically recalled how some of his programs had transformed their lives and region. The most frequently mentioned were the CCC and WPA (the interviewers asked first whether interviewees could recall any particular New Deal program and if they did, then requested

At the dedication of the REA [Rural Electrification Administration] project, Barnesville, Georgia. (Courtesy National Archives.)

specifics), and their descriptions define the import of the New Deal to the South.

When FDR took office in 1933, nearly a quarter of a million young men were hopping aboard trains in efforts to find work far from their home. This statistic was part of a larger administration concern that a whole generation of young people would come of age with little chance of employment, marriage, or hope for the future. Nearly 40 percent of those between sixteen and twenty-four were neither employed nor in school, and as the European model was showing, this army of unemployed could become problematic if a tyrant could capture its imagination. To address this situation, FDR proposed to Congress the Civilian Conservation Corps bill in March 1933 to "eliminate the threat that enforced idleness brings" to American youth. The program, which Congress passed, accepted unmarried men between the ages of seventeen and twenty-five and put them to work for six months, away from their homes, constructing elements of the nation's public environment. They were paid thirty dollars a month and received food, clothing, and shelter. Of their pay, the enrollees kept only five dollars, with the rest being automatically sent back home. Although the CCC was designed as a makeshift program, the administration was pleasantly surprised by its success. The CCC planted nearly three-quarters of all new trees before World War II and employed over two and a half million young people, pumping $670 million into the family economy.[23]

The South was part of the Fourth Corps area and had 198 camps spread throughout the region. Tennessee had 33 camps, while Georgia had 32 and Alabama 17. The entire Fourth Corps area was to employ about forty thousand men a year, with about two hundred men per camp. Several of those who served in the South recalled their experiences with reverence. Sam Davis went to the CCC after the passing of his father, and the twenty-five dollars he sent home every month enabled his mother to "buy the children clothes and things they needed for the house." When Roy Patterson went into the corps, he did so hoping to save the money he sent home so that he could marry his sweetheart, Lucille. His mother sent him a letter that begged his forgiveness because she had to spend some of the money so his "daddy could buy something he needed." Patterson told her not to worry because the family came first. Henry Clark tried several times to get enrolled but was turned down because his family was not in need. He even offered to work and "send the money back to some needy family," but to no avail. Henry Felton's brother went into the three C's, and the money sent home helped his mother "exist." Anne Pierce's father could not find steady work and was on and off work programs, so her brother joined the CCC. The money he sent home ensured that the family "could eat and have a place to sleep." Lena Stimpson's brother also assumed the role as primary breadwinner, quitting school at sixteen and lying about his age to join the CCC. While her mother was brokenhearted over his leaving school, the family "needed things," and with the CCC, the son "could make something" to support the family.[24]

The work of the CCC was recalled as hard but fulfilling. John R. Beach, sporting a U.S. CCC tattoo on his arm, recalled being outfitted in World War I–era U.S. Army clothing and being sent to work at Fort Monroe, Virginia. He lived in a tent while building barracks and was assigned to be part of a surveying crew. He spent his time in the corps working in the George Washington National Forest in Virginia. Sam Davis's time in the CCC was spent building fire trails and recreation areas and planting trees in the Great Smoky Mountains. He believed that he was well fed for his efforts, as each worker received "five sandwiches each for lunch." Roy Patterson recalled that his CCC outfit from Fort McPherson in Georgia had to cut a fire break through a swamp by digging "trenches eighty feet wide and just as straight as your eye could see." They dug out trees by hand because there were no "bulldozers in those days." Instead, a young man they called "the climber" would scramble to the top of the tree to secure a rope to the top. With the dirt near the roots already dug out, the rope was connected to a "big road machine" and pulled down. The CCC boys would then "cut them up and burn them."[25]

Although most of the informants were not employed by the CCC, they nevertheless related stories of what they remembered about the agency. This provides a glimpse into how many southerners came to view the CCC and what effect they believed it had on their communities. Most regarded the CCC as a positive program primarily because it helped give people, as Willie Clackum recalled, "their pride back." As each graduating class emerged from high school, they entered a marketplace that offered few opportunities, and as Ptleene Chapman remembered, "they'd just go to the CC[C] camps for a job." Several of those interviewed called the CCC a "blessing" because, as Ernest Porter recalled, the three C's took the young men off the streets and put them in camps where they "stayed busy." Charles Clayton recalled that from his home in Etowah, Tennessee, he would witness "trainloads, maybe fifteen cars, coaches [filled] with these boys, just teenagers from the cities." He would meet the enrollees at the train depot in his truck and drive them to the CCC camp in the mountains, where they were clothed, fed, and worked. The CCC "kept all the young boys" who could get in, remembered Lowell Bean, "off the street [and] gave them a place to live and something to eat." But it was not relief, as most agreed with Albert Cicero's accounting—"they would really come in and work. Those guys worked."[26]

Several people told stories of how they were affected by these CCC boys. Delmas Easterwood's husband had the CCC boys stationed near Malore, Alabama, rebuild their pasture fence. Lois Scroggins's husband, a barber in Villa Rica, Georgia, was pleased by the proximity of the camp to his business, because with haircuts going for "ten or fifteen cents" each, "business was good" with the CCC boys. Gladys Partridge's family near Lake Martin in Alabama would come down from their mountain home and sell their "vegetables . . . milk, eggs, and chickens" to the CCC. Perhaps many communities were more like those in and around the North Dakota area where Genevieve Meredith grew up. She recalled the adults in her area reacting to the CCC with both excitement and concern. On one hand, the camp brought jobs and money to the area, but on the other, parents were concerned about the "bad reputation" many of the CCC boys had. If people "had girls old enough to date," she recalled, they would try "to keep them away from the boys."[27]

Nearly all those who recalled the three C's linked the corps to the rebirth of the nation's forests. "They literally lived in tents," recalled Geneva Ariail, and "did much of their work" to reforest and clear the "undergrowth in the forests." Theirs was a task for the future—Miriam Merrell told her interviewer that the CCC is why the South has "all of the pine trees today." Some were able to recall more specific CCC creations, such as Delano Lake in Georgia and "a lot of camping areas around Pine Mountain," according to M. B. Guy. For Lita Vance, recalling the CCC brought back memories of growing up in Carrollton, Georgia, and witnessing the corps activities. She listed with pride the things built by the CCC, including the "big old rock gym over there on [Route] 27 North," as well as a swimming pool. To her and others, these activities became living testaments to the positive activities of the New Deal in their communities and among their friends and neighbors. The result was plain to Hub Waters in central Georgia: "it got money flowing and the farming really got better." Everybody appeared to have benefited from the CCC one way or another.[28]

The other program most mentioned was the WPA. Created in 1935 as a work relief program, the WPA sought to employ those who were still unable to find work in the private sector, but in a manner that did not directly compete with business and industry and helped build confidence and hope in the American system of government. Over the span of its existence (1935–1942), the WPA pumped $11.5 billion into the national economy and provided temporary employment to over eight and a half million Americans. In the South, this translated into hundreds of thousands of jobs and hundreds of millions of dollars that transformed the region. The WPA built or refurbished thousands of schools, laid thousands of miles of roads, and constructed hundreds of bridges, sanitation lines, airports, recreation facilities, and much more, right in the South. The infusion of money meant that people could, according to Geneva Ariail, "feel like they were doing an honest day's work and getting paid for it."[29]

Most of the respondents recalled the WPA in much the same manner as they had the CCC: a benefit to families, to communities, and to country. When Merrill Horton graduated from high school, he tried to get on the WPA but was refused because they told him there were "so many married men with families and children" who needed work. While disappointed, Horton understood that individual sacrifices were necessary for the country to emerge from the dark days of the Depression, and this was his small role in that process. Others retold stories of their own family situations, such as Clifford Oxford's unemployed pharmacist father. Thrown out of work by the Depression, he worked for nearly a year for the WPA. Oxford remembered that "it was the only paying job [his dad] could find in order for [the family] to survive and pay the rent." Clare Doherty's father faced similar problems after he lost his business. He first tried to get something else going by borrowing a wagon and selling vegetables, but after this venture failed, he joined the WPA. Although not used to hard labor, he learned how to lay brick and worked with the project building roads. He did not make a lot of money, Doherty recalled, "but he made enough that we didn't starve . . . and [paid] our rent."[30]

Many recalled how the WPA helped them more directly. Gladys H. Burroughs's husband worked on the WPA shortly after they married in 1935, "because, you know, in the country that was about all the jobs there were." Sarah Riddle's husband also worked for the WPA, helping to clear the way for building roads. He was not paid much, she recalled, but it was better than the wages he had received picking cotton—thirty cents for every one hundred pounds. Allan Furline remembered that his wages went from "making fifty cents a day to two dollars a day" building roads with the WPA. The fifty-cents-a-day wage must have been standard for unskilled white laborers, because many recalled the same wage. Delmas Easterwood's husband worked with the WPA in Roanoke, Virginia, to "pour the streets of

Roanoke" for "twenty-five cents an hour [which] was a great improvement over making fifty cents a day!" Making roads back then was a bit different than it is now, recalled Josephine Taff: "Tractors, and these big old things to work on the roads, they didn't have them. They worked [with] mules, picks and shovels." The work was not reserved for white workers, as Madie Myers recalled that around Columbus, Georgia, the WPA "gave men jobs, colored men." She was unsure whether white folks were part of the WPA or any government program: "I don't know if it was [just] in the black area but I know the WPA was something that had a lot of people working on it." E. LeRoy Jordan was one of those "colored men" in the area working on the WPA. He recalled getting on the WPA to help clear the land for building roads in and around Fort Benning, outside Columbus, Georgia. They only worked "one or two day[s] a week," and they had to bring their own tools. In Jordan's case, he brought a shovel.[31]

Some recalled the WPA in a more personal manner. Geneva Stewart remembered that one time a "man and his wife [came] and stayed with us while her husband worked on that WPA" in Carrollton, Georgia. The wife stayed at the house and minded Stewart's children while she and her husband went to work in the textile mill. The couple "didn't pay no board" but lived there while he did work for the WPA. Naomi Jean Bowden's mother worked as a supervisor in a WPA sewing project, in which the "government gave them the cloth" and the clothing that they made was given to "whoever needed 'em." Sylvia Selman worked in a WPA nursery school in Rome, Georgia, so that the children's parents could work. "We gave them their lunch and they had a little cot to sleep on," she recalled, "and we gave them snacks before their mothers came for them." For her, the project signaled "hope" and that the government "would do something to help them."[32]

Several stories came from those whose lives were changed by the WPA. Lillian Wrinkle grew up in the small town of Benton, Tennessee, with a dream of one day going to college. Graduating from high school in 1939, she spent the year looking for a way out of Benton, but with neither transportation nor opportunity, hope was dimming. "Finally the chance came" for her to travel the fifteen miles to Cleveland, Tennessee, as a neighbor who was a teacher at a local CCC camp offered to take her to Cleveland to sign up for the WPA. She worked as the teacher's aide in the camp, helping to teach the CCC boys to "read and write." When the camp disbanded, she left the program and signed on with the National Youth Administration (NYA) to realize her dream of going "to business school." For William Gordon, a black man in central Georgia, the Depression meant that he worked for ten cents a day with meals and a place to stay. Gordon placed the blame on Hoover, saying the president made it so "poor people who depended on the white man, he keep you hungry so you could work a little more." Times were tough, but with FDR came food and a "work program, the WPA." Gordon made twenty dollars and ten cents every two weeks, he recalled, and he credited Roosevelt with being "the best president . . . for the people."[33]

Most of those interviewed viewed the WPA as a positive project that gave aid to folks who needed it and left behind a stronger nation. Stella Bowie said that the WPA projects in the area of Jacksonville, Florida, during the 1930s "gave men something to work for and have a little money and have a little dignity left." She believed that the terminal unemployment of the primary breadwinner in many families was detrimental not only to the recovery of the country but also to the people who made up the country. Even as the people saw the good in the WPA, however, they related jokes about the project. Young Lester of Atlanta said that the WPA "was the first time shovels had been invented with seats on them." Paul Maddox, also of Atlanta, told his interviewer about a terrible accident on a road the WPA was working on. It seemed that "termites ate up the handles on the shovels they were using" to lean on, causing the roadworkers to fall and hurt themselves. James Harper said that some folks believed the WPA had more people than jobs, leading them to change the name to "We Piddle Around."[34]

Maybe this perception was held more firmly by those in the cities, as few jokes or criticisms of the WPA came from informants from rural areas. Among these people, there was little criticism of the WPA or any New Deal program as being soft or coddling workers. Many agreed with Lizzie Johnson of Bowdon, Georgia, in her assessment of the project. In recalling her brother's WPA employment, she said, "Folks didn't have no jobs or nothing and he would work on the roads" with the WPA. The labor was hard, but the family appreciated his ability to bring home some money. Lois Scroggins of neighboring Villa Rica, Georgia, pointed to the community benefits of the program: "They built a swimming pool and a regular recreation place" for the people to use, which helped bring folks "out of the dumps." Tom Skelton worked at a service station in rural Carnseville, Georgia, that also served as the WPA morning headquarters. Around 4 a.m. every weekday, the crew assembled while attending to that area's roads. He talked to the men—some from his area but many others from all over Georgia—and determined that without the WPA, "we would have fought among ourselves, because it had [gotten] to that point" of survival.

He labeled those he met in the early morning as "good honest working people [who] were caught" in a cycle that trapped them in poverty. Without the WPA, Skelton said, "they would have starved."[35]

The people knew how to work and understood that it was difficult. Getting a living had always been a difficult daily task in rural areas, as the traditional employers—agriculture and textiles—worked their people hard for low wages. And with the economic crisis, there were fewer jobs and even lower wages. As a result, most rural southerners had tremendous respect for the New Deal programs, particularly as efforts to improve their working experiences. One such program was the National Industrial Recovery Administration (NIRA). Created in 1933 as the linchpin to economic recovery, the program suspended antitrust laws to give business and industry the opportunity to create cartels to lower costs and risks in exchange for following general guidelines established by the federal government. Launched with much fanfare, including parades and other festive celebrations, NIRA became the first New Deal program to come into the South. Some of those interviewed remembered the Blue Eagle (the symbol of NIRA), primarily as it affected their wages. Maurice Sponcler recalled when NIRA raised the minimum wage in 1934 at the textile mill in Newnan, Georgia, from $6.60 a day to $12.00. The owner assembled the employees and told them that they were "going to have to double their efforts" or the mill would go out of business. But Sponcler said, NIRA "helped the mill get on its feet and make money." George Potts worked in the same mill sixty hours a week for seven to eight dollars a week. When FDR wrote the legislation that became NIRA, Potts's hours were cut to eight a day while his pay doubled. He found it funny in retrospect that the owners complained "they were going to go broke"; the mill continued to operate well into the 1990s. For Lillian Chambers, who was employed in a textile mill near Rome, Georgia, the NIRA initiative to cut hours and raise wages meant that "we was rich people then [because] you had a little money you could spend every now and then." Bessie Fowler also worked in this mill and explained that before NIRA, not only did the people have to work twelve hours, they also had to fill "a quota" to get the full pay. With the introduction of NIRA, however, hours were cut to eight and the quota eliminated. She remained thankful, as the transformation allowed her more time to spend with her family. Lynna Vaugh worked fifty-five hours a week for $5.60 in the mill before FDR. After NIRA went into effect, the mill "couldn't employ a person over forty hours without paying them time and a half and they had to pay them at least forty cents a hour to work." The changes transformed her way of life.[36]

Clause 7(a) was also part of the NIRA legislation; this clause gave workers the right to organize and bargain collectively through representatives of their own choosing. What is surprising is how few recalled 7(a), problems with NIRA, or the Great Textile Strike of 1934. The South represented a significant portion of the textile industry in the 1930s; nearly 65 percent of the cotton spindles in 1937 were located in Georgia, Alabama, and the Carolinas. The early part of the decade was a tense time for the textile industry, as mill operators' use of the stretch-out—adding work to some workers' loads while laying off others—encouraged walkouts, strikes, and violence from Alabama to the Carolinas. When NIRA was passed, unions such as the American Federation of Labor's United Textile Workers were excited by the potential. However, by 1934 it had become clear that most complaints filed by workers and the union about textile company violations regarding hours and the minimum wage were being ignored by the National Industrial Relations Board, set up to enforce the NIRA codes. In July 1934, about 22,000 textile workers in Alabama went on strike over items the NIRA rules were supposed to ensure—minimum wage, reduced workweek, and union rights. Throughout the summer, tensions between the workers and managers increased, culminating on September 4, 1934, when nearly 400,000 textile workers, half of whom were in the South, walked off their jobs. The Great Textile Strike, one of the nation's largest, forced the governors of Georgia, the Carolinas, and Alabama to call out their state militias. Violence ensued—seven strikers were killed in Honea Path, South Carolina, and many others were beaten, bayoneted, and teargassed throughout the region. At the end of the month, FDR offered to step in and create a mediation board to deal with some of the issues, resulting in the abandonment of the strike on October 3. The problems exposed as a result of the walkout would not be adequately dealt with until after the passage of the Wagner Act in 1935. But even with this stronger legislation, the concerted effort of the Congress of Industrial Organizations (CIO), beginning in 1937, organized less than 7 percent of the South's 350,000 textile workers by the end of the decade. Out of all the interviews, only one person mentioned this situation, although many recalled working in mills, living in mill towns, or having parents or family who were in the mills. Joseph Foster recalled the "violence at the time" as the "corporations were fighting" the work of the unions. But, he recalled, the companies were forced to accept that "wages went up and the forty hour week." That was the extent of those who admitted to recalling anything that resembled worker/management violence.[37]

Most of the informants instead chose to recall how the New Deal programs were part of the transformation and reformation taking place in the midst of the crisis. Because the New Deal brought a level of self-respect and pride to a people in desperate need of hope, many individuals focused on the positive attributes of the New Deal and credited FDR with making it feel as though they were part of the recovery. Ada Kane recalled how working with the National Youth Administration (NYA) changed her life. Working in the zoology lab cleaning slides, she helped earn her way through college. But she said the experience was more than just that—"it was much more important that [I] felt like I was doing something and earning something." Lucy Wagner was hired by the school district of Forsyth, Georgia, in 1937 to teach school under a federal government initiative that paid her fifty dollars a month and was matched by the county. Not only was she glad to have a job, but also the pay made her feel as though she "was rich." George Weaver went to work for the Farm Security Administration in Calhoun, Georgia, "trying to rehabilitate [farmers and] help them from losing their farms to mortgage foreclosures." Wyolene Warren recalled a destitute woman in the community whom the WPA aided by helping her set up a public kinder-garten: "She was a wonderful teacher [to] all my children." Margaret Askew of Carrollton, Georgia, recalled that if one was a farmer and made less than five hundred dollars a year, "the government gave you fifty pounds of cotton" to make your own mattress. Delmas Easterwood remembered that "one of the other social workers . . . showed us how to make cotton mattresses . . . at the school building and we made mattresses one whole day." Dora Hol-combe and her family from Elijay, Georgia, made her own mattress this way and remembered that "we was real thrilled about having a mattress [and not having] to pull that straw to make beds out of."[38]

The federal government made inroads into the South through a variety of programs designed not only to meet the immediate needs of the people through jobs but also to introduce new methods, technologies, and ways of being that might help break the cycle of poverty and exploitation. One project, which was later used during World War II, involved traveling can-neries designed to assist in preserving food. Winnie Murphee recalled that a "woman" set up a "big cannery just out in the open" near Heflin, Ala-bama, with pressure cookers—"trying to help people." Maggie Jones was that woman; as the supervisor for the Public Works Administration (PWA) canning center, she "canned 1,700 cans of food for the people that were on relief." She explained that as part of the relief effort in Alabama, the people were to raise "food in their gardens where they would have something to live on and they didn't know how to take care of it and so Mildred Bynum

[Jones's boss] and I supervised the [canning] center." It helped, Jones said, because it "gave everybody who worked there . . . something to eat and something to look forward to."[39]

These types of efforts were not lost on those who were helped. The people understood that this was a new way of governing and that a reformation was taking place within their communities and the nation. No longer were the people going to be ignored. Viola Elder of Carrollton, Georgia, recalled that the federal relief effort gave her and her family clothes and food because they could not find work to support themselves. Roosevelt, she said, "made it better where people could get some help, you know, even if they didn't have a job." Audrey Willingham perhaps put it best when discussing FDR's programs to help low-income Americans get homes: "I remember he helped the people who couldn't help themselves."[40]

There were few critical assessments of the New Deal or Roosevelt among those interviewed. Many people in the South "loved him . . . almost to the point of worshipping him," according to Norma Brumback of Gadsden, Alabama. But some "hated him worse than death." Those who fell into the latter category voiced their disdain for three reasons: the New Deal made people lazy, it went against the individualist American credo, and it was socialism. Dorothy Askin, whose family benefited from the NYA, was critical of the New Deal because the people on relief "were frowned on as being lazy, incompetent leeches, [and were] shunned by ordinary folk." F. C. Dougherty of Floyd County, Georgia, complained that the New Deal programs "started the giveaway programs . . . giving people everything and not working for it." The New Deal was wrong, Oscar Heimerich believed, because a "person had to earn [his own] living and the New Deal was devised to give people something for nothing." This led to a society in which the American people believed "that the government owed them a living." Carroll County's Odus Duffey said, "I think he was the starting of all this white and black mixing," and Edgar Rhodes pointed to the programs causing "us to get a little closer to socialism."[41]

It is interesting to note that one program rarely mentioned is the Agricultural Adjustment Act (AAA). Although the rural South was agricultural and was hit hard by the decline in farm prices, few of those interviewed chose to recall this program—perhaps because it helped to force them off the land (as many were employed at one level or another of tenancy) and that was not a positive memory. Certainly, since many were involved in agricultural pursuits, they had to have run up against AAA regulators in the region, but their silence on the topic suggests their belief that it did not have a positive effect on their way of life. The question that invited discussion concerning the New Deal simply asked what programs the interviewees could recall or which ones affected their lives. Even though most respondents did not become part of the CCC or the WPA, since these programs were viewed socially as positive, their mention suggests the type of unity of purpose that was associated with FDR and the New Deal. The same holds true for the informants' recall of NIRA; a few recalled what it was, but most of them had little understanding of what it did or how it operated.[42]

The critics of the New Deal and FDR were in the extreme minority. While some may have not liked one particular program or felt that the president had not done enough about another issue, overwhelmingly those interviewed saw FDR and his programs as saviors in their lives, their communities, and their country. They saw in FDR someone who was willing to do what was necessary to get the country, as Raymond Giles said, "back on our feet." That meant taking on "the big dogs in New York" and making sure that the benefits of society were evenly distributed. Dolly Hancock "felt like he was going to be a president that would help the working class people," while E. LeRoy Jordan reflected that FDR clearly was "for the workin' class people." They pointed to FDR's New Deal programs as evidence of his commitment to them. These programs "changed everything," Allan Furline believed, by restoring "faith in the workers by letting them work for their food." Roosevelt "put people to work," Leonard Crenshaw said, so that they could, as Helen Rakeshaw added, keep "from going hungry and [keep] their families together."[43]

Perhaps this last comment, more than any other, helps to explain why Roosevelt so appealed to the working people. His programs "opened up jobs for people" and allowed their families to survive, said Maggie Robinson. In their understanding, before he was president, no one cared for the poor or the rural people. When elected, "he went in there and said he was going to help," recalled Lizzie Johnson of Bowdon, Georgia, and "he passed a law so that everybody working were suppose[d] to pay their hand thirteen dollars and thirty-three cents a week." As a laborer in the local Sewell textile mill, this was a vast improvement in wages and guaranteed a better life for her and her children. Many of those interviewed credited FDR with the advent of better working hours as well. "He changed the working hours to eight hours a day," recalled Geneva Stuart, giving more people work in "three shifts" and more time for the family. Lillian Chambers credited him with bringing in the union at her job in Rome, Georgia, which meant better wages and more free time for her family. For the young family headed by

Woodrow and Frances Maffet living in Monroe, Georgia, without the aid of FDR and the change in work rules, they did not "believe [they] would have ever made it" through the hard times. It is interesting to note again that these wage and hour benefits were mentioned without the corresponding inclusion of union activities or the Wagner Act. Instead, FDR is credited with the improvement in their quality of life, which may suggest a more modern, antiunion position held by the informants.[44]

What the interviews do reveal is a nearly universal adoration of Roosevelt and his New Deal. Henry Clark still believed that FDR was "the greatest man we ever knew" when interviewed fifty years after his death. When pressed as to why he adored Roosevelt, Lee Weaver said that Roosevelt knew what he was doing and "took politics out of managing the people." People came to love the president for what they believed he was doing. Almedia Wray responded to the question of what was her impression of FDR with a simple "I loved him, honey." Bessie Birdsong explained (perhaps for both her and all those others who loved Roosevelt) that his programs liberated the people and country: "If you didn't like Roosevelt," she said, "you better not say anything about it because they'd be somebody ready to fight you!"[45]

The people's support of Roosevelt, at least in their recollections, sometimes invoked religious symbolism. Jennie Kilburn called him "an idol . . . a savior of the land." Nell Everett saw him as a "savior" who "was going to save the world." Anne Pierce viewed him as a "Godsend," and Stewart Hull "thought he was a God-sent man," even though Hull had a job and did not benefit from any of the New Deal programs. Perhaps this adoration came from what Charles Ricks of Soperton, Georgia, called FDR's ability to "relieve the anxiety and the fear of the people." Ricks felt that the president was "blessed with some kind of gift to know what to do and how to do it." Lucy Wagner of Jasper, Georgia, simply saw him as "an angel that was sent down from God and Heaven . . . [to bring] peace and security to our country." Annie Mae Cook recalled her grandmother saying FDR was like "Moses leading our country out of the wilderness." These metaphors are not unique, as others, such as Braudis Barrett, likened FDR's leadership to helping lead "us out of the wilderness." For Geneva Ariail, the folks she knew in the area around Commerce, Georgia, "likened him almost to a god because he had saved them."[46]

Those interviewed were quick to point out why they held FDR and his programs in such high regard. When he was elected, remembered Magolalene Martin of Atlanta, FDR "made it where people who didn't have nothing could get a little more than they did have to start with." She meant specifically the influence and voice of the people in government. "He fixed it where you could have more of a say-so in government, when you didn't have none at all before." This was a "big change," said Ann Curry, and FDR made it so that people could "have jobs and things" and were not simply ignored because they were poor. It was his commitment to the people that created a more optimistic view of the future, even in the midst of crisis. Folks "didn't make a big living" on the New Deal, remembered Sewell Barron, but the programs "gave us an idea to look for in the future and something to carry us day to day."[47]

Because of this reformation, many of those interviewed saw FDR's policies as revolutionary, primarily because, as George Stoval said, they "put people to work." Roosevelt's rhetoric that everyone had to contribute to the recovery and that no person would be left behind resonated with those interviewed, as they saw his programs as a way to be part of the process. It created excitement among them because they felt that government, under the aegis of FDR, was on their side. "I think it made a lot of difference to the ways of the country," recalled Carroll County's Isabel Hester, because the programs "created better jobs for people." The government was finally, the interviews reveal, on their side.[48]

They were also aware of FDR's critics, which only steeled them in their loyalty. Norma Brumback knew that "the rich people" did not like the fact that FDR was "passing so many acts for the little man" and were trying to make it seem as though he were a bad president. Frank Hudson also pointed to "the capitalists . . . who controlled the national banks" as the ones trying to make it seem as though Roosevelt were destroying the American system. But a new way of thinking about America was emerging, and this excited many of those interviewed. Bill Curtis knew that FDR was "stretching the powers of government quite a bit" but also believed that this was necessary for the country's survival. The revolutionary programs and FDR's appeal to the people were not lost on them, as they witnessed the emergence of a new type of government. "It caused a different way of thinking," said Charles Ricks; "it caused people to have a different view about the government" and what government could and could not do. Some, such as Miriam Merrell, thought that "the New Deal was very socialistic," but with so many people out of work and "hobos riding the rails all the time trying to find jobs," Roosevelt "had to do something and do it quick."[49]

The larger purpose of FDR's programs was not lost in these individuals' recollections, for many respondents understood that the New Deal was necessary so that other, less democratic, solutions could be avoided. Urban Farnsworth believed that the radicalism of FDR's programs prevented the country from turning to communism. "I think it really pulled us out of a bad hole," he said. Without these drastic measures, which demanded "government stepping in to rescue the country," according to Earnest Pierce, the likelihood of recovery or preserving the American system of government was in jeopardy. "You wonder," recalled Louis Dickey, "if we hadn't have had . . . somebody the people had confidence in what would have happened to our government." Paul Morgan knew what would have happened: "if Roosevelt hadn't been elected president . . . we would have changed types of government." Regardless of the radical nature of the programs and the growing influence of the federal government, the people saw these solutions as necessary for the survival of the American way of life. Paul Maddox qualified his comments about Roosevelt by identifying himself as a Republican, even as he credited FDR with not only saving the country from the likes of "an Adolf Hitler" but also making sure that the country would remain committed to the "free enterprise system."[50]

What forced FDR to take such drastic action was the desperate nature of American society in the 1930s. Most people have difficulty understanding the depth of the country's impoverishment during the era, choosing instead to hear and see it as a nostalgic recollection. Even when interviewed, some people described the era as part of their martyred past, with some hardship, but generally as a time when there was little crime, prices were low, and everyone worked together. What makes these oral histories interesting is the dearth of people who fail to reflect on either the dire straits of the country or the importance of FDR's New Deal. "It might not have been the greatest thing under the sun," recalled Ed Isakson about the many New Deal programs, "but it sure was great in that particular time."[51]

Historical memory sometimes blurs our understanding of the past. Certainly these recollections regarding FDR and the New Deal underwent some revision from the Depression era to the time in which the stories were told. But several issues reveal themselves that suggest that while memory may fade, core ideals remain. In nearly all the interviews, the people believed that FDR and the New Deal had helped them. The manner in which they had been assisted varied. While some had been aided through direct relief or employment and recalled specific programs such as the CCC or the WPA, few had actually worked for the programs. Many of those who related stories about the New Deal recalled the benefits the programs had brought to the people, the local community, and the country as a whole.

This speaks to the success of the New Deal, as it rehabilitated the un-employed and encouraged belief in a more hopeful future. The programs that affected some personally were recalled with great fondness, with each respondent suggesting that the New Deal and FDR saw them as people first and casualties of the collapse second. The interviews reveal a pride that arose from both the individuals' sacrifices and the assistance, as though the privations meant something larger than not having enough food or cloth-ing—that their sacrifices and the assistance provided by the government proved the greatness of the republic and its people. The recollections of the people point to the effectiveness of FDR's goal of building hope through government intervention to salvage democracy (and capitalism) by creating a government ethos that was inclusive both in granting the rights to food, shelter, and work to all people and in demanding that everyone had to work together to make this American dream a reality.

"THE FINER THINGS OF LIFE WERE A LITTLE BIT SCARCE"

Accommodating Consumption

When Ann Rehberg recalled the Great Depression in rural Grady County, Georgia, she admitted that the family never went without food or basic supplies. As farmers, they grew and made most of what they needed. But she nevertheless remembered that the "finer things of life were a little bit scarce at the time." Lacking the money they knew they needed to experience a better way of being, many tried to make it seem as though the lack of luxuries did not matter. But their words and memories reveal their ambiguity. "It was happy times," said Mary McClain, when neighbors visited and church was the central focus of her life. Yet she and others completed these memories with "even though there wasn't any money." They were aware that their experience, although in memory laced with happiness, came as a result of their inability to consume—they would say, "You don't have to have money to have a good time," even as the larger social structure was saying, through advertising or government action, the very opposite. Helen Vasant placed this duality in context during her interview, saying that "in the midst of hard times you don't always realize you are struggling. When you look back and compare it to what you have got today . . . we didn't realize how much we suffered in the midst of it." Yet the structure of her recollection shows that she did indeed understand that she and others lacked those things that identified the good life, and these things came from money that they did not have.[1]

Their recollections were strategies employed to soften the harsh realities of the past and soften the transitions they were inextricably caught up in. Many rural residents understood that their traditional ways were either in the process of being replaced or were gone altogether. As Gary Cross convincingly argues in his *All-Consuming Century*, during the first third of the last century a new social ideal emerged that connected what people consumed with their perceived roles in society. This consumerism both redefined democracy, as equality came to be defined by the choices of consumption, and "allowed Americans to free themselves from their old, relatively secure but closed communities" and enter the open and individualistic mass American society. During the Depression era, as capitalism was at its nadir, advertisers, bankers, factory owners, and even the government made the advantages of consumerism known to the people and sold them new, better, and more modern products to lay the "groundwork for a full-scale ideology of consumers' democracy after World War II."[2]

This new American way of life began to permeate their consciousnesses, and their desire to be part of this new way of being brought conflicting feelings of failure, guilt, pride, and patriotism. Many came to realize, as Lela Knight recalled, that "the things we wanted every day were not beyond our reach if we wanted them bad enough." It was this type of conflict—want versus need—that defined the new consumerism and was at the heart of the transition in the new South. In the midst of economic and social crisis, new patterns were replacing old ones; as is typical of this modernist shift, the people were torn between the traditions of the past and the ideals of the future.[3]

With the realities of hard times all around, it must have been difficult to be optimistic. Yet, as Mary McClain recalled, the folks around her in rural Georgia were all in the "same shape," and although they lacked many of the luxuries of today—such as "refrigerators, electric lights," and "washing machines"—they maintained a positive outlook on the future. "[We] didn't give up hope," she said.[4]

Part of this optimism reflected the effective mix of politics and propaganda that was Roosevelt's New Deal. Right from the start, he and his advisors came to understand that while their programs were able to infuse money into the economy, their larger purpose was to encourage a sense of hope in a society overwhelmed with images of hopelessness. How could one offset the image of soup kitchens, of run-down houses and buildings, of vagrants wandering the country in search of work, food, or a future? The Depression era challenged the citizens to rediscover the meaning of America, and FDR and his administrators saw the larger purpose of their programs tied to this reformation. Linked explicitly to the New Deal's complex mixture of political, economic, and social activism was an underlying appeal to nationalism. Unlike the hyperpatriotism of, for example, Germany during the same period, American nationalism linked the economic crisis with an appeal for inclusion. This meant accepting the concept of consumption

Lunchtime for these Georgia peach pickers. (Courtesy Library of Congress.)

as part of a citizen's social responsibility. Increasingly, as historian Charles McGovern argues, the "American people . . . came to equate the consumer with the citizen, a consumer standard of living with democracy, and the full participation in such an economy of spending and accumulation with being an American." Although the process had been under way since the turn of the twentieth century, only during the Depression did the trinity of politics, advertising, and ideology allow for the proliferation and acceptance of this more modernist conception of the consumer's role in society. Advertisers increasingly came to suggest that buying a commodity represented more than just satisfying a need, that it was linked to the larger social concept McGovern labels "the individual's civic role." In a complex way, consumption was enjoined to suffrage, for to choose a commodity meant the citizen was voting for the company that produced it and, in a larger context, the society that encouraged its production. Not consuming meant being outside the accepted ideals and indicated inferior social and political status. "Consumption," McGovern writes, "was a symbol of American social democracy and the engine of social equality." The mantra of the new era suggested that the best way to be a good American was to consume, and to not consume might contribute to the downfall of the republic.[5]

Lawrence Glickman has examined how workers played a key role in this new consumerism by linking the ideals of collective labor with the emergence of the modern consumer-directed economy. In the early part of the century, as their identity as workers took on an increasingly complex patina, they abandoned the call for the release from wage slavery and the acceptance of socialism and instead sought to help create a "republic of wage earners" contributing to the greater good of all America.[6]

The American South lagged in the adoption and acceptance of this new role for workers. The 1936 *Report on Economic Conditions of the South* paints a desperate portrait of the region. With regards to labor, the authors suggest that "northern producers and distributors are losing profits and northern workers are losing work because the South cannot afford to buy their goods." Because of low wages paid to workers and the often temporary nature of their employ, many southern workers were attracted to returning to the farm, which weakened the market. In the last year of the study (1935), yearly per capita wages in the South were less than half that for the rest of the country. These low wages and lack of economic stimulus were not a Depression by-product, the report concluded, but a terminal condition of the region. If the situation could not be rectified, the ability of the New Deal or any other program to succeed was judged highly doubtful.[7]

"It was not just me and my wife, but everyone had a hard time," remembered Harvey Bray. Living in Franklin County, Georgia, at the time, he and those around him "didn't expect much." Most informants echoed Walt Wilson's recollection that the lack of money "bothered all parts of your life, couldn't get no candy, chewin' gum, . . . no job, . . . couldn't do nothin'." The situation affected all parts of their lives. It had a negative impact on Larry Carroll's ability to date, as the "ten cent show and a nickel Coke" was more money than he or his family could spare. In her interview, Jennie Kilburn lamented that despite things being so cheap back then, there was barely enough "to feed and clothe" her family. Annie Priest perhaps described the situation best when she said that "it was just living. It was hard to make a living back then."[8]

Things were tough in the rural South. The problems outlined by the 1936 report pale in comparison to the recollections of those who lived through the time period. Ada Hardin was widowed with seven children during the 1930s, and while her family always had food to eat, she was always aware of things she could not provide. "We had to work hard and do without a lot of things . . . that were wanted." In nearly all the interviews, the informants were able to recall specific prices paid for coffee, flour, sugar, bread, and a whole host of other commodities. These recollections included the prices of not only food products (which, it can be argued, are needs) but also automobiles, movies, cigarettes, Cokes, and a host of other items not essential for survival. While most informants brought up the prices to remind the interviewer how cheap things were in the 1930s compared to the early 1990s, most also echoed Horace Maynard from Lawrenceville, Georgia, in asserting that "the cost of living was cheap . . . but you didn't have money to buy it with. Food was cheap, but you didn't have the money." Ruby Henry was in Atlanta at the time and recalled forgoing a nickel Coke so that she could "buy milk." It bothered her, because she knew there were things she wanted, but the family simply "had to do without." Most of those who lived and worked in the rural South went from day to day, just as Nellie Blackwelder did: "We had to do with what we had, no money to spend [and] barely enough money to buy you a pair of shoes and your clothes to keep warm." Cantankerous A. B. Baughtman responded to the question "what was the cost of living like, as in buying stuff" with "well, they whatn't no cost to it. You didn't, whatn't nothin' to buy. You didn't have nothin' to buy it with." Josephine Taff fondly recalled riding with her father to the country store several times a year during the latter part of the 1920s. By the '30s, however, the trips had become less and less frequent, until finally she "just pretty well stayed home because [the family] had nothing to spend." Henry Clark's family continued to trade at the country store several times a year in northwestern Alabama, but they bought very little, often "a piece of cheese or a sack of crackers . . . or fruit."[9]

If these recollections were unique, one might see the phenomenon as a type of reverse nostalgia. But in the hundreds of interviews collected, most informants recall similar stories of having to do without those commodities they wanted. It was not as if they were out of the consumerist loop and so were unaware of those things they lacked. Nor were they happy and satisfied because they were not sophisticated enough to know what they lacked. That they knew and understood they were deficient as consumers and Americans points to their internalized guilt. "Well," said Sewell Barron, "we learned to live without the things that we thought we had to have but couldn't afford."[10]

There was an understanding among those interviewed that they wanted to buy but lacked the means to fulfill this desire. In Melissa Walker's examination of rural farm women in Tennessee during this period, she points out that some women in the countryside attempted to mimic the consumptive behavior of those from the towns and cities—"consumption was tangible proof of their success"—yet few were able to "adopt these trappings of middle-class life." This brought about a variety of emotions, from an uneasy sense of failure and guilt to a proud resilience. People understood that there were things they should consume, items that would make their lives more comfortable and perhaps happier, yet they were conflicted over what to do. Thelma Moncus recalled the effect on her father during the crisis, as the children knew that he could not provide the things they felt were necessary for their happiness. "My daddy was out of work a lot," she recalled. This meant money was tight and tensions were sometimes high. "Well, it made us all feel bad and nervous and my mother and father were nervous [because] we couldn't have things like the other children." Jean Buidrillard writes that "man-as-consumer considers the experience of pleasure an obligation," like a "duty." Pleasure is connected to consumption, as work, wages, and experience create an atmosphere for purchasing those things that might bring happiness. The interconnection between consumption and happiness, or even citizenship, is at the core of Thelma's parents' feelings of nervousness, for their inability to consume challenged their understanding of happiness and raised questions concerning their ability to raise a family. The ability to buy the things your family needed to be considered happy was not unequivocally connected to a better standard of living but to a sense of empowerment, participation, and being. It identified the consumer as American.[11]

Those interviewed were aware of being unable to fulfill their wants. "We wanted other things," Lena Stimpson recalled of her family life in the 1930s. As farmers, they were not "as happy as we wanted to be, we wanted more for the family." Many of the things that were supposed to be part of the normal household were missing, as many recollected. Grover Hardin pointed out that "some poor people didn't even have a sewing machine! They made clothes with just an ordinary hand needle and thread." Nowhere in his statement was there an understanding that just a generation or so earlier in his town of Redbag, Alabama, everyone used a needle and thread. Catherine Bohne's sister-in-law was an avid smoker but had to give up the luxury of cigarettes while living with Catherine and Catherine's husband. Instead, she would "get the butt" of a tossed-away cigarette and make it her own. Ruth Rhymer walked "ten thousand miles" in all sorts of weather because she and her family did not have the money for a car. But she asserted that this did not make her feel inadequate, as "hardly nobody had cars" back then. Ann

Rehberg's father did have enough money to buy a car. In fact, he paid cash. The result was that "it cost him a lot of friends and he lost his first election as judge [in Grady County, Georgia] because of it." Bessie Birdsong did what many folks who had little money did: window-shop. Living in Atlanta during the 1930s, she and a friend would take a quarter and spend the day going into stores to "look at the merchandise we couldn't buy." They would return home about the same time their children would come home from school. Ed Isakson recalled that his mother loved to window-shop during the 1930s. She would take two sandwiches with her and spend the entire day shopping in Atlanta without spending a dime: "you didn't have money to buy [so] you'd look in there at the merchandise."[12]

Wanting, but also understanding that one could not consume, created feelings of inadequacy, guilt, or depression. Dolly Hancock did not want to be part of this underclass, shunning those activities of her family that placed her in a position of being viewed as poor. For example, she "wouldn't be caught dead in a wagon." In the middle of the decade, she "marr[ied] up" and had an electric refrigerator. Travis Dorrough felt that the inability of his parents to provide meant they were "down at the very bottom of the barrel." He remembered them going into grocery stores with no money and only a promise to pay in the future. But the manner in which he recalled their situation underscored his own sense of hopeless desperation: "I'll pay you for this [when I get some money] but I cannot go home and see my children crying, hungry and going to bed hungry."[13]

To not be able to consume, to be happy, and to be American naturally brought forth feelings of guilt and hopelessness. Mary Jackson's parents tried to shield the family from the hardships they were experiencing, but she knew that "there were things that we needed that we just couldn't afford." Ethel Shockley agreed, noting that the worst part of the Depression was "just not having things we really wanted" and witnessing the sense of failure on her parents' faces. Henry Green recalled that these situations made people increasingly "frustrated and angry." Not having any money to spend while at the same time wanting to consume was difficult to manage. Gene Autry remembered being so hard up for money that he would go to the local store and watch others drinking Cokes and eating candy bars: "[I] wanted one so bad and didn't have a nickel to buy it. That's a bad shape to be in." George Weaver's family learned to get by, like so many others, with less. But he also witnessed the larger toll it was taking, generating an "inferiority complex from being in real poverty." Lee Weaver's family likewise did all they could to make ends meet, but he also recalled that "many people

A hitchhiking family waiting along the highway in Macon, Georgia. (Courtesy Library of Congress.)

laughed at us" because of some of the strategies they employed on the small farm to survive. This sense of shame permeates many of the interviews, particularly those of high school–aged individuals competing within their peer group for validation. "It was not a happy time for me growing up as a school student," recalled A. Young Lester. His father "didn't have enough money" for books, lunches, and the other things Young felt he needed to go to high school. By the time he was fourteen, he had to start working to "put myself through high school." But his grades suffered; he "barely got by" in his studies. Annie Priest's "daddy couldn't afford books," so she had to quit school. One of the more interesting stories underscores the sense of futility and hopelessness and at the same time introduces the ideology of pride. Lanier Weathers did not have much growing up in Rockmills, Alabama, during the Depression. Like others, the Weathers family made do with what they had, and where everyone contributed to the family table, he and his brothers would hunt. Unfortunately, they "didn't have money to buy gun shells." Armed with "sticks and rocks," they would run down rabbits and kill them. In listening to his retelling of the story, it is hard not to hear his hopelessness—"we'd kill it with a stick and a rock."[14]

Many within the Roosevelt administration understood the interconnection between the South's underconsumption and the economic recovery. FDR wanted the South to become more integrated into the national economy, recognizing its primacy in bringing about a more centralized and planned American economy. The *Report on Economic Conditions of the South* had outlined the major problems with the rural South: a large population of tenant farmers (over 50 percent) working small parcels of land haunted by the continued erosion of the soil; an average income that was half the national average ($314 for the South, $604 nationally) and even lower for those rural folk involved in tenant farming; high school retention and literacy rates that were the lowest in the country; a lack of sanitary water supplies; underemployment permeating the region even before the Depression, and chronic unemployment, particularly among the rural farmers, after the crash; three-quarters of all the employed children in the United States between the ages of ten and fifteen (even as the region had fewer children proportionately); high interest rates and local levies resulting partly from the fact that the region's banks held only 11 percent of deposited monies. The report identified the rural South as the "low-income belt . . . of sickness, misery, and unnecessary death." Yet for all of its negative economic and social analysis, the report concluded that the South was the "nation's greatest untapped market." The people there wanted to purchase "houses, radios, butter, beef, vegetables, milk, eggs, dresses, shirts, [and] shoes."[15]

The South was linked to the rest of the country in this regard, as the American economy came to be driven by consumer industries during the first third of the century. Higher wages were sought as capable of satisfying an ever-increasing list of needs. Historian Lawrence Glickman argues that as workers accepted the ideal of wage labor, they actively helped construct the consumer culture that developed, by "redefining wages in consumerist terms." Their wages and what they purchased came to be seen as part of the ongoing redefinition of working-class life in America and part of the larger engine of commerce. Their participation in the economy became almost a civic duty. The consumerist ideology brought with it a new republicanism, in which the right to buy and define oneself through consumption suggested an equality in the marketplace and, by extension, within the whole of the American landscape.[16]

Many observers during the Depression era—whether sociologists, consumer advocates, or government officials—recognized that the new economy had accepted the expanded idea of "need" beyond food, clothing, and shelter to include entertainment, transportation, and occasional "luxury" items. But as Ernest Porter recalled, "the money just wasn't there" after you paid for all the necessities; "You just didn't have money for these extra things."[17]

Money, both as a wage and as a symbol, thus underwent redefinition. It came to be seen as a just reward for services provided and as a means by which to consume those commodities once reserved for the elites. Not that the worker or rural farmer sought out caviar, Cadillacs, and the like, but people did come to view their money as a means of defining themselves outside their class. Money, and the choices it availed, allowed the consumer to create identity through consumption. What one wanted was no longer seen within the more frugal lens of the earlier era but came to be valued as a justifiable pursuit. Viviana A. Zelizer explores *The Social Meaning of Money* and concludes that the "modern consumer society turned the spending of money not only into a central economic practice but into a dynamic, complex cultural and social activity." One had the right to consume. "The first curtains I ever got, I was so proud of them" because they suggested success, recalled Opal Hunter. She collected and peddled walnuts to acquire the money for the three panels. When they went up, she thought they "were something." Money meant something. Cornelia Presley recalled that she once "dropped a nickel . . . in the grass and spent an hour trying to find it and never could find it and it's like losing a fortune almost 'cause you could buy a great big old hamburger . . . and eat good!"[18]

Presley's understanding of the value of that nickel was part of a more complex transformation of the meaning of work and money intertwined with modernity. Consumption became the vital link in the connection between production and the maintenance of the economy. Akin to the organizational ideas that linked the factory setting to its workers and urban areas to its residents, the unification of consumer and producer allowed for better organization and planning of the economy. "Consumption," Jean Baudrillard explains, "is a system which assures the regulation of signs and integration of the group: it is simultaneously a morality and a system of communication." The act of consuming is part of a larger structure that links the products to the consumer and by extension the social and cultural identity of the citizenry. Consumption is therefore not the frenzied desire to possess but the ideological desire to become part of the larger society.[19]

During the 1930s and the Great Depression, this new consumer consciousness achieved widespread acceptance. To suggest that the ideals of consumption achieved validity during this terrible economic crisis seems almost oxymoronic, but as the decade wore on, more people came to see the legitimacy of a consumer-directed economy. For example, the secretary of labor, James L. Davis, echoed President Roosevelt's oft-cited complaint that the nation suffered from underconsumption, suggesting that if the 7 million wage-earning women in the country and their 23 million dependents would buy a new dress, the unemployment problem in the textile and tangential industries would evaporate. Leaders in both industry and politics understood that the key to the recovery, and indeed America's future, rested on the consumption by the masses. According to Glickman, this new American way was based on the "construction of a consumerist political economy" balanced between economic consumption and political organization.[20]

Roosevelt's New Deal, especially after 1935, adopted this ethos. The organizations created, from the Works Progress Administration to the National Youth Administration, sought to put real money in the hands of the people who simply had too little to spend. Lena Stimpson remembered that because "the pay was so little," they had to save everything for food and there was no "money to spend on anything else." This forced many to save and to keep valuable resources out of the economy. Clare Doherty wanted a roasting pan so much that she scrimped and saved "nickels and pennies . . . until I had enough money to buy my roast[ing] pan." Ruby Henry saved her pennies for three months to have the sixty-nine cents necessary to buy her daughter a birthday dress. John Gillespie remembers going to the local store to just look and see, for the family never had extra money to buy anything. Whether through the legitimation of the right to collective bargaining in the Wagner Act or the wages paid to Tennessee Valley Authority (TVA) workers, the underlying ideal was to create an expanding consumer base. FDR's advisors held firm to the belief that through these work-relief efforts, the people's hope would be restored and new markets would open, stimulating private production. Mildred Williams witnessed the results in Randolph County, Alabama: "Roosevelt had a big [effect as the] standards of living started being raised. When they got a paying job [with the government,] they started buying more furniture, more food and better clothes."[21]

Many in the rural areas understood the connection between the infusion of capital and the New Deal. The administration's policies had, by 1937, focused on growing a consumer-based economy. The New Deal's many programs put "money, cash money into the hands of the people," recalled Ray Carter. "People were paid every week, [and] of course, it was necessary that they spend what they got." A clear change came in the midst of the Depression era. Historian Meg Jacobs argues that the class reformation that took place during the 1930s pitted the advertisers' holdover 1920s view of the consumer economy, which sought to extend the middle-class markets by catering to women portrayed as frivolous, against a working-class economy focused on mass consumption and the production of cheap, yet quality, goods. This contest played itself out in the New Deal, as it "regarded the organization of consumers as workers as necessary halves" for the maintenance of a prosperous political economy. With the government and its policies behind them, the people thus came to want the emerging consumer culture, which promised "mass-produced abundance" and became linked to the American way of life.[22]

Jacobs and other historians have generally studied the Northeast, Midwest, or West to detail the acceptance of this policy. Often the focus is on the factory worker or other members of the traditional working class. Yet in rural areas throughout the South, this transition came with some tension. Ted Ownsby's examination of the emergence of a consumer culture in Mississippi argues that the traditional ideology of thrift, barter, and creating necessities conflicted with the increasingly powerful credo of consumption. By the time of the great crash, many rural southerners understood and accepted this new way of satisfying their needs. Mildred Williams, who spent the Depression years in rural Randolph County, Alabama, linked this new ethos with the larger economic recovery, stating that FDR's "idea . . . was to get the farmers out of the country and into the towns where they could have lights and electricity and a payday, a paycheck, every week." To many in the rural South, this modern connection was tied to electricity: "you know when we got electricity . . . it made it better," said a man named Rogers. Growing up on a small farm in Georgia, he recognized that his family could not afford all the things that electricity could provide, but they were able to get a refrigerator, paying a "little at a time." The arrival of electricity opened up a new system of wants for the rural residents. Former conveniences such as the wood stove and the icebox fell by the wayside, doing away with related traditional farm chores. "When electricity came along," recalled Stewart Hull, "well, uh, that almost did away with the ax." His understanding of the electrification of the area was "out of this world" and made him feel as if the whole family "had moved to town." The rural folk also understood the interconnectedness between electricity and the growth of the economy, in allowing families such as Emma Wallace's to "get more of the things [they] hadn't had." The arrival of electricity in these rural areas began in earnest after 1935 with the passage of the Rural Electrification Act (REA). Margaret Askew told her interviewer that now she could not "imagine not having electricity" and the things it brought, such as the radio and refrigerator. Electricity changed her world and helped her family in getting "all of those nice things that we don't even think of." The items of the modern economy became, in the minds of many in the South, normal, expected, and necessary.[23]

As the New Deal's policies affected rural areas, people such as Era Dennis found that they could "buy tractors . . . [and] insecticides" to grow better crops and make a "better income." This newfound power meant they could "spend and . . . buy more." The change was seen not as radical, according to Charles Clayton of Etowah, Tennessee, but as "reasonable." With the electricity from the TVA and other REA projects, the ability of ordinary people to buy washers, radios, ranges, refrigerators, and other commodities improved. And as the "cash flow got better," according to Ray Carter, "the whole world came back together."[24]

This renewed economy also encouraged national chains to make inroads into traditional neighborhood markets. Lizabeth Cohen's innovative study of the transition of Chicago's working-class neighborhoods argues that even as the chain stores and their mass-produced items entered the local marketplace, the members of the ethnic working class worked to retain their sense of identity. They did not become, as the advertisers might have hoped, simply the middle-class consumer ideal but instead used their buying power to negotiate within and accommodate the new economy. Those interviewed from the rural South saw their situation in much the same manner. Traditionally, transactions were written in each customer's record book to be paid when they "sold their first bale of cotton," according to Lee Weaver, whose family ran a small general store. Farmers would sell their crops and livestock and take the credit and buy the things they needed but could not produce on their own—including "sugar, coffee, and salt"—from locally owned stores. But these stores increasingly felt the pressure to compete with the newer chain stores such as Piggly Wiggly, where George Maddox remembers being able to "buy three and four bags [of groceries] for five to ten dollars." This new store, the first in the small town of Griffin, Georgia, meant significant change for the locals, even as it had to adapt to the needs of the community. While the "little corner grocery stores," where you told the counter people what you wanted and they gathered them, continued to compete, as the 1930s wore on, recalled Nell Everett, the newer grocery stores made it easier to shop: "you could walk up and down and pick up the groceries if you wanted." Increasingly, the new models replaced the old ones, and competition between the chain stores and local groceries ensued. In Monroe, Georgia, the national chain grocer A&P competed with local "modern" grocer Rogers. Both offered low prices and improved selection, but to Francis Maffet the canned goods made all the difference. "That was a big deal for us to get that can goods" for under ten cents a can, she recalled.[25]

Like those of Cohen's Chicago, the people in the rural areas continued to retain their traditional ways even as the ideals of modernity were changing the daily patterns of being. They appeared to understand that the barter network was quickly becoming a thing of the past and that they were increasingly being asked to become part of a larger, more modern economy. But in light of the lack of money and work in these areas, some traditional economic patterns remained part of their daily experience. One of the most fundamental of these traditional patterns was the recognition that their lack of money meant they had to be careful about spending. Many wives and mothers found themselves responsible for earmarking funds for necessary purchases, such as children's clothing or shoes. Brenita Reid was trying to raise her family near Roopville, Georgia, and found it difficult to make ends meet. "Times were so tight," she recalled, that the money she earned had to go to buy the children "decent" clothing for church and school.[26]

Having extra money for clothes or other items not considered necessities was a luxury most lacked. Buying things at a store was "like an outside world" to John Gillespie in Heard County. The family raised all the food they needed, and clothes were traded for once a year. Whatever money people were able to generate was carefully thought about before spending. "If you got a little money in your hand," Clara Knowlton recalled, "you would hold it so tight" and carefully decide what to spend it on, for you did not know when you might get more. Many of those interviewed echoed Velma Morgan's assessment of money during the Depression era. To her and the people she knew, the lack of money meant they had better "take care . . . and save . . . because they knew that they might have to go through it again in days to come." The uncertainty of the future was reflected in their understanding of the value and importance of the money they did not have. Martelle Payne sounded like many who lived through the era in saying that "once you live through a depression, you learn the value of money, or the value of anything you own." They were well aware that their lack of money, which a generation before might have caused little difficulty, had come to mean hardship and frugality. "We didn't have money to buy many new clothes," recalled Ploma Morrow of Bartow County, Georgia. While some may have tried to make their own clothes, they found that even that task was too expensive and, according to James Beavers, had to make "do with things that we had."[27]

Saving money, putting it aside for important purchases, or simply sacrificing needs became the norm for many of these folk during this economic crisis. The price of goods was reasonable enough, Clara Knowlton felt, "but you didn't have anything to buy it with." Charity Thomas would take her husband's old shirts and pants and make clothes for her children. "We['d] find anything to wrap them up in." Looking around their communities, they understood that others were in the same boat and found solace in this collective identity. Some, like Ruth Pickett, adjusted to the fact that "people just didn't have money to spend and they had to make do with what they had." She did not harbor ill will toward those who did have money, nor did she look down upon those with less. Everyone, she believed, was in the same crisis situation.[28]

While most agreed with Guy Knight's assessment from Gwinnett County—"there just wasn't any such thing as money at all"—some saw the problem as the result of the wealthy hanging on to their money. "They wouldn't turn it loose," recalled Mildred Hammond, and their selfishness "was the reason why much money wasn't circulating." Inez Parkerson agreed that the undefined "they" were responsible for the money crisis. She and her family would take a calf, fatten him up on "melon rinds," then try to sell him. But with no money in circulation, they ended up slaughtering and eating the beef themselves. "They killed the currency [and the] few got hold of it and the rest of them had to do without," she concluded.[29]

The limited amount of currency in circulation encouraged many of these rural folk to revert to the more traditional method of barter. An overwhelming number of those interviewed recalled trading items from their farms for goods at the store. Ralph McCain's mother would send him down to the store with a dozen eggs in exchange for a "can of salmons and a box of soda and a box of salt." The relative ease with which they traded for goods suggests that the ideals of the modern economy, which tied their consumption into a national network of economic growth, had not taken deep root. The rural South was not alone in this retention of the barter system or in its desire to remain somewhat detached from the modern consumer-directed economy emerging during the era. Daniel Horowitz points out in *The Morality of Spending* that during the economic crisis, while many in FDR's administration and within private industry were suggesting that the new economic model focus on the national consumer and the opening up of ignored markets, others hoped that the "failure of the economic system" would allow for more regional and less materialistic economies to emerge. Critics including Stuart Chase, Alfred M. Bingham, and Robert and Helen Lynd decried the encroachment of capital into the lives of many American citizens, fearing the conformity of consumption. The Lynds' 1937 study, *Middletown in Transition*, described a community where the conforming effects of the modern economy encouraged residents to work so that they might consume.[30]

What these critics of the modern consumer-based economy hoped was that the economic crisis might slow the advance of this centralized and conformist new model. Their pleas fell on deaf ears, however, as most Americans and their leadership continued to march to the drumbeat of the modern economic model. Even as rural southerners utilized the barter system to acquire necessities, they understood that this situation was temporary. When Delmas Easterwood described trading peanuts for flour at the country store, she defensively told the interviewer that it was because there was a "shortage of money to buy." Dot Robinson framed her description of the barter in which she and her family participated in much the same light. "There wasn't much pay to anything," she recalled, so you would take your surplus eggs, milk, or cheese to the local store and "exchange for your commodities that you needed." Many of the informants described their participation in the barter system in this manner: "we had no money, but we raised vegetables and had a cow" and would trade them for other items not produced on the farm, according to Sidney Clotfelter. Many of those interviewed discussed that they grew their own food, but for other necessities such as coffee, tobacco, and cloth, they had to trade. Interesting, nearly all of them recall trading eggs. "If you had extra eggs you would take them to town," said Mildred Garlich, "and exchange them for groceries." Henry Arnold remembered, "When we needed coffee, tea, sugar . . . we would take a dozen eggs . . . and swap it." Gladys Burroughs's mother would trade her eggs "to get material to make [her] dresses."[31] So many of the informants talk about this egg bartering that it both suggests the pervasiveness of the practice and makes one wonder what store owners did with all those eggs!

Local stores no doubt absorbed the eggs and other traded items at a loss to help those in their communities. As a tenant farmer, Cecil Tate described the process in his interview. Growing cotton "didn't bring but two to three cents a pound," he observed. He continued, "Then if you sold any you had to pay your debt for what you bought [like] sugar, flour, and coffee. For the year you would have to go make arrangements to buy your stuff on credit at the big store in town, and buy your fertilizer. And then [when you] sold your cotton you had to pay that. Then what was left over . . . you would take it out in clothes and they wasn't going to give [it to] you in money." Violet Lowe recalled the struggles of her father, who would work day in and day out in the tenant field raising cotton for the family. When it was harvested, he "would take the bale of cotton to the gin and get it baled and ready to sell, go sell it on the market, and bring back the money for what we had already eaten." The structure of the town or country store had been set in the latter part of the nineteenth century and represented a significant drain on the southern economy. The years leading up to the Depression saw some changes coming to the rural South with this regard, but with the economic crash, many areas reverted to the older practices. Guy Knight recalled that he and his family got most of what they needed by trading with the local store. But the structure of the store remained fixed in the earlier era, so that the owner controlled consumption by "fetching" what the customer wanted: "you had to tell them what you wanted and they would get it. There wasn't no price on anything . . . they'd add it up on pencil and paper."[32]

The local storekeepers relied on this informal credit system both for control and to assist their neighbors, whom they knew to be in dire straits.

Cotton Sharecroppers, Greene County, Georgia. (Courtesy Library of Congress.)

Edwin Harman recalled his father's country store in Carrollton, Georgia, during the 1930s and spoke of how the store provided the locals "with groceries for the whole year." After the harvest in the fall, the farmers would come in and try to make amends by paying off their tabs, but with the price of cotton, they were "getting a little bit farther behind every year." The store owners would take nearly anything in exchange, from cotton to eggs, to make their own ends meet. Mabel LeFeure's family grocery gave a "lot of credit which we would never collect." Her husband felt connected to the locals and tried to "help everyone." These country stores understood their community role and tried, as much as possible, to help through bartering eggs, taking cotton in exchange for money, or simply allowing the store to be used as a local meeting place. Mary Jackson's family would go to the local country store on Saturdays to trade eggs and peanuts for family necessities, and while there, the adults would stand around talking about "everything that was going on and why things were like they were."[33]

These country venues, involved in a larger struggle for survival with the increased proliferation of chain stores, tried as best they could to meet the needs of the local population. Many times they simply created an alternative exchange system because of the lack of money in circulation. Often this meant that crops replaced money. Sarah Riddle remembered that her farmer husband would work in the fields and take their surplus corn to trade at the local store for "flour, or lard, or sugar, coffee, anything you know." With two children at home, things were tight; she and her husband were appreciative that the "peddler," as she called him, was willing to trade. Even medical doctors in the country took trade in exchange for services. We "didn't have money for one thing to pay for the doctoring," so Guy Knight's family offered the doctor chickens, produce, milk, cheese, "whatever you could pay them with." When William Worley's second son was born during the hard times of the early 1930s, the local doctor charged him twenty dollars for the delivery. Unable to pay, he and the doctor agreed to settle the debt with cotton seed, which the doctor really did not need because he also lived on a farm and grew his own cotton. But both sides agreed to the transfer, and the debt was cleared.[34]

The rural folk also actively traded with rolling stores. Long part of rural American life, these traveling general stores brought modern commodities to the country folk. Jessie Pierce experienced the Depression decade just outside the town of Bowdon, Georgia, and relied on the "rolling stores that came around." These peddlers bartered with the rural folk and traded commercial items such as soap, flour, and coffee for chickens and eggs. In Glen, Georgia, the "peddler came through once a week and bought anything you had to sell," said Myrtle Hall, and always "saved her a couple of bars" of hand soap. She and others waited for these traveling stores and saw them as a connection to the outside world.[35]

More than anything else, these rural folk dealt with their lack of money by believing that "everybody was poor but it didn't matter because we were all poor." While they bartered, saved, and sacrificed to make ends meet, they saw their position in almost patriotic terms, as if their hard times were connected to the larger democracy. In recalling these hard times, again and again the respondents placed their economic hardship in context with the unity it wrought. "I didn't have nothin'," said Guy Gordon, "didn't nobody else, so we're all in the same boat." This sense of unity helped diffuse any class tension that may have developed. Perhaps the attitude that "no one seemed to be angry [because] they all just realized that everyone else was in the same state that they were in," as recalled by Nell Lovelady of her experience in Decatur, Alabama, was an accommodation strategy designed to ease the guilt of their poverty. The Depression brought these people together; rather than complain, they accepted less. In fact, that they had less became a mark of pride. "We had the best time," Mary McClain said; "you don't have to have cars and money." The pride and unity was linked to the simplicity it brought. "It was hard to raise ten cents," said Whitley Morris, but rather than worry about it, he recalled, "[we] just took it in stride and went on our way and enjoyed life." But though they may have made the best of the situation, they were well aware that they lacked, that they were suffering, and that there were commodities available outside their reach. Violet Scott laughed when asked if she had money to spend during the 1930s, saying, "we never had money to buy nothing with . . . we didn't have money, period." But, she continued, "it didn't hurt any of us, I think we prospered from it." Her inability to consume created a sort of bond, much akin to foxhole friendships during war, in which deprivation and fear help boost the courage of soldiers in battle. "You learned how to do without," she said, "put[ting] things together that you wouldn't think about before."[36]

The lack of money did create a sense of guilt and failure, yet it also served to remind people of the more important things in life. Many of the interviewees told of their families and communities growing closer in the struggle. Since everyone seemed to be in the same situation, they relied on each other for support. James Thompson recalled that his family never went hungry, and while the food "might not have been exactly what we wanted," they were glad to have something to eat. The era was difficult, he said, and there was "lots of hard work, but we lived good." Violet Lowe put a more direct positive spin on her recollections when she said that "one of the good things was that it (the lack of money) made us love our families and to be closer to them, and to cherish the things we had and not dream about the things we didn't have."[37]

However, this type of recollection appears to be more a product of nostalgia than reality. Most of the interviewees described how the ideology of consumption colored their Depression-era experiences. Far from being detached from the modern ideas of production and consumption, those in the rural South were keen to understand their position and created a variety of strategies to offset their inability to consume. Their perceived sense of guilt, failure, or pride defined the Depression era and became the cornerstone of the next epoch—World War II—during which they would once again sacrifice for the greater good. The experiences of the Great Depression thus serve as the foundation for the emergence of modern America, particularly the ideals and attitudes regarding consumption.

A central theme in most of the interviews is the desire to retain one's pride amidst the hardship. Many felt that even though times were tough, their spirits could not be broken. "We didn't have everything we wanted," recalled Viola Bass, "but we didn't go hungry." This type of optimistic resolve permeates most of the interviews—we were down but not out. Henri P. Herron remembered that "we had to give up a lot of things . . . but we never really wanted for anything." Whatever they needed, they made or grew or found a way to substitute something else for it. Opal Jackson of Newnan, Georgia, remembered that there were "hard times" where they ate what they grew: "we didn't even know what a hamburger was or a wienie or nothing like that." Louise Smith's mother would have her and her sisters look through the Sears Roebuck catalog and pick out dresses they liked. Then she would "make me a dress like the one in the catalog," Louise said. Ruby Henry recalled making her daughter's clothes for first grade. She took her own skirts and with a "single edge razor blade ripped the seams" out and made two school dresses. Ernest Porter's son was attending Tech High School in Atlanta in the middle part of the 1930s and was unable to attend dances because of a lack of funds. The boy joined the ROTC in his sophomore year and wore the uniform every "Monday through Thursday" because they did not have money for school clothes. Bessie Birdsong recalled how "proud" she was when she finally saved the "$1.98" for a new pair of shoes.[38]

This sense of pride suggests an awareness that the traditional rural way of life was being replaced by a more modern one. Even though many residents of the South were unable to participate fully, they recognized their future in this new world of consumption. Nevertheless, while waiting for jobs to open up and the southern rural economy to catch up to that of the rest of the nation, rural southerners relied heavily on traditional ways of living, as the next chapter describes.

4

"I WAS JUST FIXIN' TO TELL HER ABOUT THE WASHIN'!"

The Meaning of Daily Life

Paul Thompson's excellent work on oral history suggests that the life narrative approach is one of the best formats for oral historians. The style and design of this type of interview allows informants to feel comfortable in the experience and therefore better able not only to recall facts about the past but also to convey their emotions or consciousness.[1] The task of getting people to open up is complicated by time and by the influence of history, as both of these tend to modify some memories. By listing the everyday activities, however, and allowing the informants to describe in fond detail the experiences of their daily past, we get a glimpse into their lives; these views help to define the social and economic conditions of their lives during this period. Perhaps an interviewee's ability to recall political or economic situations is skewed by the conforming effect of history, but the situations of their daily experiences, personal and real, provide a clearer picture of how the people in this study saw and explained their daily lives. This approach broadens the ability to analyze the nature and influence of consumption, ideology, capital, space, time, leisure, and much more. In essence, allowing them the space to define their daily and often overlooked experiences creates a more complete picture of the larger issues of Depression-era America. In the earlier chapters, the interweaving of informants' voices created a symbolic unity of consciousness on the issues of work, government, and consumption. Their extended discourse on making candy or soap or on how they created and stored food helps to better frame those unified voices—providing a way to discern from the few the ideals of the many. One of the central purposes of this study is to provide an understanding of the interconnection between memory and history—and these vignettes serve to bridge that gap. Therefore, in this and the following chapter, the voices of the people will be

Sharecropper and son. (Courtesy Library of Congress.)

foremost, thus allowing them to tell their stories more fully and in this way introduce a personal nuance to the Depression era.

In November 1991, Kelly Sullivan sat down with her husband's grandparents Bernell and Zead Sullivan to ask them questions about their time together in western Georgia during the Depression era. Her father-in-law, Richard, and his brother Ray were also present. She started the interview off easily by getting Bernell (Grandma) and Zead (Papa) to talk about their wedding in 1932. From this auspicious beginning, we are privy to their world and can see into the lives of many rural southerners.

Kelly: You were married in 1932, right?

Papa: We was married on the 8th day of December.

Kelly: Well, I mean, like what was it . . . what was it like?

Grandma: It [was] cold like it is today.

Ray: Did y'all have a place to go to?

Papa: We went to the preacher's house.

Kelly: You went where?

Grandma: To Preacher Bates's house.

Kelly: For dinner or something?

Grandma: No, to get married. About this time in the evening.

Papa: Ol' Chill couldn't eat the biscuits. Hell, he didn't eat none of them biscuits. Chill couldn't eat them biscuits.

Grandma: He'd pass the biscuits down and ol' Chill got that one.

Kelly: Chill?

Grandma: Chill's their dog. Let's see, Earl Pierce and Ruby, Zead and Mom and Dad, Elsie and R.E. and Louise.

Kelly: What do you mean, you all went home (after the wedding and dinner)?

Richard: What do you mean, you spent the night with your family?

Grandma: Slept in the same room with my Mom and Dad.

Richard: Good lord, what a honeymoon!

Grandma: We ain't never had no honeymoon.

Papa: We had a honeymoon!

Grandma: When?

Papa: When we went to bed with your Mom and Dad. That's a honeymoon.

Kelly: Well, I mean like were all your sisters and brothers there?

Papa: All of hers was.

Grandma: Mom and Dad slept in one room with us and Louise, I think. Oscar, Rosco, naw . . .

The Meaning of Daily Life

87

Papa: Oscar, E.C. . . .

Grandma: E.C., Uncle Lee, and Bennie. R.E., Elsie, and Louise was in the other two rooms.

Papa: R.E., Elsie, and Louise was in bed with your Mom and Dad.

Grandma: R.E., Elsie, and Louise wouldn't be in bed.

Papa: I SAID Louise!!!! You said Elsie and R.E. and Louise in the other rooms . . .

Grandma: I said in another room.

Papa: Aunt Ruby was in the bed with R.E. and Louise, wouldn't she?

Grandma: Yeah.

Kelly: That's pretty nifty. Well, I mean what happened next? Did y'all get up the next morning and make biscuits and have breakfast and all that kind of good stuff?

Papa: Yeah, cooked biscuits, ham, eggs, sausage. Back then everybody had something like that.

Kelly: Well, what did you do the next day? The day after you got married, what'd you do?

Papa: Went in the big woods and over to my place and ate dinner over there and went back over to her Maw's. We went home with 'em.

Grandma: I don't remember much about it.

Papa: I got up and it was cold, I mean COLD and had to pull corn with her father.

Kelly: Pull corn?

Papa: Pick corn, pull corn . . . had to tote it out, the damn trees so thick you couldn't drive a wagon.

Grandma: There was so many trees in the field that you couldn't drive a wagon through.

Kelly: In the fields?

Papa: Yeah, made the damn best corn like bottom corn.

Grandma: Some of 'em he'd thin 'em and then later we'd come back and cut 'em for dry firewood.

Richard: That's interesting, the first day after y'all was married, y'all started workin'.

Kelly: What day did y'all get married on, Saturday?

Grandma: No, it was Friday . . . the last day of our license. Like to let 'em run out on account of Dad. My Dad didn't want us to get married 'cause he wanted me to help him gather up their crop.

Kelly: What, did you have to get married before a certain time after you . . .

Grandma: We's supposed to get married the first of November, sometime in November. Dad wanted me to stay at home long enough to help get their crop gathered up and Zead said "that's why I want her to help me too!" So I had to gather up two crops! And that's how the license about run out and Mrs. Sullivan said, "Zead, you not gon' fool that girl. You messin' up on it if you do. You better a be goin' and get her while you can. She might say hell with him, I don't want him!" And we's in a topless T-Model and freezin' to death.

Kelly: Oh my goodness!

Papa: Hell, it was cold, I mean . . .

Kelly: Y'all go to the preacher's house in that?

Papa: Yeah . . .

Kelly: With the top down?

Grandma: It didn't have no top on it, it done got so old.

Kelly: What all happened from there? I mean, y'all had kids and y'all had a farm and . . . when did y'all get a house? Y'all stayed with your Mom and Dad the first night and then you went to see (Zead's) Mom and Dad.

Grandma: In the summer. Well, Zead had a house rented and dad said, "Y'all just let that house go and let someone else have it. I'm gon' get the hay out of that little house up yonder"—a little two room house and was gon' let us move in[to] it. Well, we's over at Mrs. Sullivan's one day and Zead was heppin' [helping] get the hay out of the house where we could move in and we could see from over there, where we lived, and I's sittin' in the kitchen door and here goes two wagons up the road. Dad and them was moving in[to] the two room house and left the three room house and hall for us!

Kelly: Really, why?

Grandma: Well, it was like this, ah, it was a little later than this and Zead had to go over to Duff's and get our bed and our stove and everything and bring it in and it was dark when he got there and he forgot to get the rails and we had to sleep in the floor on a mattress.

Kelly: Well, where was the stuff?

Grandma: At Duff's, Zead's brother.

Kelly: OK, and he had furniture over there?

Grandma: Yeah, and he had some syrup and stuff to eat over there and when he went to get it, he didn't have no syrup. Duff 'n' 'em had eat it for breakfast and Eunice had made syrup cakes and syrup candy and Zead didn't even had none. You've seen so'gum [sorghum] syrup, ain't you?

Kelly: Yeah, I know what it is.

Grandma: That stuff's high now . . .

Papa: I priced some the other day at . . . if I had a syrup mill I'd get rich. Five dollars a quart. That's twenty dollars a gallon.

Grandma: Now it is, but back then you could get [it] for nothin' nearly.

Papa: Fifty cents a quart . . . I mean fifty cents a gallon!

Grandma: We had the big house and they had the little house and they had, let's see . . . there's Mom and Dad, Elsie and R.E, and Louise, Oscar and Rosco.

Kelly: Why did they give y'all the big one, [if] it was just the two of you?

Grandma: I don't know! Well, they had a big barn up here to put the cows in and they could see after the calves up there. Dad had 150 acres of land. We lived on the fifty acres and they lived on the 100 acres.

Papa: And another . . .

Grandma: He said before we got married, "well, the first one to get married will have the pick of the land. The girls get 50 acres—I mean 25 acres of land. He had that 100 acres of land up there and he's gon' give the boys a mule. They give E.C. and Bennie a mule.

Kelly: When they got married?

Grandma: Yeah . . .

Kelly: Well, you got fifty instead of 25 . . .

Grandma: I didn't even get nothin'.

Papa: Yeah you did, Maw got hell!!

Kelly: I thought you said that . . .

Grandma: He *said* but he didn't. See, when I got married I didn't get nothin' but a calf. And then I had to pull the calf away from the cow from the day it was born 'till it got to be a big calf.

Kelly: Why did he give you a calf?

Grandma: And Zead had the cotton seeds to feed the calf a growin' up.

Kelly: Cottonseed?

Grandma: Yeah. And Zead had a heifer too. So we had a heifer apiece when we got married. And Mrs. Green's ol' cow knocked my cow in a ditch and pulled her leg and she couldn't get up and I sold that cow for $14 . . . you can't buy a calf now for $14.

Kelly: Well . . .

Grandma: You can't buy a tit off a cow for that!!

In this brief exchange, one sees into the rural way of life that has passed by. From the empowerment of Grandma telling the story, correcting and even cutting off her husband's recollection, we see that she is defining this memory, and she will have nothing alter the way it is told. We also view the nature of gender in its time, as well as class and the simple customs associated with getting married and setting up a household. The conversation continued with a discussion of the birth of their first child in 1937 and how Grandma's "little wood stove had four eyes" and that she made all sorts of delicious food. She told Kelly that in the late fall, they would pick as much of the cotton as possible, "burrs" and all.

Grandma: If you couldn't get out there and pick it, you just drug you a . . . you pick about half a bale nearly in a day by pulling the burrs and all off. . .

Kelly: Oh, instead of picking just the cotton out . . .

Grandma: Picking the cotton out of the burr. You picked the whole thing, cause you could just snatch it off. If you got sticks that long it didn't matter . . .

Kelly: And then y'all would [clean] it inside?

Grandma: In the house. We'd pile it up in one room, in the corner, and then we'd get around the fireplace and burn the burrs while we's pickin' the cotton. We have went to bale up cotton and picked up snakes in the cotton . . . and in the house too. And we didn't think nothing about it. I mean rattlesnakes too!!

Kelly: Oh, OK, if you thought it was going to rain . . .

Grandma: Yeah, if it looked like it was goin' to rain you'd grab a bag and go to pickin' that cotton and pulling it off burrs and all.

Kelly: Didn't that hurt your hands?

Grandma: It didn't hurt as bad to pull the burrs off than it did to pick it. When you grab it at first them little sharp burrs would get your hand.

The interviewer, Kelly, was flabbergasted by what she was hearing: how difficult their life was and yet how honest and prideful Grandma seemed to be in retelling the story. This part of the interview concluded with Grandma explaining that the neighbors would help each other pick the last of the cotton and sit by the burr fire making bales. When there was no more cotton to pick, the women would sit around making quilts for the winter, sometimes getting three or four done in a day.

> Grandma: There'd be so many people around and the young people would be around and they'd be sittin' 5, 4, and 5 up and down one side. One would start at this square and skip a square and you'd have plenty of room to sew. It's be all the way around. I've seen 10 and 12 kids—girls . . .
> Kelly: But the girls did it, no men?
> Grandma: If the men didn't have nothin' to do!! They's out huntin' and cuttin' wood and doing their jobs!![2]

The Sullivans' story of the early years of their marriage provides a glimpse into the lived experiences of rural Georgians in a time of transition. One can see in Kelly's sometimes-incredulous response her difficulty in framing their lives, as the narration seems far removed from what she had come to know about the past or her in-laws. A mature woman at the time of the interview, she was awestruck by some of the stories, and what began as an interview quickly became a conversation. In the process, the elder Sullivans relayed details about social customs, living arrangements, housing, work, agriculture, gender, and folk- and foodways. This information provides a more complex look into the context and structure of their daily lives. What was it that they valued? How did they negotiate between work and leisure? How did they define "power" within their relationship and in relation to the larger community? Many of the oral histories from this collection reflect this type of detail. Many do not, as some of those interviewed sought to satisfy the interviewer by providing almost scripted answers. But for those who did choose to engage in a conversation about the past, a telling document was left behind for their families, for students, and for scholars.

One of the more interesting means of seeing into people's worlds is to examine their foodways. Scholars have begun to analyze the meaning of food, diet, and cooking as a way to explore the larger social and political issues of the era. What people eat tells us what they can afford and where they place value within the marketplace. How they prepare their food underscores the role and influence of technology—a wood stove versus a gas stove, for example. Foodways can reveal the informant's world in a way that discussing politics and work cannot, as food can reflect values, habits, and attitudes, particularly of a regional population.[3]

Roxie Etheridge said, "I'd cook for the children—they didn't have no lunchroom, and I'd cook for 'em gunny sacks full . . . I guess you don't know gunny sacks. They were flour sacks. But I would dry fruit. I guess you don't know what dried fruit [is], but I'd dry fruit, two big ol' gunny sacks full. One gunny sack full of apples, one of peaches. That's what I'd can 'cause we didn't have no deep freeze and I'd can stuff, we just didn't can it all [because] we had no place to store it. It was rough."[4] Gene Autry's "aunt had three acres of peas—black-eyed peas—planted down on her property. They were just ruinin' so she told us if we would come down there and pick them we could have them. So we went down there and picked about four or five of these great big old cotton-seed sacks full of black-eyed peas. We took 'em home and got them out there on the driveway and beat the hulls off of them, got all the little peas out of them. You know what we're going to have for dinner and supper—peas. Breakfast in the morning."[5] All Ruby Henry could recall having "for lunch was fried potatoes and biscuits and the biscuits I didn't have no milk to make them with and they would be so hard I didn't want anybody at work to see them and I would go out to the water fountain and eat out there so I could wash 'em down. [I] would have choked to death if I hadn't had water."[6]

It has been well documented that during the Depression, American families learned to "make do" with what they had. This tendency to reuse, save, conserve, and recycle was reinforced with the country's entrance into World War II. Urban middle-class women learned to stretch the family budget by making their own clothes or baking their own bread. Poor and working-class urban families had fewer luxuries with regard to the family budget, and their stories often reflect a more survivalist approach to food. For rural folks, which most of those interviewed for this study represent, the Depression era did not necessitate a return to or relearning of past food preparation or storage techniques, as most people were still utilizing traditional methods; southern food preparation was modernized because of the internal migrations of the war. Because most of the rural South lacked electricity and therefore refrigeration, the food crops had to be canned, smoked, or pickled.[7]

Wayne Copeland and Myrtle McCormick recalled with fondness something called "streak o' lean":

Yeah, we raised everything we ate. Very little stuff did we have to go to the store and buy. Coffee and sugar was the main things we had to buy. The ol' middlin' meat, you know what middlin' meat is? That's the part up on the side that has a streak of lean in it. A lot of people used to call it a streak of lean. Then the fatback was under the belly. That was all fat, no lean in that at all . . . You'd take a piece of streak of lean and slice it real thin and fry it out and use the grease, you know, for what we used to call saw-mill gravy or thickenin' gravy.[8]

Most of the meat you could get back then was this old streak-o-lean. They didn't have no way of keeping meat. They didn't have these freezers and all that and when you killed a hog it had to be real cold weather. We would salt that meat and let it lay overnight. Then you had a big ol' meat box. We'd pack that meat and put down a layer of salt and a layer of meat. Most of the time you had to take the back-bone and spareribs and cook all of that up in jars and can it. You'd fry your sausage in patties and pack these one-half gallon fruit jars with sausage, pour [in] grease and all. It was good. Boil that backbone [and pull] that meat off the bone and pack it in these jars and it was good meat.[9]

Jewel Cheek remembered drying "food on a scaffold outside on a piece of aluminum tin and put the cut peaches on it, and cut apples. We peeled apples and not the peaches. We dried them all. I have not made pies in a long time. We had plums, peaches, apples, pears. We had every kind of fruit, cherries and everything."[10] Jim Teague described with vivid recall making sauerkraut:

Some of us'd go and take the cabbage from the garden, we'd go through the process of getting [them] ready. Quartering them up and getting the center part out. Then you'd put them in a container. It was an ap-paratus that was made from a hoe; you'd curve it out in an S shape [and] it was sharpened on the edge of it, put a handle on it. You'd put those cabbage quarters in this container and take this thing and start chopping those cabbages up. When you got the cabbages chopped up [the women] would do something to that, put it in a churn and process it and then it made kraut. It was like pickles, that's what it was. When it got to that stage they'd take it from the container to the stove, put it in a big pan on top of a wood-fired stove. They'd cook that to a certain degree then they could can it. Then they preserved it for the winter.[11]

The smokehouse and its preservation value meant a lot to Robert C. Johnson and Marguritte Lilly:

We had the whole bit—chickens, cows, hogs, and mules. It was about as near self-sustaining as you can get. As far as being independent, we would grown our own pork and each winter we'd kill and cure out the pork and hang it in the smokehouse and take the lean part of the carcass and the sausage and fix it up and hang it. My mother would take real thin cloth and make a little bag and—it's be about that thick or a little thicker—and put sausages [in it] and flatten it out and hang it in the smokehouse and when we needed any sausage we'd cut one of those and skin the cloth back off it, and boy, it was good eatin' I'll tell you.[12]

All we needed from the store was sugar and flour and coffee because we carried our own corn to the mill for our meal. And we cooked off the fat from the hogs and made up pork sausage and put the sausages patties in layers and in the grease that we cooked from the fat of the hogs. And they kept the whole year through. We smoked our meat in the smokehouse and wrapped it and put it away and cut it whenever we needed it.[13]

Steve Dearing remembered a recipe for poor man's sausage that his family served: "We ate buttered cornbread and syrup a lot of times for breakfast. Back then they'd raise these whipper-wheel peas they called them—these little speckled peas—and we'd eat them three times a day. We'd eat 'em at lunch and at suppertime and if she had any left she'd mash them up and put sage and peppers and things in them and fry them up for sausage. You couldn't hardly tell the difference between that and sausage. We just had it hard."[14]

Most of the informants had pleasant tales to tell about their way of life. One of the more intriguing involved the process of making candy. There were two types they recalled making (both from sorghum syrup): ribbon and taffy. Violet Scott told her young interviewer that there's "no tellin' what they make [your candy] out of." For her era it was simple: "we'd pull the coals out [of the fire] and make a good coal bed and then set a skillet on

Mr. Foster with home-cured meat. (Courtesy Library of Congress.)

there and we'd make candy. We'd cook syrup and make syrup candy and it was *so* good."[15] That so many recalled making candy reflects both their nostalgia for the past and the very real situation of rural life in the Depression era in the South. Lacking the varieties of popular amusements available in the cities, rural people created their own entertainment, either with family and neighbors or through their churches. Candy making was also recalled as a social gathering where young men and women in the area could mingle and get to know each other. The frequency of this recall is indicative of what they valued as rural Americans—family, sharing, and visiting. John Gillespie remembered making the candy as part of the courting process:

> You would cook sugar and boil it until it got to a certain degree and then you would choose a partner which was usually this girl, you know, and you would get out there and you would get a bunch of that stuff in a ball and you would start twisting it like elastic and just keep on and keep stretching it until you get it out to about like you wanted it and you would twist it about half a turn and lay it on the table and

it would get hard. It was like we called stick candy now. You would take something and break it and chew it. Sugar candy was what it was really. When you got [it], it would be just like chewing gum. Then you and your partner would just start pulling at it and you would twist and pull it, twist and pull it and it would just keep stretching like elastic until you got it as long as you wanted it and then you would give it about a half turn. I don't know why, I guess it made it look pretty, I reckon. Then you laid it on a table and let it get cold and it would be hard. That was all the candy you had.[16]

Edna Mann recalled the candy-making times as a way to introduce her young interviewer to the simpler ways of the past:

... we would have candy pullings. Have you ever heard of that? It was made out of syrup. You know, we had raise[d] syrup cane. We had plenty of syrup and they would cook it somehow or another but I can't remember how they did it. But they would cook it and they would keep pulling and pulling it and twisting it and then you'd eat the syrup and a lot of times we put peanuts in it and just things like that. And then they [as part of the candy pullings], a lot of people would have dances for young people to go to dance. Maybe this person would have a dance at his house one time and another person would have it and then we'd all go to dances and dance.[17]

Erma Dennis saw the joy of the pullings as part of her connection to the larger community:

We'd gather together, you know, the young people and go to a certain neighbor's house and they'd cook it and we'd, you know, make taffy that way or peanut brittle. Make popcorn balls. They'd put it in a slightly greased plate. Pour so much in there and let it cool where you could handle it. And there's two—like I'd have it stretched out here and you'd reach in there ... over here and you'd just pull it. Then you stretched it out on something and when it hardened, you could take a knife and just crack it.[18]

When Wendy Weathers interviewed her grandparents, Rozelle and Lanier Weathers, she was amazed by their ability to recall their late teens and twenties. She was also interested in the types of things they did for fun.

Wendy: How did you cook?
R&L: Wood stove.

Wendy: Wood stove? Do you remember anything particular about that? Did you ever have any fires?

Lanier: Uh, no. We had that old wood stove and the mill come and they give us our wood stove. Had to go over there and cut our wood off the company land and haul it home. That's the way we got stove wood.

Wendy: Do you remember anything about cooking on a wood stove?

Rozelle: No!

Wendy: What did y'all do for fun . . . ?

Lanier: We had candy pullings . . .

Rozelle: Parties, we had parties . . .

Wendy: Tell me about these candy pullings. What did you do?

Lanier: It was just like a party only you cook . . . take ribbon cane syrup and cook it down and make candy out of it and you pull it. Get you a partner and pull candy.

Rozelle: Sort of like taffy.

Lanier: Grease your hands with butter. Pull it out that way, she'd reach and get it this way and pull it that way and you'd reach and get it that way and pull.

Wendy: It was kind of like tug of war?

Lanier: Yeah . . .

Rozelle: It was really like taffy-like. I think that's what they called it. It got hard, it turned, it got hard, didn't it?

Lanier: Yes, it changed colors. When it first gets done it's red and the more you pull it the lighter it got.

Rozelle: It turns white almost.

Lanier: Yes, it turns white and you can make popcorn balls.

Wendy: Popcorn balls?

Lanier: Yes. Pop your corn and have that syrup candy and when they're 'bout done, roll your popcorn in it. Make a ball out of it and have a popcorn ball.[19]

The discussion of the candy-making process reveals the many social layers that were a part of the food- and folkways of the rural South during this era. The closeness of the community seemed to play a paramount role in the socialization of young people. It also suggests that the expansion of consumerism among the youth, even though historically prevalent, did not fully overtake the more basic folkways of the community. These small-town and rural people knew about candy bars and even wanted to buy some

Mrs. L. Smith making her own soap on their farm in Carroll County, Georgia. (Courtesy Library of Congress.)

when they visited the five-and-dime, but the few instances in which they recalled specific brand names with regards to candy, they did so in a way that reflects the scarcity of these luxuries and a type of envy that suggests an expectation of desire rather than real want. In all of the interviews that included stories about taffy pulls, porch music parties, and other community affairs, there were none who found them alienating, boring, or meaningless. Perhaps this is because only those with positive memories told of these situations. However, there were several questions designed to get at how the informants viewed leisure and what they did for entertainment, and no one said a negative thing about these occasions, which to the interviewers in the early 1990s had to sound like quaint, old-fashioned folkways.

Another folkway that many of the informants seemed particularly proud of was soap-making. Many recalled that they used homemade soap but gave few other details. Others were more specific. Brenita Reid and Sarah Riddle described the steps they went through:

> Yeah, I used to make soap. I had a fireplace where I burned oak wood and saved the ashes. James built me a contraption about that wide and that high (she demonstrates with her hands) but it stood on legs.

And I'd save the ashes and pour 'em in that thing and keep 'em covered up—keep it from raining in it—with a piece of tin. When spring come, I would rake out a hole in there and pour water in there to catch that lye. I made lots of soap."[20]

Yeah, we made the lye in the soap out of ashes dripped . . . You fix an old barrel and save your ashes through the winter and then in the spring you would take and pour water in the barrel of ashes and it'd drip down and make lye. And you'd put it in a pot with some grease—put water and grease—yeah and it make . . . all the old grease they could save. You know, the old fat meat they couldn't use. They put that in there and it turned it into soap. You'd cut that like bars of soap. And it would just make the clothes so pretty and clean.[21]

Men were less sure of the steps, and like earlier assessments which addressed the differences in which they recalled the past, their understanding of the process differed from the women. Note how John Gillespie and Frank Winn's recollections reveal they wanted to impress their interviewer that they knew how to make soap but relied more on non-homemade lye:

We made our own soap and everything! You would use what we called pot-ashes. Empty ashes out of the fireplace and bought something, I don't know, some kind of chemical to put in it and boiled it and then you let it get cold and cut it into bars like you'd want it. It'd take your hide off [when] you were getting a bath.[22]

No, I don't remember the recipe. You had ashes and you had lye. You'd burn oak wood, get ashes, and buy the lye at the store. You could get a big can for ten cents! I don't know how they mixed it up now, but it would come out a bar of soap. A big yellow bar of soap.[23]

What is interesting about the recollections regarding soap is that women recalled how to make it while men had a harder time identifying exactly how to do it. Small-town and rural women were responsible for such tasks, and men rarely played an active role in this part of running the household. Women were more likely to discuss the varieties of things they did to maintain the household, which often revolved around caring for the children, working around the stove, and cleaning. Ima Burns remembers these as the happiest times of my life. Yeah it was wonderful. Couldn't have been no happier. I had one [baby] when I was eighteen, then two years [later] I had another one, that was nineteen, twenty, twenty-two, twenty-four, that would be three or four children. My goodness! Every two years I would have children and well, there ain't nothin' to tell. I don't know nothin' about nothin'. I had babies, just babies, babies. I used to put a box up on, you know, what these a [...] what you get oranges and apples in, these crates, wooden boxes that have partitions in the middle. Yeah, well, we put that up on the wall and put our dishes in that crate. Well, I had two of them I think, and I put some in one and somethin' else in the other one for shelves, for our cabinets. We didn't have cabinets.[24]

When women such as Mrs. Ralph McCain, Dorothy Hill, and Geneva Mack told of their household chores, they did so with great detail to impress upon their younger interviewer the difficulty of their lives:

We used flat irons. You put them on the stove. We had a big stove. We kept that iron on the back of it and when you started to iron clothes you moved them out towards the front where they would get good and hot. You had your ironing board set up in the kitchen where you could get to it and iron clothes. [The ironing board] was made from a big plank with a quilt wrapped around it and a sheet. We all knew we had to work. We had things each of us had to do. Brought in stove wood and would draw water and fill all the buckets up and keep the tub filled up for bath water. Bring bath water in to heat on the stove.[25]

We cooked on a wooden coal [stove]. They called them a coal range during that time, that was what we had. The stove had iron discs, like an eye on the stove. It had a thing across the top they called the warmer. After you cooked your food you could put it up there and keep it warm. What they called the oven was down under the stove. You put your wood and coal in that and made the fire and that heated the stove and that's where we baked—in the oven.[26]

Now we had a coal and wood stove but it had something on it you called a reservoir. I guess it held about three gallons of water. You got the water from the well, we had a well, we didn't have a hydrant. We had a well in our yard. We'd draw the water and then we had a bucket. You keep this reservoir full of water and when you make up your fire in this stove to cook the dinner or breakfast or what have you, this water would get hot. Then you had a dishpan that you wash your dishes in. We didn't have sinks. There was a table that had two dishpans. This dishpan you wash your dishes in there and this dishpan right here you scald them in hot water and then you dry them.[27]

Other women—including Thelma Hughes, Virginia Thelan, Myrtle McCormick, and Ophelia Dearing—compared their experiences to those of the modern world both to detail how far society has come and to underscore the privation of their world:

We didn't know what a disposable diaper was! Mothers in this day and time don't know what it is to have babies and have to wash diapers. Scrub them on a board, put them in a wash pot and boil them. Then you take, it would be a cloth bag, a cloth flour bag, and we'd wash that and make something out of it for the kids or dish towels or something like that. Guano used to come out in cloth bags and we'd take that and make things and it used to be, guano would come in coarse white bags and we'd sew 'em together and make a sheet and it was rough sleeping under them guano sacks. And you didn't have beds like you do now. You had a straw bed. And we'd make a—you take shucks [cornhusks] and make you a mop. You'd have boards with holes in it and you'd put shucks and put them through and that's what you had to do. We didn't have linoleum, we just had to scrub the floor. It wouldn't take long, you know, you would use the same board—just take out the old shucks and put in some new. It would last a good long time. And, we didn't have washing powders like they do now. You'd take white sand and put it on the floors to scrub the floors and it would make pretty white floors too![28]

We didn't have a vacuum cleaner or a carpet sweeper. Nothing. So what we did was we tore, we wet newspapers and tore them into strips and put them on the rug and then we swept them up. See, that kept the dust down. When we got all the paper swept, the rug was nice and clean.[29]

We had these old washtubs made out of big old barrels and we had these big old wash pots where we had to wash the clothes and then put them in the wash pot and boil them and take them up from the big tubs of water and rinse them and squeeze them. Everything had to be done with your hands. Then we'd hang them on a clothesline.[30]

The way we had to wash, we'd have to scrub the clothes in soapy water with soap in an old rub-board. Then we'd take them to a battle-block. It would be a thing about this big around, and while they was wet and soapy just beat them with a stick and then put them in a pot and boil them. We beat the dirt out of them and then put them in a pot and boil them and after we boiled them take them out and rinse them in tubs and all and then you'd hang them out. We didn't know what a washing machine or dryer or anything like that was.[31]

Women had it hard, as Katherine Melton reminds us: "[Women] mostly washed and ironed and did our housework because we didn't have anything electric. We had a well you draw you[r] water from and boiled your clothes. You had a line to hang them on. Kept you busy doing what chore you had to do as well as cooking. We didn't have a lot of snick-snacking and sandwiches like we do now. We just had vegetables and boiled stuff."[32]

Men recalled the hard work they did around the house—such as cutting wood and digging a well. Scott Gregory's grandfather Jim Teague relayed to him the nature of these day-to-day affairs:

Scott: Did you and your brothers do all the lumbering?
Jim: Oh, we had to have some other people, but we did most of it.
Scott: How was your saw powered?
Jim: By steam engine.
Scott: Gasoline steam?
Jim: No, it was steam—fire. Boiler with a steam engine sitting up on top of it. And the boiler provided the steam for it. It was steam operated all the way.
Scott: What did you use for fuel, coal or wood?
Jim: Wood. The slabs that come from the logs, the leftovers. The waste product. 'Course, they don't have no waste product now. They use even the bark and everything else! They got a market for it, a product they make out of it. When we was in the business, you know, you got to cut a slab off the side of the log. You got to cut off four sides before you ever get it down to where you started ripping your, whatever size it'll make, sixes, eights, tens, whatever. You'd saw it up, depends on whatever size the firebox was in your boiler. You

fired the boiler with that part of the wood. Generate steam, drive that engine. It sets right on top of the boiler too. And the boiler was on wheels. 'Course, then all your logs had to be brought in. You didn't cut over a very big area and drag the logs in. You'd cut in a certain area, then you'd pick up and move the whole mill and set it up somewhere else where it was in the center or closely to the area where you was going to bring logs in from. You'd move it from time to time.

Scott: So you had a portable . . .

Jim: It was very portable. And the boiler in the engine combination was on wheels where you could revert the power to driving the wheels to move things. That's what moved it from one location to another when it come time to relocate.[33]

Henry Clark told his interviewer that after he married, he and his sixteen-year-old bride had nothing—"nobody gave us nothing." His wife's father had some land, and Henry found an abandoned farmhouse out on the land and spent the next several weeks cutting "timber and rebuil[ding] it." When they moved in, they had a "bed, with the cookstove in the kitchen."[34]

That men and women had certain tasks and recalled their specific roles is as important as the descriptions they provided in their interviews. Women were able to recall more facts about home life and told their stories as they related to the family, almost outside of themselves. This conforms to the scholarship concerning women and memory, which suggests that women often voice family issues over self and often downplay their contributions as simply running the household. The men interviewed for this study, in contrast, recalled few stories of home life or cooking (other than what they remembered of their mother) and chose to instead talk about the rough work life they faced and the time they spent in the fields. Rarely did they deviate from themselves in the conversation concerning their contribution to the family, and hardly ever did they include their wives. This conforms to the scholarship on memory and gender, for men tend to recall their ability to work and provide for their families without much mention of actual family life.[35]

Dating and the early stages of marriage reveal another division between the recollections of men and women. The men who addressed the issue of dating or the establishment of a home after marriage focused on the financial aspects. How much the date cost, what types of activities they did, or how they came to get a place to live as newlyweds were the primary recollections of men. For women, their memories conjured up more of the social aspect of courtship and the privation of just starting out.

Louis Swint described the basic primping he found necessary for rural men: "And so we didn't have no bath tubs or convenient toilets or nothin'. Nothin' like that. We had outdoor toilets and had a tin tub to bathe in. And holler out on Friday nights 'rainbow on a nasty night.' That was bath night. And Saturday night we'd go to see a girl 'cause that was the only time that we'd have a bath."[36]

Women provided a more complete picture. When asked what they did on dates, Mary McClain replied,

> Well, we just had to walk to church or walk to the neighbors [to] be with other couples. We would all get out in the road just going from one house to another. Maybe there would be eight or ten couples. We just liked being together, have fun, like you all would get together. We would just have to go to each other's house. We didn't have anything to do, play games. We would go swimming. Lots of Saturday evenings we would go down to the creek and it would be full, just about every young couple in the county would be down there swimming, playing, jumping in that water. Mostly just being together, that's about all because there wasn't nowhere to go.[37]

Courtship in the rural areas was still done within the neighborhood or through the church. John Baggett recalled that in the area around Douglasville, Georgia, the neighbors would do something he called "sittin' to bedtime." Friends and family would stop by for a porch visit and in this way be introduced to potential suitors. This was how Marie Sanderlin first met the man who became her husband. Later, they continued to talk near the fence that separated the two properties. This was the only way she was going to meet a man, as she "wasn't allowed to date" and "never had any dates." An orphan being raised by her aunt, she faced strict rules. She married the neighbor after "he spoke to my aunt about wanting to marry me. . . . I just married him," she concluded.[38]

Isabel Hester's recollection of early married life in Carroll County, Georgia, reveals the hardships a new family faced in the midst of the Depression:

> I married December 25, 1930, right in the middle of the Depression. We lived in the house with his parents the first year. That fall we worked the land on halves. That fall after he paid his due on our bill

and everything, he had ten dollars out of his cotton crop. He took that ten dollars and bought us a little four-eyed stove. A cookstove, four chairs, and a set a dishes, and an iron bedstand for ten dollars. That's what we started housekeeping with. We had an old orange crate. The oranges used to come out of Florida in a wooden crate. We had an orange crate and he tacked that up on the wall. That's where I put my dishes ... We had chickens that run out in the yard. There was cracks in the floor you could stick your finger through. My oldest daughter was born that year, 1933. He took old soda sacks, they were paper lined, and went under the house and nailed those sacks up between the sleepers to keep the air in with that new baby. . . . I read a lot and pieced quilts. I had either five or seven quilts that I pieced and when I was engaged to be married, my momma helped me quilt them. I had my quilts when I got married. We had to use quilts for cover back then. We made sheets out of flour sacks. We saved flour sacks.[39]

Jackie Garlich interviewed her grandmother Mildred Garlich and asked about the days leading up to Mildred's marriage in 1935.

Jackie: How did you meet your husband?

Mildred: We met in 1929 at a baseball game. We wanted to get married, but we had no money. Back then there was no credit. You didn't buy anything on credit unless your family could help you out. You had to save your money to buy anything. By 1935 things got a little better. We saved enough to buy a set of kitchen furniture—a maple table plus four chairs—a little porcelain table, a divan, a chair, a bed and a dresser, and, by the way, I still have every piece and I still use them! I remember the only thing that we borrowed money for was a team of horses, he borrowed the money from his dad, and we paid everything back.

Jackie: When you did get married, what was the wedding like?

Mildred: Well, it was quite different from today. I had an aunt who was a dressmaker who had sewn for people. So she made my wedding dress and it was white moray. Do you know what moray is? Well it was quite popular in those days. Oh, I think it was called watered silk. There is a sheen to it, a kind of design to it. So she made my dress and I guess she made the bridesmaids' dresses too. My aunt baked a wedding cake, an angel food cake. We had our reception in the Methodist church. My bouquet was made out of snowballs—these were big white flowers. I also had orange blossoms mixed in with the greenery to add color. With this, we put a ribbon around to bring the bouquet together. The neighbors brought food to the house, everyone worked together. We killed chickens and had fried chicken and potato salad. Everyone contributed for the reception.

Jackie: So you didn't have a honeymoon?

Mildred: No, but we did have a dance. We had one room where we moved the furniture so we could dance. His cousin and a friend played the accordion and a banjo and played songs like "Let Me Call You Sweetheart" and songs that were popular then.[40]

Jim Teague recalled that they "played a lot of horseshoes. That was one of the big sports on Sunday afternoon, sometimes all day Sunday." This activity, like candy making, was part of a larger organized youth activity. "The young people," he continued, "would congregate at someone's house in the community, preferably where they had a fine oak grove—a lot of shade—and you build a horseshoe court and just get out there and play horseshoes all day long."[41]

Community activities brought the people in the area together for both courtship and other reasons. Ellen Litwicki convincingly argues that the creation of more than twenty-five secular holidays between 1865 and 1920 brought unity and focus to diverse groups of urban dwellers. These public holidays were in part a reaction to the changing ways of life that were affecting many within the working and middle classes, and they were designed to display a particular group's identity or vision of America.[42] In rural areas, the church and the many gatherings at people's homes served similar purposes. In communities that lacked the ethnic diversity or working-class mass of the urban North, get-togethers—formal and informal—brought together community members both to maintain their way of life and to reinforce their vision of the nation. In their celebrations, parades and banners were replaced with taffy pulls, horseshoes, and porch-sitting. While not as elaborate, these activities nonetheless served the same purpose and brought disparate people together for a shared goal.

For many of the informants, the best times they recalled dealt with neighbors, visiting, and music. Allen Furline told his interviewer that his "fun and entertainment came for a few minutes each evening, as we sat on the porch or around the fire in the winter time and talked about what we had done and told stories and maybe a joke occasionally. And on a Saturday evening a neighbor or two would come over and we'd sit around and laugh and tell stories."[43] This sense of community also held that nearly everyone played some sort of instrument or tried to entertain the neighbors. As William Gordon observed, this form of entertainment was also discussed with regards to privation: "Well, the best I could afford was a harmonica. They called it a mouth organ. If I was lucky, I could get a second-hand guitar . . . we were always having square dances at least once a week at somebody's house. We were having a square dance. We had for music for these square dances a banjo, fiddle, guitar, and maybe once in a while, a mandolin."[44]

Imogene Florence told her story about music virtually unaware of the complex racial situation she described: "Colored folks could sing like you never heard in your life. They had no music, they sang a capella. But, they sang gospel music. Daddy would bring them home on Saturday night after he would close the store and they would sing out on the back of the truck in the driveway until they just gave out and that was fun."[45]

These events, like many others in the rural South, provided opportunities for the young people to mix, mingle, and, as many hoped, meet their mate. In an era and region where close contact was frowned upon, Raymond Giles told his interviewer that dancing allowed for some acceptable female contact: "Yeah, what it was is hugging one another and dancing. You know, how you dance with the music. The fiddle's going, something like that. That's about all we did. There was nothing else."[46] Isabel Hester fell in love with her husband at one of these socials:

> We'd have singings a lot of times on Saturday nights and Sunday nights. Now we always had prayer meetings in the community every Sunday night, and that's where I first saw my husband. I played the organ, too. There was one of the preachers, Jimmy Lee Shadinger, the one that married me and my husband. When he came to our prayer meetings he wouldn't let nobody play for his singing except for me. So, I was playing that night and I turned around and saw this good looking young man sitting back in the back of the room and I thought "Oh Lord, there's my sweetheart." That was during Christmas week. He didn't come to see me until the first Saturday night in February. We went together from February 'til Christmas before we got married.[47]

Although some of the informants mentioned what was called "hillbilly music" back then, when they were asked to recall music from the time, they tended to focus on these local gatherings of neighbors, at which those who could played for the community. Perhaps the lack of electricity discouraged them from listening to the radio, as Louise Smith told her interviewer: "I can remember we did not have a radio because no electricity. They did have radios with batteries, but not transistor batteries but I can remember like big car batteries. We did not have the money to buy a radio. The music was, we had a good time, the neighbors would sit up to midnight talking, laughing. They would bring their guitars and fiddles and mandolin and they would have a good time."[48] Interestingly, this lack of modern sensibility did not apply to all of the informants. Many—including J. B. Campbell, Joe Salituro, Al Leiker, and Nell Everett—recalled with vivid detail the songs and bands of the Swing era:

Oh yeah! They had what you call big-name band[s]. There's not no such thing now, but they went all over the country—college graduations, nightclubs, hotels, and things, Guy Lombardo, all like that. They really put out some good music.[49]

The music of the era was one thing I remember very well. Of course it was a time when Frank Sinatra was coming on very strong, and the big bands of Tommy Dorsey, and Jimmy Dorsey, and it was, for music it was a wonderful era.[50]

The first music I began to take note of was probably, maybe, the beginning of the big band sounds such as Paul Whiteman. My favorite though came along during the late thirties, early forties, with the sound of the big band such as Glenn Miller, Tommy Dorsey, Jimmy Dorsey, and band[s] of that caliber. It's still my favorite.[51]

That was a big band era. That was Bing Crosby and Perry Como and that's when we did the jitterbug. Big bands would play and people would dance. You wouldn't go out like with tables and all. We had dances, school dances. We had nice ones. We had parties in our homes. We went to different people's houses. We didn't have a lot of refreshments. When we went, we'd have punch and some cake, something like that. We never had—it just didn't cost much. I danced a lot. We did a lot of dancing; we went to people's homes. We had fun. That was a party and we danced. There were Victrolas and records and we'd dance to the records. Or if somebody played the piano, and there was one there, we would dance to that. Or sometimes we would turn on the radio because big bands played on there so if we got it at the right time we danced to that. We did pretty much what kids have always done, just talked and walk[ed] to somebody's house.[52]

This connected them to their generation, even as they were outside the norm in many other ways. Frank Favors recalled how music affected him, a young black man in Summerville, Georgia: "Well, about the last of the Depression they put in these jukeboxes and we could go to the café and go in the back door and they would have a little room back there for the black people and they would have a jukebox back there and if you had a dime or a nickel, you could play it. I believe it was Louis Armstrong and Cab Calloway, I believe them two were the main singers then."[53]

Sometimes it is hard to imagine the way of life many within the rural South led. This is particularly true when it comes to health care. The acceptance of modern health care has, to a certain extent, wiped clean the folk history of family medicine, in which women were responsible for the general health care for the family. There were some country doctors, Mildred Williams told her young interviewer, but when "somebody on the farm got sick or a neighbor got sick, even if it was typhoid or pneumonia or malaria, people would go and sit at night and administer the medicine and put wet towels on them or whatever needed done." The doctor would come by and check on those who were ailing, but it was up to family and the community to monitor their care. The idea of going to the hospital was tantamount to an admission of death: "If you went to the hospital . . . they knew you were fixing to die because everybody stayed at home." Guy Knight concurred, telling his young interviewer that "if you went to a doctor, it was really serious. And if you went to the hospital, you might as well say good-bye because you were gonna die."[54] Frances Clements described in some detail how she protected her children:

I know there was an epidemic of diarrhea come through and just about every baby caught it and Lorene was my baby. She was born in 1939. The lady that lived next door to me had twins and they caught it. I took mine to the doctor and he told me to get my prescription filled and told me to take her home and get some fresh oranges and squeeze them, roll them and squeeze them and strain the juice through a strainer or a clean cloth and take rice and cook it for five hours and mix with the juice and take her off of all milk and everything else. I think it was for 24 hours, which I did and he said she'll get alright and I carried her to the doctor on Tuesday and Sunday she was alright.

Ruby Henry recalled her birthing experience,

I washed diapers for the others, well, the others had helped me with mine whenever she was so sick, because she was so sick you couldn't hardly do your work and take care of them. My husband worked on the second shift and he left the house at 2:30 p.m. and he would get back home about 12:00 a.m. and from the time he left home until the next morning she had had 14 movements and he told me to take her to the doctor . . . and I had to walk out and go to the hospital myself, but I stayed there as long as I could. When I had been in the hospital eighteen minutes, everything was over. The doctor even asked me, "Mrs. Henry, how in the world did you ever get in here?" I said, well, there is an attorney that lives next door to me, and the lady that lives in the house with me came with me, my baby was sick and my husband had to stay with her. He said, "I mean in here." I said, I walked in here. He said, "My God! I don't see how in the world you did." He told me "don't you even move a toe till they can get you to the emergency room," and the doctor was mean to me, he had just gotten back off of his vacation, and I was praying and he told me to shut my mouth, that God wasn't doing that, he was. I shut my mouth but I didn't quit praying, I just prayed to myself.[55]

Clements's and Henry's assessments of doctors and hospitals also rang true for most of the male informants, who identified either their mother or their wife as the primary health care provider and talked about the varieties of home remedies available. Guy Knight recalled some specific folk remedies:

If you got really burned bad we'd go out in the woods and find these . . . bamboo briars and you'd get these leaves off and take 'em home and momma'd make a salve. I got scars on me right now, 'cause I was meltin' a piece of rubber one time and dropped it on my hand. Old hands are getting so wrinkled now that you can hardly see it. If you got cut real bad or anything, momma'd just run and get some old spider webs and soot out of the chimney or whatever and stick it on there. And your scar would always turn out black, when it healed up. It was black because of the soot, but it stopped the bleeding. And we always had bad nosebleeds, most of us did. They'd tell you stick a pair of scissors down your back and lay 'em down behind the back and that's supposed to stop it. And you know, you might laugh about it, but nine times out of ten your nose would stop bleeding.[56]

Isabel Hester's description of labor was enough to perhaps frighten her young female interviewer out of having children:

When my first was born (1933) the doctor stayed there two nights and gave me all kinds of medication he could. So there was this fella that lived up off old [Georgia State Route] 27 going back towards Clem by the name of Cheyenne Morgan. He was a bootlegger. Doctor Otto was my doctor. My husband's name was Byron. The doctor told Byron "I've given her all the medication I can give her. Can you go to Cheyenne Morgan's and get her some whiskey?" So he went to the people we were living with and got a mule and went to Cheyenne Morgan's. He gave [him] a Coca-Cola bottle full. He told him what he wanted it for because he knew my husband didn't drink and he didn't make him pay for it. I don't know how much he gave me, but he sweetened it and put it in some water and I drank it and she was born about twenty minutes after. Then his daddy came in after she was born and turned up that Coca-Cola bottle and drank every drop of it. Byron told him, "Dad, I got that for medicine." "Well, you could get some more." So he drank it. His daddy was bad to drink.[57]

If corn liquor was one remedy, Frances Clements described another: "Only had a doctor if contagious disease were prevalent to get shots. If we stepped on a nail, Mamma put our foot in a pan of kerosene or turpentine and that was all the doctoring we got."[58] Brenita Reid described an old reliable from the era:

We didn't have no medicine, just castor oil. Castor oil and turpentine and this old black drought. Y'all don't know nothin' about that. When my children would get colds and I'd call 'em, Harvey hid. He'd always try to run and hide. He'd fly. Sometimes he'd get out and run down across the field. I gave him so much. Well, that was all we had. Yeah, that's what I had to [help] the children. Castor oil and put me two or three drops of turpentine in it. You could come to the store and get you a box of black drought. It wouldn't cost but a quarter. We kept some of it all the time. Harvey, he'd run and he'd hide, he took so much of it. He'd see me with that bottle and down across the field he'd go. Naw, we didn't have no medicine. I guess they might have had the drug store but we wasn't able to buy it. A lot of folks wasn't. There was an herb down in the woods—I don't see none of it now, I guess it got plowed up or dying out or something—call it scurvy grass. People used to go out and get it. A lot of us used to go a-fishin' and come down through the woods and dig up some scurvy grass and carry it home and wash all the dirt and grit off of it. Tie it up and hang it up. It was just like a laxative. It was good for colds. You could boil some water, pour over it, and steam it and drink it.[59]

There was a certain undefinable joy or pleasure the informants got out of telling these stories. The informants used a mixture of nostalgia for an imagined past and a desire to share with their younger interviewers tidbits that defined their daily life. Oral history, as Linda Shopes reminds us, is nothing if not "good stories" and could "obscure the workings of political and cultural power." But given that the chapters before address these issues, these recollections have a different ring to them. The level of community solidarity that comes through, the reliance on and reference to family, the idealization of the simplicity of their lives all help to paint a clearer picture of southern rural American life during the Depression era. The primacy of validity or "truth" within these narratives is overshadowed by the themes of self-reliance, hard work, and practicality that shine through. The people in this section are defining their world not in reference to something like work, government, or consumption but in relation to themselves. These are perhaps the most personal stories, for the informants hide little in describing the manner in which they existed during the era. Their stories remind the reader of the power of memory and the meanings associated with place and even class. They saw themselves (even as many later became city dwellers and middle class) as rural and poor, and the values associated with this experience helped shape how they saw the past and its meaning. For the interviewers and those reading these recollections, the picture of the past becomes more colorful, complete, and in many ways, real.[60]

5

"WE THOUGHT THEY WAS GOOD OL' DAYS BACK THEN"

Tales of Privation and Hope

When Susan Lockaby interviewed her grandfather Fred Lockaby about his experiences during the 1930s, he prefaced his recollections by reminding her (and us) of the subjective nature of his memory: "Them was the good ol' days I used to call 'em, but I wouldn't want to live back then. We thought they was good ol' days back then." Mr. Lockaby frames this chapter by reminding us that not all of what the informants remember about the era was truth in the universal sense of the word; some was reflective of the larger meanings associated with the difficult times. Some stories and memories that have a grounding of truth take on larger and more symbolic meaning as they are retold to those who did not experience the situation. In this way, the stories form a symbolic meaning outlining the basic lessons that many of those who lived through the era came to accept as definitive American values. Tales of economic collapse and privation were nearly always followed by stories describing people helping each other or the positive values associated with hard work. In this way, the responses in this section serve as a jeremiad of sorts, as they recount lessons learned through the struggles of the era. Sometimes larger than life, oftentimes delivered with greater lessons in mind, the stories that follow document the pervasiveness of the idea that the struggles of the Depression era, real or less than real, made the American people stronger and reinforced the values that would carry the country through World War II and the struggles afterward.[1]

One of the most pervasive of the informants' stories concerns the stock market and bank crashes of the early 1930s. Roy Patterson recalled,

> I forgot just when the banks crashed in '29 or '30. Papa had about $250.00 in the bank down in Douglasville—we heard that they had crashed—men was jumping off of the Austell Building and the Hurt Building committing suicide because they woke up and the stock

market had crashed and they did not have anything . . . all of their money was gone and they just committed suicide. But we walked to Douglasville when we heard it had crashed and closed the bank. Went down there and Mr. McLardy—he and my daddy had went to school together when they was boys around Villa Rica—and my daddy called him by his first name. We got down there and the people were standing around, ladies with little children—some of the ladies were crying—and my daddy called him by the first name. He was standing in the doorway at the bank and my daddy said "I come after my money." He said, "Jack, I am sorry, there ain't no money here." I imagine that they loaned it all out and they hadn't paid it back. It was sad to see all them people [learning] what little money they had was gone.[2]

Within this recollection are all the ingredients that point to the larger meaning Patterson was trying to get across. In the retelling, he made the situation personal (his father had money in the bank and knew the owner), connected it to the larger context (people jumping off buildings and committing suicide, as occurred in New York City and Atlanta), and conjured up images of privation and fear (women with crying children). He combined all the basic elements of the Depression in one story to convey to his young interviewer not just the situation but also the meaning of the era. People were sad, confused, yet somehow connected. Louis Dickey and Pat Inpecoven shared this story formation:

. . . when the Depression came he owed five thousand dollars. Well, they were going to take it [property] away from him for the five thousand dollars. There was some people that were going around buying up mortgages from the banks and they were about to foreclose on it. My dad told the banker that he had enough [life] insurance money that he could pay him off, but if he used it that he was only to take the banker with him when he went. In other words, threatened to kill the banker and kill himself.

Our banks were broke. The bankers, most of them, committed suicide. They just couldn't stand seeing what had happened to all of their clients and themselves. A lot of them committed suicide. Yeah, several of them did. Several of my best friends did, because not only did they lose everything they had but . . . everybody else did too. All their friends that they had recommended to their banks for years—friends of the families for generations.[3]

House in which cotton farmer has lived for fifty years. (Courtesy Library of Congress.)

Shirley Spruill painted a vivid image filled with Depression-era images:

> Money! Money was it. In news or in the papers the worst thing I think happened was, I can't remember how many, but I have read, jumped out of the Empire State Building each day to commit suicide. Bankers and the wealthy men just couldn't take it and I noticed where I remember reading that they said the bankers and professors and everybody wore holes in the bottom of their shoes. And it was soup lines so long till it take from one meal to the other for them all to go through the soup line.[4]

George Pope and Don Lowler connected the situation to the uncertainty of the future:

> Well, I guess the mood overall was very low, because everyone was wondering what was going to happen and what was going to become the outcome of, you might say the bankrupt[ing] of the world because we had banks that were closing. We had a neighbor that had about $5,000 in the bank and her husband had died and that was her life

savings and when the bank closed they closed and gave her 40 cents on the dollar.[5]

The mood was at first, I guess it would be anger, that we'd get in this kind of shape . . . the country would. But then it was fear that, you know, 'cause people were committing suicide 'cause they couldn't pay their debts. People jumping out of tall buildings and shooting themselves.[6]

For others, such as Jefferson Brock, the closings were personal: "I was married on June 11, 1931. I made a deposit on Friday night and on Monday, the bank failed. So it is safe to say that it was not a good time. That was the depression."[7] Similarly, Horace Bright recalled, "And I had, uh, 4 dollars and I think it was the best I can remember; 4 dollars and 35 cents in the bank when he closed the bank, and I never did get my 4 dollars and 35 cents."[8] The collapse of the banks made Bertha Hicks afraid for her family:

We had a bank in our town and if I remember correctly it was First Federal, I'm not positive that was the name of the bank but the president of this bank was a very good friend of my father's and 2 days before the bank closed he came to my father and told my father that the bank was going to go bust. And my daddy went to town and got his money out of the bank and back in those days they had cans for inner tube patching—if you had a car the tires had inner tubes and they had those cans of patching to tape it on to the inner tube. So he took his money out of the bank and rolled it up and put it in this inner tube can and hid it under the house. Of course, nosey me found the can and I was having a ball playing with the money. I can remember it was a lot of robberies; people taking things from the others back in those days. A lot of people from the north; the gangsters would come to our town, our part of the county. We lived back off the highway; they would pull off our little road into the pine trees and sleep in their cars and then after they would rest and sleep, they would come to our house and want food. There were several times I can remember my daddy going out the back door before my mom would start to feed them and they would not know he was around anywhere because he was outside with his gun waiting for them to make an attempt to rob us and he would stay to watch the barn all night when people was parked in the woods like that. It was a frightful time.[9]

Obviously, these stories are embellished a bit to accentuate the larger meaning they were trying to convey. Through the use of images and ideas that leave little room for alternative interpretations by the listener, the stories resonate with the fear and uncertainty that defined the entire era. As Bertha Hicks said, "It was a frightful time."

The narratives describing the onset of the Depression and the fear and confusion it brought serve as a foundation for other stories told, the design of which is less about conveying historical truths and more laden with other social meanings. The crash—which certainly created fear and led to a lack of money and opportunity—was painted as a dire portrait. Yet within this desperate situation, larger life lessons were learned. One of the most frequently retold focused on the value and meaning of money. Cecil Tate tried to impart to his interviewer how important money had been to him and his family:

> We had to kill them rabbits. We could get nine Monarch shotgun shells for a quarter, and you better not miss none. If you missed them you [had to buy] them at the Rollin' Store for a nickel apiece. And if you caught one in a rabbit—boy, you could get a dime for it. You learned to shoot a gun and even today when I pull the trigger, I'm going to hit what I'm aiming at. Oh yeah, we ate them rabbits—them "Hoover Hogs." And it was hard times. I would plow a pair of mules from sun up to sun down for $5 a day. And have to take it in peas or corn or cotton seeds. I didn't get no money.[10]

Laurel Haskins and Billy Stephenson grew up understanding the value of even the smallest amount of money and retold their stories as testaments to their frugality:

> I practically always saved mine (money) and until I had enough to do something. But I would say, at least half of the time my savings went back to my parents who needed it to buy bread. This would happen quite often. Or maybe it would cost a dollar to go to the doctor, take the baby to the doctor. Mom might only have fifty cents or so and we girls would dig out the rest of the money.[11]

> For instance, we had to economize on everything that we did. One of the things we did was when a customer was not in the store, my father would cut out the lights. Each light down the center aisle had a pull string socket. When a customer came in, he would go down

the aisle and pull on the lights. When the customer would leave, he would go back and cut the lights out again. Next door was another business, which at that time was a drug store. As you know, a drug store is very dependent upon the telephone and electricity. It became necessary to cut a hole in the wall in order for the drug store to use the same phone we used. When we had a phone call, they would pass the telephone over to us, and when we would receive phone calls for the drug store, we would pass the phone back to them. This seems to be very unusual, but everyone at that time was economizing in every way that they could.[12]

Many of the recollections in which the interviewer did not focus on a specific historical instance allowed the informants to create their own responses outside of the confines of the question. These responses contain elements that sought to detail the larger meaning behind the struggles and privations of the Depression era. As the stories above and those to follow detail, many are closely connected to an American storytelling tradition: the tall tale. Unlike the more classic tall tales from the mid-nineteenth century, which use comedic "fact" to exaggerate a story, the tales retold here tend to use privation to exaggerate a story. The storytellers utilized the basic storytelling formula of setting the stage, making it personal, and then finishing with an ending whose meaning could not be mistaken. In this way, the stories may also resemble allegories, as they seek to relay information on several levels—the real and the imagined. Understanding the symbolic meanings in their stories, the informants used the interview to tell not just what occurred but also how what happened had larger social, and perhaps even sacred, meaning. But rather than explicitly outlining these other meanings, the informants chose to weave the symbols associated with these meanings into their particular tall tales or allegorical stories.[13] "Listen" as James Peterson and Essi Whitely spin their tales:

During the depression, in Tacoma, I got a job in a Dodge garage. They let me sleep in the used cars in the back. The job I got was washing cars on the wash rack. I had one shirt, I would wash it in the harsh car soap, and tack it on the wall, instead of ironing, since there were no irons. While I was there, I was so hungry I went three days without eating. I was desperate, almost as desperate as those men jumping out of the windows. I found a dime on the street and picked it up. It looked like a million dollars. I went down the street to a donut shop where I had gone before when I had a dime. They would give you a cup of coffee and a donut for 10 cents. I went right down there and my favorite lady was working; she was a wise cookie; she knew that things were rough for me. I plunked the dime down and said "I'll take whatever this will buy me." She started pouring coffee and gave me a donut. She kept filling my coffee and filling me with donuts until I thought I was going to die. I ate so much I got so sick. After spending that wonderful dime and eating those wonderful donuts I went out into the alley and heaved it up.[14]

The hardest thing I remember: We had a neighbor. The boy took pneumonia. He was nineteen or twenty. He took pneumonia and died. And the man who owned his home had two cows and a pair of mules. And he couldn't get no money to bury that boy. Nowhere was there any money to bury that boy.[15]

Rose Conerly tried to convey both the personal and the larger social problems that came with the Depression:

One afternoon my husband and I was coming from a ball game; it was one Sunday afternoon. And, uh, about 4 p.m. we met a couple and they had a little baby on their shoulder and one quilt. They didn't have a suitcase and I don't know why they didn't. And Mitt said, it was coming up a big cloud and he said, "Where you folks going?" Said, "We don't know." He said, "You don't know?" They said, "No, we got kicked out of our house. We couldn't pay the rent and we just walking." Mitt said (they had a little baby!) a little baby on their shoulder and I didn't see nothing for that baby. It had a quilt. And Mitt said there was [a] store right up the road there a little ways, go on up there and get in it because there is coming up a bad storm. I've always wondered what happened to those people.[16]

Z. A. Sullivan remembered her lack of money in a way that would surely impress any interviewer:

And during that time my father died and we had no money to come down here to Georgia [from New York City]. And my husband's employer bought my ticket. And um, oh, they bought my ticket to come see my father's funeral. And my sister-in-law bought me a dress and a hat. But we were so long in getting off and the train—so slow that it was a day—no, a day and a half before I left New York. And um, so, um, I did not get to see him. He was buried in the morning. And we had to take the milk train from Savannah over to Dublin—over in a country station out there. So, therefore, I missed his funeral. He was buried in the morning.[17]

Inez Parkerson's narrative combined all the elements of a Depression story, from lack of food to outdoor toilets to walking miles for a penny:

Well, my home life was . . . rough. We didn't have it easy. We had to grow everything we ate, make everything we wore, wash clothes on a rubboard, cut wood, carry wood for the fire. We didn't have bathrooms, we had a little bathroom outdoors. We didn't have bathtubs, we had to take baths in a tin tub. But the wages were down with it. Just like it is now. You could get a nickel for a dozen eggs back then. But what you'd get out of them you'd have to take and trade. Now you can't get a piece of bubble gum for that. I've took an egg and walked five miles to meet a peddler and get one penny out of it. Few clothes to wear. I had two dresses . . . I wore one, one day and the one the next . . . washed them on weekends.[18]

Magdolene Martin and her cousins would hang around the railroad yards and truck depots looking for castaway food or coal:

We would go up there and get, ok, like when the trucks come in from Florida with the produce we would uh . . . when they come up we would take oranges and apples off the truck and uh . . . Sometimes the fruit that was already inside the place, they would put that out in the garbage for the fresh stuff. We would go out there and dive over in them garbage cans and get it. Sometimes the man . . . the boys come in on the truck with the driver, they would see us and throw out fresh fruit off the truck, you know, and stuff like that. We also—at the corner of Hunter, which is now Martin Luther King, then it was Hunter Street. At the corner of Hunter and Butler Street, the railroad tracks go 'cross there, you know, [the] railroad. We would go up there in the winter and set and set on the stoop 'til the folks would unload the boxcars. You know, putting that coal on the truck so it delivers to different houses, and every time it was an incline and every time the trucks go to come down the incline the trucks be piled up with coals so it would fall off. We'd have our sacks and we'd set there and when the coal fell off on the road, honey all of us children would be there grabbing coal, lumps of coal, putting it in our sacks. We tote those coals on our back right in front of there, you could look down over in there, just lean up on that wall and look down on the railroad. And between the railroad tracks it was a white man who use[d] to set there. Everyday, six days a week. He didn't have no legs. And he would draw pictures (religious pictures) in the sand. In the sandy area. He would draw pictures in the sand. People would throw money down there to him. But all that down there was stores. We used to walk that railroad; we'd get on up there, that's where we would pick up the coal at.[19]

Lema Mason saw the effect the lack of work and money had in her community and also the unity that developed:

You lost all your pride and everything else during that. Then something else. There was a poor family that lived not two miles from us. It was a big family and the father got sick. He had double pneumonia I think. Some of the neighbors went over there and he was sleeping on the floor on just a little pallet. He hadn't had a doctor and they saw that Dr. Burgess got down there. Dr. Burgess passed the word around that people better get with it and see about that family. Some of the men cut a big load of firewood and took firewood to 'em. Some took warm blankets and quilts. Some took some of their canned fruit. They took food and everything. Dr. Burgess went and didn't charge 'em a cent. He went to check him, he had high fevers, but he got well and plowed a mule.[20]

Money meant something to Geneva Stewart because she had so little of it:

And it was really hard times. I can remember that, at that time, one time we was sharecropping and uh, I had made my little girl a dress. I sewed, you know, made their clothes. And I had a little boy—he was about four, I guess, or three. And uh, some woman had given me material for him to make a little suit out of. And I wanted to make him a little shirt to go with it. And there used to be a material called pongi. It was pretty. Kind of a light tan. And I was down in the smokehouse one day and uh, picking off peanuts and I heard something rattle and I thought that sounded like a dime. You know, like a dime, and sure enough it was. And I took that money and bought some material out of that dime to make him a little shirt to wear with his little suit. I was so proud of that, I didn't know what to do. And I took them to church, them wearing them little clothes.[21]

Some of the stories the informants told reflect the reality of their lives but are narrated in a manner that attempts to convey privation, elicit pity, or document pride. These informants were consciously trying to get the interviewers (and us) to see their lives as poor and, in contrast with the more modern era of the interview, without luxury. However, given that they were country folk, what they described is how they lived and had lived for several generations; some of these experiences at the time held little association with poverty or privation. Consider Thelma Hughes's recollection of how she had to clean: "I washed in a washtub. I had a scrub board and a black pot. I would boil them outdoors. Well, I didn't have any kitchen appliances, nothing electric; in fact, we didn't have any lights. We had big old smoothing irons and we'd heat water on the stove to take a bath in and take a bath in a wash tub, a number 2 washtub, and drew water."[22] One can hear in this response Hughes's desire to see her young granddaughter-interviewer's look of incredulousness and her hope that the girl would then ask, "Golly, Grandma, you mean you washed in an old washtub?" Her interviewer did not take the bait, however, and the interview continued. This tactic was used by quite a few informants in the hope of impressing upon their interviewers the severity of the crisis or, as Ima Burns said, "Oh, I guess ... these children, my grandchildren, I get so irritated with them sometimes I just wish I could call back thirty [fifty] years ago, let them see what it was like, yeah, and let them, I just wish they could live one year, just one year, like I had to live. They'd appreciate life."[23]

This type of story, designed to get the interviewer to see the 1930s as a difficult time and to place the informant into the hardships, was often offset by tales of privation that reflected more realistically not just the level of poverty but also the mood of hopelessness and fear. Sometimes these stories were stretched a bit to give them more power, so things that had perhaps happened once or twice were retold in a way that was meant to suggest that they had happened daily. Consider Janice Skelton's and Cecil Tate's tales:

I have actually seen, and this is not a joke, I have seen men, 35 to 45 to 55 years old, walk during the winter months. It's cold, walk 10 to 15 miles, barefoot, to work on WPA to get that one dollar. They did not have, could not afford to buy, shoes for all of them. And he would, the man would, go without shoes so that the children could have shoes or something. I've actually seen that. I've seen them come in, in the winter time, and [their] feet would be so cold that we would go get—well, where you greased the car, you had rags and so forth, or to clean windshields—we didn't know what a paper towel was. We cleaned it with a rag. We would go get those towels, let them wrap their feet up in them 'til they could get warm. And they would go out and work all day if it was raining bad, just like that. Barefooted. Maybe they didn't even have a coat, nothing but their shirt and pants—overalls.[24]

The school I went to I had to walk two miles to school and in the mud. And the school had a three-room schoolhouse, a potbelly stove, and the desk was homemade, and there was two to the desk. The three rooms just went through the sixth grade. And we had a cloak room on each side, the boys went to one side and girls went to the other side. We put our milk and cornbread in there with baked potatoes and rabbits—which we called "Hoover hogs." That's what we had to eat. If you get close to the railroad you could of seen a man and his wife, and two or three kids, or however as many as he had. Would be on a flat boxcar riding or in a boxcar, and if you were a sittin''n looking out, they would be a hoboin', a man and his whole family. You couldn't buy or steal a job, there would be no such thing, you just didn't get no money.[25]

Norma Brumback retold a story that no doubt had been told many times, as it follows a strict story format:

There was a night school in our neighborhood, I think they were around all over the country, for the purpose of teaching illiterates to read. They were mostly men, all of them were men or just boys, any-where from 16, 17, 18 years old. I had two friends who taught school there and I went down to the school with them a time or two. One big, overgrown, red-headed boy named Willie said to Mary one night, "Miss Mary, I bet I done something today you didn't do." Mary said, "What was that, Willie?" He said, "I taken a bath. The CCC wrote me a letter and said they was gonna send for me sometime soon, so I thought I'd just go ahead and take my bath and be ready when they called."[26]

Clara Mae Knowlton first detailed how tough things were and then quickly distanced herself from these more radical solutions to the situation: "The Hoover days were tight, I'm going to tell you now. Times were so tight

Father of landless sharecropper family. (Courtesy Library of Congress.)

that women began to work on the streets, but along in then all we did was work on the farm."[27] Many of the stories were personal but relied on other people's experiences, based upon hearsay. Consider how Edgar Rhodes and Maggie Tiller told their stories:

> Our next-door neighbor came to my daddy one day and said, "Mr. Ed, I got to have some work [cause] we don't have any food to eat. And I'll work for any amount of money that you feel you can pay." So, he worked for us; I recall at $3 a week and the first time that he drew his pay he went home and told his wife that he didn't mind eatin' pinto beans for breakfast, dinner, and supper, but he was damn tired of 'em for dessert. So, I think he got some dessert.[28]

> I mean people were losing their jobs like flies falling off the table. And a lot of them, especially the young ones, not only couldn't find jobs and did lose them, but the ones who were young married ones, couldn't afford to pay the rent wherever they lived and they had to break up housekeeping and live with the parents and most every household you

saw had more than one family. Oh, they just all came back home and it was real rough.[29]

While framed in hard times, the stories also reflected a sort of humor, as in the way Claude Davis described the hardships: "The home life was rough, no jobs, the living was made on the farm because the jobs were gone in the cities and even the rabbits packed their lunch and went up on the mountain, the top of it."[30] Another theme is togetherness, as in Mrs. Charles Trimby's recollection:

> People moved in with their families, two and three families living in one house. Actually there wasn't as many homeless people back then but there would have been if they hadn't doubled up. Relatives took care of them. There were several soup lines and people would only get one meal a day. Men came to work so weak that they couldn't hardly work. What money they [the workers] could get a hold of they bought food for the children. Yes, stealing, not murder or anything like that; a lot of stealing. They would steal milk bottles, when milk came in glass bottles, they would go back and get the deposit on the bottles. If you left a car out, you could always figure that somebody would get your gas that night. I looked out one day, I was doing laundry, I looked out on the clothes line and they were all gone. I guess people needed them to wear. Some reason or another I didn't mind.[31]

That the woman above (who gave her name only as Mrs. Trimby) didn't seem to mind that people were taking things from her and her neighbors reflects another sort of symbolism that many informants relayed to their interviewers. Perhaps without realizing it, in recalling their experiences during the Depression era, they liberally used allegories to suggest a larger meaning. The type of allegory they used was not the strict classic definition in which words have exact meaning, but a more modern one in which the symbolic meaning of the words takes on a larger and more social meaning. And being southern, as Jan Whitt points out in her study of the allegory and southern writers, their use of this type of allegory is connected to their Calvinist Protestant faith. Unlike their northern counterparts, they did not hold to the "myth of innocence and success" but instead saw their situation within the context of past difficulties and a "longing for deliverance." In this way, the retelling of their lived experiences that conveys meaning outside the historical objective reality works like a parable, which Sallie McFague reminds us is nothing more than an "extended metaphor." These stories are meant to convey lessons about the experience to help the listener or reader get a sense of the larger meaning behind the struggle.[32] Even though things were hard, difficult, and bad, they were instructive to those who lived through the hardship, teaching them life lessons in equality, hard work, sharing, working together, and never forgetting the larger meaning of life. The informants told of how people pulled together, not just to document the past but also to suggest the lack of unity that they saw as part of their late-twentieth-century world. Rita Beine recalled that

> farmers were not looking for jobs; they were too busy doing their own farming. On rare occasions, if a farmer had all his farming done before the end of the season, one farmer may hire another farmer's son to do extra work for him. That was rare. Farmers got together to do their harvesting. But if a farmer who had no boys, as my father didn't have at that time, he did have a small son but too small to do farm work, he would go to the train stations where the hobos would be riding. Then he would interview them to see if any of them had any experience in farming. He rarely ever found someone that ever had farm experience, but he often brought home someone to do the simple chores around the farm like feeding the hogs, putting in feed for the cattle and the horses, and so on, so that dad could stay out in the field from daylight till dark. During that time, we farmed with horses and not with tractors, until the beginning of WWII. Again, we were not looking for work; we sometimes needed help. And it was the city people who were looking for work. I think just thinking back today the thing I remember most are those hoboes riding the trains. Every time I think about the Depression, I think of men riding the rails. And it's a very depressing thing to me. I think that it is the most depressing thing of anything that I have experienced, because I know now that many of those men never went back to their homes, they never had jobs to go back to.[33]

The hardships they endured became badges of courage, not issues of shame. "I can think back over the Depression and I am proud that we survived it," recalled Sam Davis. "You had to be tough to survive and you had to be able to work and be willing to work. If you were, then you could make it."[34]

Other stories practically tell themselves. Josephine Taff told her tale in an almost exhausted manner:

I was married when I was thirteen years old. I was living down here at the Taffs' where they live now. And we had people that come there, that their shoes were wore out, begging to work for thirty-five cents a day. And that is when the PWA was on the roads. They were working with mules, shovels, and picks. I picked cotton, I hoed cotton, I pulled footer. I plied the tractor, anything that come in the farming life, I was in on it. The hard times, we had hard times. I could tell you a lot, but I won't. You may not like it. Honey, I've been when it is freezing cold and didn't have a thing on but a little old thin dress. In the Depression time right down yonder [referring to the place she lives], didn't have nothing to buy, no underclothes, and didn't have none. Because I bought it for my little old young-uns and done without myself and went cold. A lot of times I've been under the floor, where we put the potatoes for the winter, to try to save our Irish potatoes and I was gravelling it out, no bigger than that [about the size of a silver dollar] so we could have something to eat. And one day while I was down there, Uncle Jack Taff come and he, I reckoned he had saved money or something, it was on Sunday. All we had to eat was them little Irish potatoes and biscuits. And my husband made me get up and make the kids leave together and to cover it up, so that he wouldn't know how little we had to eat.[35]

Norma Brumback described a typical Hooverville in Alabama:

These little shacks that were built up in a little wooded area, out of Gadsden a little piece, out on the edge of town there, they were made of, men built them themselves. They were made out of tar paper, pieces of metal, tin roofing, and pieces of lumber that were just, they'd find them anywhere they could, you know. They made them. They were about, I'd say not over nine or ten by nine [feet]. That was the size of them. Yes, just more or less like a little shed to get in. There were a number of them in this one little place. Just ever so many of them. It was a sight to see. I expect there were twelve or fifteen or maybe more in that group, and it was named Hoovertown. That's what the people called it, Hoovertown.[36]

Other stories were just as heartbreaking. Stella Bowie detailed the personal effect the Depression had on her:

Well, to start with, I was engaged about that time and we were going to get married, and we didn't pay too much attention to the change.

We knew there had been a crash in '29, but it was later that we were affected by it. All the young people were happy and my husband to be and I were saving money. I was working at the telephone company and he and my father were working at General Outdoor. We were doing okay. We weren't making the money like they do now, but we made enough because prices weren't then like they are today. I got sick and had an operation, so I waited a year to get married. But, about the time we got married, we didn't realize it, but the Depression was really coming on. We had been paying on our furniture and had quite a bit paid on it. We moved into this apartment, it was a nice apartment. We were getting along real well and about six months after we were married, General Outdoor just went out of business. My father and my husband were out of work and that's when the trouble began. We had to move out of that apartment into a little house, but we still had our furniture. We had our furniture almost paid for. My husband could not find work and what he did find, paid very little money. We couldn't keep up the payments on our furniture, so we lost it every bit. So, then we moved into another little furnished apartment. We were having a hard time—a real hard time.[37]

John R. Beach told the following story to his young interviewer to convey the seriousness and pervasiveness of the hardship, even as some, via government assistance, had hope for the future.

They had bread lines, especially after it got real bad when the factories closed down. The government would have bread lines and all they would do is—you would go get in lines three blocks long that would go all the way around buildings. And, by the time you got there, they would give you a cup of soup, which was watered down; a very thin soup, and a piece of bread. That was the only way people could eat; they didn't have no food! They just got into bread lines. To give you an example: In the CCC camp, the mountaineers that lived all around there would come down there every night to look for the leftovers after we had eaten supper. We would take our mess kits and scrape them into the trash can and most of the boys knew they were there to get food, so they would get more than they should have just to rake it into the garbage for the mountaineers. I did that one night with a big piece of meat, and three men, one of the bloodiest fights I had ever seen, fought over that piece of meat with their wives and children standing around waiting to see who would get the piece of meat. That was the God's truth; I saw that. That's how tough it was.[38]

In Beach's story, we see both urban and rural descriptions of the Depression. Most of the informants were from rural areas of the South, so their stories of privation tended to focus on strangers coming through town or by their farm, or their own personal struggles. Some informants, however, did recall the urban scenes that are often visually more associated with the Depression. In these recollections, they tell of bread and soup lines but do so in a way that tries to impart to the interviewer the dire circumstances of those trying to get something to eat, as Preacher Cain described: "They had established soup kitchens here in Atlanta and I passed this particular soup kitchen and I bet there were 300 people in that line and that freezing rain to get something to eat just to keep soul and body together. And I said 'Oh God, why?' Here was the land of plenty and they was gonna destroy, and did destroy, a lot of different things—wheat and cotton. They're starving to death and can't hardly exist. And I still don't have the answer to this."[39] That people were hungry and forced to stand in line for food was among the more vivid and emotional recollections for both Bessie Mae Chandler Birdsong and Viola Elder:

> It's terrible to see people standing in line to get food. We had soup kitchens, they called them then. Lot of people didn't have anything to eat. Women didn't wear stockings, they didn't have any. We went bare-legged and we didn't wear hats.[40]

> We were very poor, 'cause you know there wasn't no jobs hardly and a lot of times we didn't have food, we had, we had to go to this soup kitchen that they had, and the bigger family you had the more food you got, and so we always got two big buckets of soup and maybe we would get two or three loafs of breads, we called them pones of bread then. It wasn't what we call them today, pones of bread, it was the bread that wasn't sliced, you had to cut [it] yourself or pull it out, break it and eat it.[41]

Some, such as a Mrs. Wasdin, did what they could to help others: "And when I lost my job, I did help some before I got another place in a lawyers' office in Atlanta. Between jobs I helped with the poor people—the food lines. I helped some; I didn't cook. I didn't know how to cook. But I helped stringing beans and different things. The only thing I could do."[42] E. B. (Preacher) Cane retold his story with even more effect:

Let me just tell you this little incident. I told you that I had a job and had an old '27 Pontiac Oldsmobile that I drove to and from work. One morning I was going to work in the winter time and it was drizzling rain and freezing, and in the city of Atlanta they established what were called soup kitchens. People could go by and get vegetable soup to sustain life. I drove by this place one morning in the freezing rain and estimated 300 people in line standing in the freezing rain from the age of six to seventy. They were all waiting in line to get soup in order to sustain life. It was rough going.[43]

Recollections such as these reveal the narrative structure of the informants' stories. They were far less interested in relaying historical information than in telling the story. They were trying to get the students to understand the totality of the situation by both placing themselves into the situation and revealing the larger societal hardship. Through these stories, they established a pattern of understanding between themselves and the interviewers. This connection enhanced the respect the students had toward their subjects and allowed for freer and more open conversations. Many of the interviewers were related to those they interviewed, and this situation may have been one of only a handful of times in which the relative was given the space to tell what he or she had experienced. This empowerment allowed them to use the storytelling format to guarantee that their young relations would understand the larger moral lessons from the era. This relationship was not reserved for only family, however, as the oral histories reveal that many of the informants used the storytelling format to communicate what they saw as the more important lessons of the Depression era. Maurice Sponcler, a student at Georgia Tech in Atlanta at the time, related one such story: "One of the things that I remember so well, that really brought the Depression home to me, was this boy named Qualls that dropped dead on the street in Atlanta. He was a student at Tech. He dropped dead on the street and, when they performed an autopsy, they had found out he had starved to death. Of course that made a great impression on every student at Tech. The fraternities up there opened up their tables so that anybody that was hungry could come in and get a meal, whenever they wanted."[44] Annie Louise Curry told her interviewer that people

had to do the best we could, a lot of times we sat up and did without. We didn't have anything to eat. Nowhere to get none. We go around to some white people's houses sometimes, they let us sweep the yard and they would give us milk and butter, cold bread a lot of times. I clean up the kitchen and things they give me for helping. We were glad to get it 'cause we didn't have nothing. If you had to lay down hungry one or two nights you would thank evil, know you would. You would have been used to plenty to eat and everything, then they cut it down, you don't have anything to eat [and] you got to do what the man tell you to do, not what your mama or daddy tell you what to do. If you got a little baby and if you got another little baby then the two little children stay at the house by themselves.[45]

Some hardships were almost too difficult to describe to the interviewer; the stories, though rarely about the experiences of the informants, tried to relay the desperation and fear. Marjorie Batson, for example, told of "a family that were living in a trailer, actually, it was a hunting camp, or something on out the road a few miles from us. And this man had been arrested for shooting a rabbit out of season, and it turned out that he had this family, he had a wife, a little boy, a little girl, and she was expecting a baby, and they were from out in Kansas, or someplace, I don't know. I don't know just how they happened to get there, but anyway, they did."[46] Virginia Thelan told a heart-wrenching tale of poverty, death, and despair: "The thing that stands out in my mind was that there was a little boy that died in school and when they investigated they found out that he had starved to death. His family only had corn on the cob to eat and they were trying to cook it over a kerosene lamp. And that just stuck in my mind. That poor little boy was sitting right there and nobody knew he was starving to death."[47]

Hardship thus defined the era, but as Laurel Haskins remembered, so too did kindness:

One thing that sticks in my mind is about this man who had a wife and two children. He lived up on the edge of town. He had lost his job. He went up to the grocery store and asked the man to give him a sack of flour. The man told him he was sorry but he couldn't have any flour because he owed him money now. The man just picked up the flour and carried it back home. The grocery man called the sheriff and told him what the man did. So the sheriff went after him. When he got there, the woman was making dough on, what do you call those things? To make dough on? A bread tray, back then they called them bread trays. The wife was making up dough and one child was on the side eating the dough and one on the other side eating the dough because they were so hungry. The sheriff saw this and turned around and went back and paid for the flour. That stuck in my mind. People were so poor.[48]

The informants used the storytelling technique to impress upon the younger interviewers that times were very hard, and simply retelling the facts would not reveal the depth and breadth of the crisis. Even as their stories told about themselves and their own experiences, they included anecdotes to reinforce the meaning of their experiences. It is as if their own experiences lacked the power to capture the full depth of the hardship and the era, so that only with the inclusion of these other stories could the full view of the crisis come forth. This applies as well to the follow-up to these hard-luck, difficult-time stories, namely, the larger moral lesson. Given the harshness of the times, the struggle for food, work, and money certainly would have encouraged the basest of human desires to come forth. Survival is the most basic of instincts, and in the face of joblessness, homelessness, and starvation, competition among the people for the scant resources must have led to isolation, fear, and a survivalist sense of individualism. The informants established in their storytelling a structure that essentially set up the interviewer. After hearing about stories of hardship, unemployment, and hunger, the interviewer then asked more open-ended questions such as "What can you recall about the general mood or the feeling of the country or your community?" and "What do you recall best about the 1930s?" Sometimes an interchange would occur that clarified the question, and then the informant would present the larger lessons learned from the struggles, especially patience, charity, and thankfulness. Georgia Mae Calloway remembered,

> [I] could make myself happy with what I had. I never been a person to want everything I see somebody else with. I use what I got since I been grown, to benefit me and my family. And all that I couldn't get, they understood. I wasn't gonna do something against the law to try to get [something]. I found when you use what you have to your advantage, then you don't need to do something outside the law. Be thankful for what you have. Some people don't have anything, but they have to be thankful anyway. And it's a lot of people can't do any better because they don't know how. And it takes patience. You can't just sit down and say what I'm gonna, it takes patience to get anything done right. You can't hurry through nothing; if you do, you make a lot of mistakes. Then when you make those mistakes, everybody want

to put it on somebody else. But if they your mistakes, you just was to own up to them. No use trying to persecute somebody else because you made a mistake. Learn from your mistakes. And if you take time and listen, you can learn from other people's mistakes. You don't have to go that road because you see what happened. And then not only black, it's white too. So we are all just in this world together, we're gonna have to stay until time to leave.[49]

Tom Skelton had a similar perspective:

I guess the main thing I remember, there were some hard times, but there were good times, too. But a lot of times we had to do without things, we had to do the best we could, like we've already said, with whatever we had, but we learned how to cope and how to make the best of what we had, and we didn't really suffer that much. Now, some people did. But I don't remember ever suffering because of it. I can remember doing without a lot of things. But that was just part of living, and we had a good time. People enjoyed being together. I think maybe people were friendlier and were closer because of that sort of thing, you know. I can remember we used to have a good time just getting in the car and going and sitting down, well, just [to] park. Or on Saturday afternoon, just sit in the car and watch all of the people. That was our fun for Saturday afternoon. And we had a good time, and enjoyed being together.[50]

Ruth Rhymer observed,

But I guess the Depression made everybody think, and think deep, about what kind of situation we were in and if everybody didn't pull together, it would have never come back and I guess that people pulling together had a lot to do with it. Everybody pulling together. Not this one fighting with that one or that one fighting with that one like it is now. Everybody helped everybody else. Somebody would come by and ask, "Is there anything that you need? Is there anything that we can help you with?" It wasn't just one, it was so many. It was the attitude of the country. This one knew if they didn't help that one they might be in the same jinx. So everybody helped.[51]

Bessie Pendergrass was more pragmatic:

Everybody worked for what they could do and taking care of what they could. You know, like I said, people helped each other. But uh, you didn't have much, there was no telephone down there, you didn't have that back then. There wasn't much way you find [out what was happening], of course they had papers, but people wasn't able to buy the papers but many of them [did]. So you didn't get much news in or out, you didn't know much of a thing going on. But I think the Depression learned the people a thing. I think it, after the Depression it learned people to appreciate what they had more, what they didn't, they got, and what they already had. And I don't think, it just changed the people on, all the way around, everything. Things happened that never happened before that made you appreciate it. And in all, I think it was a big change in the whole world. About that time everybody figured, began to bloom out and have lots more.[52]

The struggles were part of the larger lesson of life, according to Earnest Pierce: "You make sure that they know, anything like a Depression is character building. It separates men from the boys and you can put up with a lot of things when you have to. That's what the Depression did for most people. It built character for them. There wasn't any of this easy life, you have to do things, you can do them."[53] Similarly, Jim Teague asserted, "I don't think the Depression had any detrimental effect on the majority of the people who came up in that era. I think it made better people, stronger people. I think it made them more determined."[54]

Identifying the larger societal lesson almost invariably led the informants to tell what many children, grandchildren, and anyone younger than the teller call "good ol' days" stories. These are tales retold again and again that reinforce that even though things were terrible in the past, somehow the people and larger society were better off. The values of the present cannot hold up to those of the past, because the people then were kinder, gentler, and much more open to others. Anyone who has heard these stories and tried to interject historical context knows the failure of the effort, for despite the introduction of facts contradicting this belief, the direction of the tales remains fixed in the consciousness of the tellers. Consider the following examples of the "good ol' days" theme from Dorothy Hill, Lynna Vaughn, Faye Ivey, Lizzie Johnson, Steve Dearing, and Geneva Stewart:

The best thing I think that came out was the togetherness and the unselfishness that neighbors had. Neighbors looked out for one another. We did not have to lock our houses. We did not have to let the windows down. You could go anywhere you wanted to go. You could go downtown and just tell your neighbors you were gone. You did not have to worry about anyone going in your house and taking nothing. We just pushed our door up at night and went to bed. No locks, no locks. You could go off on a trip and you would just tell your neighbors "I'm gone" and pull your door up and that's all it was to it. We slept with our doors open.[55]

Yes, I tell you if anybody got sick in the community, you know if they needed their crop plowed, the people would just go in and do it. Those things, if it hadn't been for that, because sometimes people got sick and then there were those who didn't get sick.[56]

Well, people just loved everybody. Neighbors were so close back then. There wasn't any hatred. Everybody helped each other out back then. Many a times we got in the wagon and the neighbors would be a little piece from us, and we'd spend the day with them and they would do the same. I can't understand why people just don't love each other like they did back then.[57]

I didn't see no sad people walking around. You know. Uh—most [of] the time—our neighbors had vegetables and things like that—and somebody out there needed some help—needed something, me and my mama went to the garden and carried vegetables to them. And I know one time, there was a lady that had a baby and it died, on the out- side of Ranburne, that's where I married my husband, and uh—they didn't have anything, they didn't have nothing to wrap the little baby in but an old dress or something and I went up. I said, "Mama, I'm gonna carry that little woman some vegetables." They had some more children and we made a big old pot of chicken stew and dumplings. And uh—I carried it to them and they was happy as somebody you ever seen ... but in the '30s everybody wanted to help people. Every- body wanted to help somebody that needed anything. If we had it, we divided it with them. I wasn't the only one, everybody done that. Everybody loved everybody then. I don't think they do now. Well, you can see 'em—you can see 'em—just not think about other fellows, just for theirselves.[58]

There wasn't as much crime back then 'cause nobody didn't have noth- ing for nobody else to steal. About all that was stolen was chickens and horses and something like that. You didn't have to keep the doors locked 'cause there wasn't as much crime and everything as there is now. I think there was more love of the neighbors. They'd pitch in if you had crops that had to be gathered. If you was having bad luck or something, got sick, the neighbors would all come in and pick your cotton or gather your corn or something like that. In the fall, when you got too cold, they'd get out and pick bolls and the neighbors would come in and pick the cotton out of the bolls. It was nice; they'd stay up 'til late hours of the night to help you. You wasn't afraid. Back then, I wasn't afraid to go from here to town in the dark by myself, which I would now. But back then, see, everybody was just about the same, struggling, and there wasn't any crime. Only reason you'd close the doors was to keep a dog or something like that. We didn't have to fear people, crime. As far as having material things, you didn't have material things. We just struggled to get by.[59]

We didn't think about locking your doors at night. There wasn't near as much stealing. Nothing like it is now. Seemed like people loved one another more, or maybe it's 'cause there's a lot more people now than

Mrs. Lemuel Smith and the children working in the garden. (Courtesy Library of Congress.)

there were then. But I believe times have just got worse. The people have gotten meaner and don't care. I kinda believe, see, there wasn't no such thing as this drug deal like they have now.'Course there was a lot of bootlegging takin' place. People making moonshine.[60]

What made the "ol' days" meaningful and therefore "good" to those who lived through them was the difficult lesson they learned via the hardship. The hard times framed the meaning of the rest of their lives and became one of the cornerstones of the post-1945 American identity—sacrifice. Combined with World War II, the Depression produced a generation of people who saw themselves as part of a group that understood that individuals had to sacrifice for the greater good, even if that good was uncertain. This lesson—hard work made us great and more unified—was one they took into the war, and it became a building block of the postwar consensus. The Depression, Augustus Jackson Sharpe told his interviewer, helped unify the country because everyone was "'bout . . . about the same. Everybody was about the same. We's all poor folks. One couldn't say nothin' 'bout the other 'cause we's all poor folks."[61] This meant that people worked together for what began as survival but then became a way of being, as Carter Ray and Larry Carroll related:

Money, cash money, as such, in the larger part, disappeared from our community. People helped one another. The farmers brought meat into town, and gave it to people who didn't have farms. They'd give them corn, and take it to the mill and have it ground. People in town, (we) all had gardens. We had vegetables and fruit and so forth, we ate well. I would daresay that there was not any person who came through this community and asked for a meal and left hungry. We took better care of our clothes and our shoes, and made do in a lot of cases. Generally, the people in this town managed. I know of a case where a widow lady walked out of a store, and my daddy jumped up and said, "I'll be back in a minute." He went out of the office and went down the street and came back a little later. I saw him stubbing a check and I said, "Just what does that mean?" (I was the bookkeeper). He said, "Son, don't ever tell this, but that lady that walked out of here was looking down at the sidewalk. That meant one thing, they have refused her any more credit. She's a widow with two children at home. If somebody doesn't do something about it, nothing but tragedy will come out of it." He said, "Your daddy is going to do something about it. I don't want this told, because I told them not to tell her, if she could ever pay it, they would give it to me. I trust them to do that." These are things that honorable men learned to do in this world.[62]

Just, people were out of work and desperate. In the cities they managed to get by; people took care of each other. I know here in Atlanta, a good many firemen, they shared their wages by feeding and giving shoes and one thing or another to youngsters of people who were really hard up. A lot of firemen just shared what they had with some hard up people.[63]

The times encouraged people to look beyond their own wants and consider the needs of others. Joe Johnson recalled,

There was just full of people walking back and forth, trying to catch rides, going from one town to another, trying to get a job. There was just so much joblessness and people were constantly knocking on our door wanting a handout, wanting some food. They were hungry and my mother would always try to have something to give to everybody that come there, even though we didn't have enough to eat ourselves. But she always tried to have a little something to give to anybody that come and asked for food, and it was just a, a time of rough going, so to speak, nobody had any money to spend.[64]

Laura Kolb suggested to her interviewer the reward that came from her family's compassion:

I remember one night this man came to the front door, and knocked on it. Daddy went and he said his name was Hester, and he had lost his job at a cotton mill, up in town, north of us. So, he had an old T model truck or Ford, and he had his children in there, his wife, and it was about 9 p.m. They had nowhere to stay at night. So, daddy said, "Well, I got an empty store down here that I'll let you stay in." So, he moved them in, went down there that night, and they had some mattresses. We got some blankets from the house. That's the reason people saved a lot of stuff, because they never knew when it was going to be needed by somebody else. So, he took those people down there and let those people stay in that store. It was right in the middle of town too. They stayed down there. I know it must have been 6 or 8 months before he could find a job, you know, and really get a job. Well, now, since then that man has died, and his boy was running for county commissioner one time. He told him [Daddy], "I never will forget what you did for us that time during the Depression." Now, he is an outstanding businessman himself. So, you can tell that you never know when your favors are going to be returned.[65]

One simply did not ignore the plight of others, as Al Leiker said, because it "was nothing uncommon during those days for someone to knock on your door, willing to work for one day, or whatever, just for something to eat. No one was ever turned away, and you were afraid of no one walking around in your neighborhood begging for food."[66]

Women informants particularly recalled sharing what they had and the desperation they were witness to. In their retellings, they displayed their thankfulness for not being the other and the hope that if they ever were in the position of someone looking for food or help, it would be forthcoming with the same lack of judgment. Martha Loren Scott related,

> I had two small children, and of course during that time, people just lost their jobs like they are doing now, and it was a time that you had to be careful with food and all other things too. Then there were people too that came by and you didn't refuse them any food because the men would walk from one place to another to try to find a job. There was a railroad that came from Rome to Kingston, Georgia, and it was easy for them to just come down here because there weren't any houses over there at that time. They would come by and ask him if I had anything to eat, and whatever we had, we shared it with them; sometimes, it would just be a biscuit, butter, and jelly, but it was some food for them.[67]

Many told stories of these wandering souls (or even neighbors) and stated that they felt a certain social responsibility to share what little they had. Listen to Claudia Ward, Wyolene Warren, Kathleen Bartlett, Geraldine Chadwick, and Ruby Henry share their memories:

> About the people going hungry, and tramps coming to the door— what everybody called tramps then because they were tramping from one town to another and mostly walking and riding freight trains and all of this and trying to find something to do so they could eat and send for their families, and send something back to their families. But we always had something to give for them to eat when they would stop at our house.[68]

There were lots of people that was hobos, they called them then. They come by wanting something to eat.

Did you give it to them?

Yes, I was sorry for them. Sometimes I didn't have anything cooked. One time I told them that I didn't have anything but bread and some onions, and I had some meat fried. And I gave it to them. I was ashamed to but it was better than nothing. And he sure did appreciate it, and he went down the road to catch a train. It had stopped just a little ways past the house. So he went down the road eating his bread and onion. I was sorry about it, but I guess he enjoyed it.[69]

Sometime, I can remember one time I gave nearly about every bit of our little fragments that was left over, you know, sharing it with my neighbors. And I like to give it all away, I bet a lot of people done the same thing. By trying to divide with everyone they could, you know, that didn't have any meat at that time, but when our neighbors would kill they would do us the same way, you know.[70]

At that day in time, if you stop and think about it, I was young, and those things didn't seem to worry us. My husband and I in one sense, like I said, if we had anything we'd share or if we could buy anything unusual we'd share it with our neighbor.[71]

One day I called my children to come in and eat dinner and it was 11:30 a.m. and I wanted to get through so I could set down 'cause I didn't have a washing machine. The lady next door to me had four children and her oldest one said, "Mother! When are we going to eat dinner?" She says, "Well, we are not, we ain't got nothing to eat." And I went in there and I had some soup and beans, I added water to that and fed them. I did that for months and I couldn't stand to see those children without anything.[72]

In all the interviews, I came across only a small handful of people who did not see in the past this sense of community and hope within the hardship and desperation. Paul Johnson was one of the few. He recalled, "A lot of people were in bread lines and soup lines. People were having a hard time getting food and paying for it, so that wasn't good. It just really didn't affect us badly. The story of my way of life is that I had a job, clothing, and food.

I was working as a lawyer for the RFC, so life was secure. You didn't just go up to people on the street and ask about their life. We lived in the good part of town and we just didn't have any connections to the people in the soup lines."[73]

Was his the accurate retelling of the past? Given human nature and the scant resources available during the Depression, it seems more likely that those who had money and resources kept to themselves and had few occasions to interact with or help those affected by the Depression. However, the scores of others who recall in the era a sense of community and hope cannot be overlooked as simply old-timers nostalgically looking back to a simpler time. The meaning of truth is woven within their recollections, and their stories of sharing amidst the struggle are too many to be ignored. Perhaps some were spared the ravages and lived their lives as though little had changed, but at least through the memories of the people interviewed here—who came primarily from the rural areas of Georgia, Alabama, and Tennessee—one is witness to a story of economic and social reconstruction, a time when society was changing and those caught up in the change were searching for new values and meanings within their families and communities. Their stories, these tales of privation and hope, document their search and outline the values that would take the country into the future.

CONCLUSION

"IT'S BEEN WONDERFUL TALKIN' TO YA"

Memory of Hope

Ethel Carraway concluded her interview with her grandson by thanking him for the opportunity to share her experiences during the 1930s. Married in 1935, she and her husband had a hard time of it in Birmingham, Alabama, but like many others who were part of this study, they remained focused on the positive things that came as a result. She continued, "You've brought back memories of a lot of things—if we had more time, I could tell you, uh, I never have told you and your Daddy what a real hard time we had during the Depression, but I always have had the, uh, ability to forget the past and the unpleasant things, and just think about the bright things in the future and, uh, with you growing up, and a young man, now, uh, I can understand that, uh, you're going to help change the world, too."[1] Her assessment of memory and how she recalled the past identifies the way in which this book tries to better define the collective consciousness of the people who experienced firsthand the Depression era. Central to this point is to be comfortable with the "way" they saw the past, which is neither dogmatic nor true but reflects basic core values that are associated with the larger struggle. The struggles of the era give structure to the informants' recollections and filter the historical "truth" through the larger and more subjective lens of meaning. As Joe Salituro told his grandson, "I guess I would have to say it was the closeness of all the people. When there's little money it just kinda brings people closer together. And I do remember everybody congregating in the neighborhood situation and all the families in the neighborhood were close together."[2]

Oral history allows the viewer/listener not only to hear about historical episodes of the past but also understand their meaning within the generation that experienced it and therefore defined it. In this way, we can come to understand how the collective consciousness is developed, namely, through the shared experiences and activities that give meaning to the time period rather than the specific and fixed events that chronicle the time period. Historical episodes from the Depression era, such as the New Deal activities and the expanded popularity of radio and the culture industries, are real. They happened in an orderly and, at times, reasonable manner. There is little debate about their occurrence. But what this study reveals is how these fixed events came to be valued and given meaning by those most affected by them. As time passed and the details of the historical events blurred, what those who lived through the time held onto were the larger social and more significant personal meanings. In this way, they came to frame their experiences in a manner that captured the emotional and personal ramifications even as they wrapped their recollections around the larger, more accurate historical episodes. "Wasn't much of a life during the Depression," Gene Autry began his interview; "it was a good life before and after [but] during the Depression we were like everyone else—we didn't have much of a life."[3]

The collective consciousness developed during the Depression era, at least as these five hundred or so interviews reveal, concerns the values of hard work, community, family, and social justice. The interviews give meaning to these shared values through the ability of the informants to recall the active and compassionate involvement of the federal government in their lives, to the transformation of their world brought about by the expansion of the ideals of capitalism, through the stories of jobs or lack thereof, through the emotional recollection of stories concerning brothers, sisters, mothers, fathers, relatives, neighbors, and even people they did not know but who helped frame the way in which they saw the Depression era. Their sacrifices and the larger meaning behind their privation gave form to their memories in much the same way as those who experienced the American Revolution or the Civil War came to see their collective pasts. The informants saw the era as a binding one, during which everyone was, in one way or another, in the same boat. And the unity of their memories suggests that this sense of collective identity, reinforced by the struggles of World War II, remained an important part of their personal histories, something they never forgot. What makes oral history special is that it tells us, as Alessandro Portelli has written, "less about events than about their meaning." In this way, it serves as a lens through which we can see how history imprinted individual lives and how these people became part of the Depression-era reformation. Theirs is a "shared authority" (a great term given us by Michael Frisch in his 1990 book), as their recollections reveal how they both shaped and were shaped by the events of their time and those that came afterward.[4]

Plough boy sitting on a fence after a day's work. (Courtesy Library of Congress.)

The shaping of the memories that constitute this research project was reinforced by World War II and the cold war consensus. The values of this generation, shaped in privation but defined by hope, remind us of the power of collective action, of people—strangers even—helping one another, of not having enough money or things yet finding solace in the simple and joyous experiences of friends, family, and community. Many of those interviewed complained about the modern era of the early 1990s, suggesting that the accumulation of wealth and society's overheated consumerism was eroding many of the values they had learned through their trials and tribulations. Very few wanted to return to that day, as they understood their own recall of the simple past to be nostalgia, but they did grieve the loss of the basic human values they were forced to confront during the time when their collective consciousness was formed. They remained hopeful that by sharing their stories, the torch of hope would be passed on to another generation.

NOTES

Introduction. The People Remember

1. John K. Davenport, interviewed by Lynn Queen, Nov. 4, 1991, Bindas Oral History Project (hereafter cited as BOHP), in the author's possession. Much of what this study reflects is the emerging historical discussion concerning collective memory, and while this is not the focus of *Remembering the Great Depression in the Rural South*, its theoretical underpinnings gird the argument set forth. The discussion concerning history and memory begins with Maurice Halbwachs, *On Collective Memory* (Chicago: University of Chicago Press, 1992 [orig. 1950, 1939]) and moves through a variety of disciplines, including *Realms of Memory: Rethinking the French Past*, under the direction of Pierre Nore, translated by Arthur Goldhammer (New York: Columbia University Press, 1996), 1–21; Jaclyn Jeffrey and Glendace Edwall, eds. *Memory and History: Essays on Recalling and Interpreting Experience*, (New York: University Press of America, 1994); James Wertsch, *Voices of Collective Remembering* (Cambridge: Cambridge University Press, 2002); David W. Blight, *Beyond the Battlefield: Race, Memory & the American Civil War* (Boston: University of Massachusetts Press, 2002); Diane Barthel, *Historic Preservation: Collective Memory and Historical Identity* (New Brunswick: Rutgers University Press, 1996); Gregory J. Sheperd, Jeffrey St. John, Dario Paez, and Bernard Rime, eds. *Collective Memory of Political Events: Social Psychological Perspectives* (New York: Sage, 2006).

2. John Forrest and Elizabeth Jackson, "Get Real: Empowering the Student through Oral History," *Oral History Review*, 18 (Spring 1990), 29–33; Michael H. Ebner, "Students as Oral Historians," *History Teacher* 9 (Feb. 1976), 196–201; Roger D. Long, "The Personal Dimension in Doing Oral History," *History Teacher* 24 (May 1991), 309–12; William E. Ellis, "Using the Great Depression Experience in a College American History Survey Course, *History Teacher* 25 (Nov. 1991), 87–92; Alistair Thomson, "Fifty Years On: An International Perspective on Oral History," *Journal of American History* 85 (Sept. 1998), 581–95, especially pp. 581–83; Valerie Yow, "'Do I Like Them Too Much?': Effects of the Oral History Interview in the Interviewer and Vice-Versa," *Oral History Review* 24 (Summer 1997), 55–79; Joanna Bornat, "Oral History as a Social Movement: Reminiscence and Older People," in *The Oral History Reader*, ed. Robert Perks and Alistair Thomson (London: Routledge, 1998), 189–205. I tried as best I could to keep the student/informant phrasing and punctuation intact, complete with their attempts to incorporate local color and conversational language. In the longer quotes found in the latter chapters, interviewer's statements appear in parentheses while my additions appear in brackets. Also, the

frequent use of ellipses indicate a trailing off of thought and not an indication of missing text, unless marked.

3. Many studies have focused on the South during the era, including Roger Biles, *The South and the New Deal* (Lexington: University of Kentucky Press, 1994); Pete Daniel, *Breaking the Land: The Transformation of Cotton, Tobacco, and Rice Cultures since 1880* (Chicago: University of Illinois Press, 1985); Gilbert C. Fite, *Cotton Fields No More: Southern Agriculture, 1865–1980* (Lexington: University Press of Kentucky, 1984); and George B. Tindall, *The Emergence of the New South* (Baton Rouge: Louisiana State University Press, 1967). But there are few studies that actually document the people themselves, and those few that exist are either the result of letters from the era, which tend to focus on one issue or idea, or overly represent the northern or western perspective. Among the best are Jacquelyn Dowd Hall, James Leloudis, Robert Korstad, Mary Murphy, Lu Ann Jones, and Christopher B. Daly's *Like a Family: The Making of a Southern Cotton Mill World* (Chapel Hill: University of North Carolina Press, 1987); Melissa Walker's, *All We Knew Was to Farm: Rural Women in the Upcountry South, 1919–1941* (Baltimore: Johns Hopkins University Press, 2000); and Robert McElvaine's *Down and Out in the Great Depression: Letters from the "Forgotten Man"* (Chapel Hill: University of North Carolina Press, 1983). There are others, of course, including *Up Before Daylight: Life Histories from the Alabama Writers' Project, 1938–1939*, ed. James Seay Brown Jr. (Tuscaloosa: University of Alabama Press, 1982); *Living Hard: Southern Americans in the Great Depression*, ed. John L. Robinson (University Press of America, 1981); *Such as Us: Southern Voices of the Thirties*, ed. Tom E. Terrill and Jerrold Hirsch (Chapel Hill: University of North Carolina Press, 1978); *First-Person America*, ed. Ann Banks (New York: Knopf, 1980); and Studs Terkel's, *Hard Times: An Oral History of the Great Depression* (New York: Pantheon, 1970).

4. Elizabeth Tonkin, *Narrating Our Pasts: The Social Construction of Oral History* (New York: Cambridge University Press, 1992), 1–18. Quote from p. 10. See also pp. 97–112; and Lorraine T. Dorfmann, Susan A. Murty, Ronnie J. Evans, Jerry G. Ingram, and James R. Power, "History and Identity in the Narratives of Rural Elders," *Journal of Aging Studies* 18 (2004), 188.

5. Over the past twenty years, many within feminist scholarship have suggested that the categorical separation of race, class, and gender have ignored basic philosophical concerns and led to further marginalization. As such, a new method of "seeing" into these situations, commonly labeled intersectionality, has emerged. At its core, the theories suggest that scholars cannot separate one from the other and that to better understand the complex social life that is at the core of any human activity, the scholar must try to find points of intersectionality to better illuminate the historical or social situation. For an excellent overview of the three types of intersectionality and its application, see Leslie McCall, "The Complexities of Intersectionality," *Signs: Journal of Women in Culture and Society* 30 (2005), 1771–1800.

6. Maurice Sponcler, interviewed by Dan Umbach, Sept. 14, 1990, BOHP, pp. 17–18. Italics added for emphasis.

7. Ada Kane, interviewed by Steve Starnes, May 26, 1991, BOHP, npn.

8. Paul Thompson, *The Voice of the Past: Oral History* (New York: Oxford University Press, 1988, 3rd ed.), quote from p. 23; Ronald Grele, *Envelopes of Sound: The Art of Oral History* (New York: Praeger, 1991, 2nd ed.); Michael Frisch, *A Shared Authority: Essays on the Craft and Meaning of Oral History and Public History* (Albany: State University of New York Press, 1990); Alessandro Portelli, "What Makes Oral History Different," in *The Oral History Reader*, ed. Robert Perks and Alistair Thomson, (New York: Routledge, 1998), 63–74. This reader also contains other articles relevant to the theory and method of oral history. An excellent overview of the past twenty years of oral history scholarship and debate can be found in Yow, "'Do I Like Them Too Much?'" 55–79. Yow also discusses the objective-versus-subjective debate within oral history and concludes that scholars should use the subjective nature of the research to further the objective focus of the topic. See especially pp. 77–79. See also Linda Shopes, "Making Sense of Oral History," from the Making Sense of Evidence series on *History Matters: The U.S. Survey on the Web*, located at <http://historymatters.gmu.edu>, pp. 1–23.

9. Samuel Schrager, "What Is Social in Oral History?" in *The Oral History Reader*, ed. Robert Perks and Alistair Thomson (New York: Routledge, 1998), 284–99; Mae B. Biggart, interviewed by Adam Greer, Mar. 4, 1992, BOHP, p. 6.

10. Portelli, "What Makes Oral History Different," 68–71; Emily Honig, "Striking Lives: Oral History and the Politics of Memory," *Journal of Women's History* 9 (Spring 1997), 139–57, quote from p. 140; Ronald J. Grele, "Movement without Aim: Methodological and Theoretical Problems in Oral History," in *The Oral History Reader*, ed. Robert Perks and Alistair Thomson (New York: Routledge, 1998), 38–52, particularly pp. 45–48; Barbara Allen, "Story in Oral History: Clues to Historical Consciousness," *Journal of American History* 79 (Sept. 1992), 606–11, quote from p. 606.

11. Paul Thompson reminds us of the importance of language in oral history by pointing to the theories of Jacques Lacan and the duality of unconscious language patterns and the embedded nature of gender symbols. See Paul Thompson, *Voice of the Past*, 178–79; Kathryn Anderson and Dana C. Jacks, "Learning to Listen: Interview Techniques and Analyses," in *Women's Words: The Feminist Practice of Oral History*, ed. Sherna Berger Gluck and Daphne Patai (New York: Routledge, Chapman and Hall, 1991), 11–26, quote from p. 11; Kristina Minister, "A Feminist Frame for the Oral History Interview," in *Women's Words*, 27–42; Beverly V. Romberger, "'Aunt Sophie Always Said . . .': Oral Histories of the Commonplaces Women Learned about Relating to Men," *American Behavioral Scientist* 29 (Jan./Feb. 1986), 342–67.

12. Joan Sangster, "Feminist Debates and the Use of Oral History," in *The Oral History Reader*, ed. Robert Perks and Alistair Thomson (New York: Routledge,

1998), 87–100; Honig, "Striking Lives"; Marie-Françoise Chanfrault-Duchet, "Narrative Structures, Social Models, and Symbolic Representation in the Life Story," in *Women's Words: The Feminist Practice of Oral History*, ed. Sherna Berger Gluck and Daphne Patai (New York: Routledge, Chapman and Hall, 1991), 77–92. Susan H. Armitage, with Patricia Hart and Karen Weathermon, *Women's Oral History: The "Frontiers" Reader* (Lincoln: University of Nebraska Press, 2002) is an excellent source for the development of research and analysis on issues relating to women's oral history collected from the pages of *Frontiers* from 1977 to 2001.

13. Honig, "Striking Lives"; Sangster, "Feminist Debates"; Alistair Thomson, "Fifty Years: An International Perspective on Oral History," *Journal of American History* 85 (Sept. 1998), 581–95; Valerie Yow, "'Do I Like Them Too Much?': Effects of the Oral History Interview on the Interviewer and Vice-Versa," *Oral History Review* 24 (Summer 1997), 55–79; *Women of Valor: The Struggle against the Great Depression as Told in Their Own Life Stories*, ed. Bernard Sternsher and Judith Sealander (Chicago: Ivan Dee, 1990); Gwendolyn Etter-Lewis, "Black Women's Life Stories: Reclaiming Self in Narrative Texts," in *Women's Words: The Feminist Practice of Oral History*, ed. Sherna Berger Gluck and Daphne Patai (New York: Routledge, Chapman and Hall, 1991), 43–58.

14. The study of documentary film and photography from the 1930s is very active, but interested persons should begin with William Stott's *Documentary Expression and Thirties America* (New York: Oxford University Press, 1973) and continue with Paula Rabinowitz's *They Must Be Represented: The Politics of Documentary* (New York: Verso, 1994), especially pp. 35–106, and then examine the photos found at <http://newdeal.feri.org/library/> and <http://memory.loc.gov/ammem/fsowhome.html>. Robert L. Stevens and Jared A. Fogel, "Images of the Great Depression: A Photographic Essay," *OAH Magazine of History* 15 (Summer 2001), 1–8, found at <http://www.oah.org/pubs/magazine/greatdepression/stevens-fogel.html>. All photographs are courtesy of the Library of Congress (thanks to Khadijah Camp for assistance with reproductions) or the National Archives via the Franklin D. Roosevelt Library (thanks to Mark Renovitch for assistance with reproductions). Captions and call numbers are assigned by the archive. For more on the Popular Front and its meaning, see Michael Denning, *The Cultural Front: The Laboring of American Culture in the Twentieth-century* (New York: Verso, 1996), especially pp. 115–60 and 259–82.

15. Anna B. Nilsson, interviewed by Kari Johnson, Mar. 26, 1989, BOHP, npn.

Chapter 1. "It was just hard times"

1. A. B. Baughtman, interviewed by Michael Baughtman, Nov. 7, 1990, BOHP, p. 6; Dorothy L. Hill, interviewed by Tesha Hollis, Mar. 7, 1992, BOHP, npn.

2. A number of contemporary observations detail the dire situation of the American South during the era: Rupert B. Vance, *Human Geography of the South: A Study in Regional Resources and Human Adequacy* (Chapel Hill: University of North Carolina Press, 1932); Howard W. Odum, *Southern Regions of the United States* (Cha-

pel Hill: University of North Carolina Press, 1936); Charles S. Johnson, Edwin R. Embree, and W. W. Alexander, *The Collapse of Cotton Tenancy: Summary of Field Studies and Statistical Surveys, 1933–35* (Chapel Hill: University of North Carolina Press, 1935); National Emergency Council, *Report on the Economic Conditions in the South* (Washington, D.C.: Government Printing Office, 1938). See also Donald B. Dodd and Wynelle S. Dodd, *Historical Statistics of the South, 1790–1970* (Tuscaloosa, Alabama: University of Alabama Press, 1973).

3. Mary Thaxton, interviewed by Scarlett Gaddy, Mar. 2, 1990, BOHP, p. 18; Grover Hardin, interviewed by David Scott Wyatt, Apr. 19, 1992, BOHP, npn; Vera Pulliam, interviewed by Shelby Queen, Oct. 28, 1990, BOHP, p. 1; Thomas Cairns, interviewed by Brian Newman, Nov. 24, 1993, BOHP, npn; Irene Bolding, interviewed by Robin Johns, May 25, 1991, BOHP, p. 1.

4. Mamie Camp, interviewed by Andrea Spiess, Nov. 22, 1989, BOHP, npn; Howard Spain Sr., interviewed by Richard W. Spain, Feb. 22, 1991, BOHP, npn; Bessie Pendergrass, interviewed by Chris Lewandowski, Oct. 29, 1990, BOHP, p. 6.

5. Wayne Flynt, *Poor but Proud: Alabama's Poor Whites* (Tuscaloosa: University of Alabama Press, 1989), particularly ch. 9, pp. 211–42, but the whole of the book defines this pattern; Audrey Willingham, interviewed by Jill Phillips, Oct. 12, 1991, BOHP, p. 7.

6. Mattie Walthall, interviewed by Ameisa Roberts, Feb. 24, 1991, BOHP, p. 2; Guy Knight, interviewed by Sherry Holloway, Nov. 22, 1991, BOHP, npn; Martha Scott, interviewed by Alan Weldon, May 1, 1992, BOHP, p. 1; Flynt, *Poor but Proud*, 280–96; Paul E. Mertz, *New Deal Policy and Southern Rural Poverty* (Baton Rouge: Louisiana State University Press, 1978), 5–15; Robin D. G. Kelley, *Hammer and Hoe: Alabama Communists during the Great Depression* (Chapel Hill: University of North Carolina Press, 1990), 343–50.

7. George Potts, interviewed by Rebecca L. Hoffman, May 16, 1992, BOHP, p. 5; Max Smith, interviewed by Michael Smith, May 12, 1992, BOHP, p. 2; Opal Hunter, interviewed by Donna D. Smith, Nov. 10, 1990, BOHP, npn; Henry Clark, interviewed by Leigh Wilhite, Feb. 24, 1990, BOHP, pp. 6–7; George Weaver, interviewed by Mark MacAllaster, Feb. 24, 1990, BOHP, p. 2.

8. Benny F. McKissick, interviewed by Jay Cawthon, Mar. 4, 1992, BOHP, p. 1; Louise Smith, interviewed by Kelly Bedford, May 29, 1992, BOHP, p. 1 (italics added for emphasis); National Emergency Council, *Report*, section 11, "Ownership and Use of Land," and sections 9–10, "Labor," "Women and Children"; Cornelia Presley, interviewed by Larry Irwin, Feb. 24, 1991, BOHP, p. 1; Joyce Ison, interviewed by Stephanie Ison, Nov. 10, 1990, BOHP, p. 1.

9. Roger Biles, *The South and the New Deal* (Lexington: University of Kentucky Press, 1994), 2–14, 36, 56; James Hodges, *New Deal Labor Policy and the Southern Cotton Textile Industry, 1933–1941* (Knoxville: University of Tennessee Press, 1986).

10. June Adams, interviewed by Lea Kilburn, Feb. 27, 1990, BOHP, p. 1; Joyce

McClellan, interviewed by Elsma Smith, May 23, 1992, BOHP, npn; Biles, *The South and the New Deal*, 18–19; Pearl Nix, interviewed by Lori Williams, Feb. 28, 1991, BOHP, p. 1; Mertz, *New Deal Policy*, 1–7; Pete Daniel, *Breaking the Land: The Transformation of Cotton, Tobacco, and Rice Cultures since 1880* (Chicago: University of Illinois Press, 1985), 3–22; Johnson, Embree, and Alexander, *Collapse of Cotton Tenancy*, 3–20; Gilbert C. Fite, *Cotton Fields No More: Southern Agriculture, 1865–1980* (Lexington: University Press of Kentucky, 1984), 100–129; Jenny Kilburn, interviewed by Lea Kilburn, Mar. 1, 1990, BOHP, p. 1; Catherine Hoyt Bohne, interviewed by Linda Bohne, Oct. 25, 1991, BOHP, p. 1.

11. Clarence Bowman, interviewed by Melissa Holloway, May 20, 1992, BOHP, p. 2; Beulah Johnson, interviewed by Rebecca Hartsfield, Mar. 3, 1990, BOHP, p. 3; Allan Furline, interviewed by Jeff Denney, Mar. 2, 1991, BOHP, npn.

12. Guy Knight, interviewed by Sherry Holloway, Nov. 22, 1991, BOHP, npn; George Wright, interviewed by Steven Wright, Mar. 20, 1991, BOHP, p. 6; Gene Autry, interviewed by Shannon Howard, Mar. 2, 1991, BOHP, pp. 3–4; Sam Davis, interviewed by Ruth Davis, Mar. 2, 1992, BOHP, p. 2; Raymond Giles, interviewed by Christy Calhoun, Oct. 31, 1990, BOHP, p. 14; Mac Abercrombie Sr., interviewed by Marie Horton, Nov. 22, 1991, BOHP, npn; Frank Howland, interviewed by Kristi Thompson, Nov. 11, 1990, BOHP, npn.

13. Brewer Hoyt Douglas, interviewed by Phillip Hines, May 15, 1991, BOHP, p. 3; Gene Autry, interviewed by Shannon Howard, Mar. 2, 1991, BOHP, p. 10; Martha Scott, interviewed by Alan Weldon, May 1, 1992, BOHP, npn.

14. Maurice Sponcler, interviewed by Dan Umbach, Sept. 14, 1990, BOHP, pp. 1–4; Mareena McKinley Wright, "'I never did any fieldwork, but I milked an awful lot of cows': Using Rural Women's Experience to Reconceptualize Models of Work," *Gender and Society* 9 (Apr. 1995), 216–35.

15. Annie Young, interviewed by Stephen Young, June 1, 1990, BOHP, p. 1; Jessie Pearce, unknown interviewer, 1991, BOHP, npn; Ethel Shockley, interviewed by Robert Jennings, June 1, 1990, BOHP, npn; James A. Hodges, *New Deal Labor Policy and the Southern Cotton Textile Industry, 1933–1941* (Knoxville: University of Tennessee Press, 1986); Katherine Melton, interviewed by Candi Chester, Feb. 23, 1991, BOHP, p. 1; Claudia Ward, interviewed by Michelle Mize, May 27, 1990, BOHP, npn; Joe Johnson, interviewed by John Womack, May 30, 1990, BOHP, npn.

16. Julia Kirk Blackwelder, *Women of the Great Depression: Caste and Culture in San Antonio, 1929–1939* (College Station: Texas A&M University Press, 1984); Clifford Oxford, interviewed by Brad Yearta, May 11, 1992, BOHP, p. 7.

17. Bessie Pendergrass, interviewed by Doug Buehler, Mar. 5, 1990, BOHP, npn; Arlie Hochschild, with Anne Machung, *The Second Shift* (New York: Viking Penguin Press, 1989); Pearl Johnson, interviewed by April Mitchell, Nov. 15, 1990, BOHP, npn; Olga Ragsdale, interviewed by Jeff Ragsdale, Nov. 12, 1989, BOHP, npn; Lizzie Johnson, interviewed by Yvette Hester, May 17, 1991, BOHP, npn.

18. Janet M. Hooks, *Women's Occupations through Seven Decades*, Women's Bu-

reau Bulletin 28 (Washington, D.C.: GPO, 1947); Susan Ware, *Holding Their Own: American Women in the 1930s* (Boston: Twayne, 1982), 21–53; Lois Scharf, *To Work and to Wed: Female Employment, Feminism, and the Great Depression* (Westport, Conn.: Greenwood Press, 1980), 86–109; Ruby Henry, interviewed by Brian Reeves, Oct. 30, 1990, BOHP, pp. 1–3; Bessie Mae Birdsong, interviewed by Gail Smith, Nov. 11, 1990, BOHP, p. 6; Maggie Jones, interviewed by Jennifer Crumpton, May 25, 1990, BOHP, npn; Lillian Chambers, interviewed by Kelley Chambers, Feb. 10, 1991, BOHP, p. 19; Olga Lamp, interviewed by Claudia Hoyer, May 5–9, 1991, BOHP, p. 3.

19. Elaine Tyler May, *Homeward Bound: American Families in the Cold War Era* (New York: Basic Books, 1988), 37–57. Lois Scharf's *To Wed and To Work* presents similar information but focuses specifically on the Depression era. Both are excellent windows through which to view the role of family and a woman's place during the middle part of the twentieth century.

20. Lois Scroggins, interviewed by Amie Barber, May 17, 1990, BOHP, npn; Mary Carroll, interviewed by Tammy Wright, May 13, 1992, BOHP, p. 2; Lillian Chambers, interviewed by Kelley Chambers, Feb. 10, 1991, BOHP, p. 2; Mae B. Biggart, interviewed by Adam Greer, Mar. 4, 1992, BOHP, p. 3; Lucille Campbell, interviewed by John Campbell, Oct. 20, 1990, BOHP, p. 2; Rose Conerly, interviewed by Kim Marlow, Mar. 25, 1990, BOHP, npn; Mildred Friedman, interviewed by Cari Smith, Mar. 7, 1992, BOHP, p. 3; Bessie Fowler, interviewed by Christy Gresham, Mar. 9, 1992, BOHP, pp. 4–5.

21. Melissa Walker, *All We Knew Was to Farm: Rural Women in the Upcountry South, 1919–1941* (Baltimore: Johns Hopkins University Press, 2000), especially pp. 33–80; see also *Country Women Cope with Hard Times: A Collection of Oral Histories*, ed. Carol Bleser and Melissa Walker (Columbia: University of South Carolina Press, 2004); Thelma Hughes, interviewed by Cheryl Anthony, Oct. 20, 1989, BOHP, npn; Roxie Etheridge, interviewed by Andy Mills, May 16, 1992, BOHP, npn; Geneva Stewart, interviewed by Leslie Riales, Feb. 1, 1990, BOHP, npn; Lucy Gable, interviewed by Stephanie Brown, Apr. 30, 1990, BOHP, npn.

22. Laura Hapke, *Daughters of the Great Depression: Women, Work, and Fiction in the American 1930s* (Athens: University of Georgia Press, 1995), especially pp. 1–26 and 219–24; Alice Kessler-Harris, *Out to Work: A History of Wage-Earning Women in the United States* (New York: Oxford University Press, 1982), particularly pp. 250–72; Lisa Kolb, interviewed by Jennifer Medlock, Mar. 13, 1992, BOHP, npn; Vera Pulliam, interviewed by Shelby Queen, Oct. 28, 1990, BOHP, p. 3; Alma McKinzey, interviewed by Jerry Agan, Mar. 5, 1992, BOHP, npn.

23. Irene Bolding, interviewed by Robin Johns, May 25, 1991, BOHP, npn; Merrill Horton, interviewed by Angela Wilson, May 27, 1990, BOHP, p. 5; Henry Green, interviewed by Cynthia Brackett, Nov. 17, 1991, BOHP, npn; Afton Fletcher, interviewed by Angie LaForge, Nov. 23, 1991, BOHP, pp. 13–15.

24. Vance, *Human Geography of the South*, 20–25; Odum, *Southern Regions of the*

United States, 482; Congressional Information Services (copyright 2001) for Georgia, Alabama, and Tennessee; *Nativity of the Population, For Regions, Divisions, and States: 1850 to 1990* [Part 04: 1930–1940], Bureau of Census, February 1999, pp. 85–88; Roger Biles, *The South and the New Deal* (Lexington: University of Kentucky Press, 1994), 18–22; W. T. Couch, "The Negro in the South," in *Culture in the South*, ed. Couch, 432–77; Johnson, Embree, and Alexander, *Collapse of Cotton Tenancy*, quote from p. 7; Clifton Grandison, interviewed by Rod Grandison, Nov. 13, 1991, BOHP, p. 2.

25. For an excellent overview of race and FDR, see Harvard Sitkoff, *A New Deal for Blacks* (New York: Oxford University Press, 1978); John B. Kirby, *Black Americans in the Roosevelt Era: Liberalism and Race* (Knoxville: University of Tennessee Press, 1980); Nancy L. Grant, *TVA and Black Americans* (Philadelphia: Temple University Press, 1989); and Biles, *The South and the New Deal*, ch. 6, "The New Deal and Race Relations."

26. Luisa Passerini, "Work Ideology and Consensus under Italian Fascism," in *The Oral History Reader*, ed. Robert Perks and Alistair Thomson (London: Routledge, 1998), 53–62.

27. Isabel Hester, interviewed by Michael Brock, May 29, 1991, BOHP, p. 12; Hub Waters, interviewed by David Feeney, Feb. 17, 1990, BOHP, p. 4; Maybell Loftin, interviewed by Heather Marbus, May 25, 1992, BOHP, npn.

28. Ruth Smith, interviewed by B. Blount, Feb. 17, 1991, BOHP, npn; Geneva Ariail, interviewed by Amanda Ariail, Mar. 5, 1992, BOHP, p. 6; Florence Murphy, interviewed by John Defenbaugh, Oct. 20, 1990, BOHP, p. 13.

29. Woodrow Maffet, interviewed by Brad Batchelor, Oct. 23, 1990, BOHP, pp. 6–7; Billy Patrick, interviewed by Brad Batchelor, Oct. 23, 1990, BOHP, p. 5; Ralph McCain, interviewed by Rebecca Reeves, Feb. 23, 1991, BOHP, pp. 24–25; Cornelia Presley, interviewed by Larry Irwin, Feb. 24, 1991, BOHP, npn.

30. William Gordon, interviewed by Joe Steele, Mar. 4, 1990, BOHP, p. 2; Georgia Mae Calloway, interviewed by Celena Sims, Feb. 28, 1992, BOHP, npn; Lillian Arnold, unknown interviewer, no date, BOHP, npn; Ossie Barlow, interviewed by Sharmon Colbert, Feb. 27, 1991, BOHP, npn; Addie Baynard, interviewed by Sharmon Colbert, Feb. 27, 1991, BOHP, npn.

31. Georgia Mae Calloway, interviewed by Celena Sims, Feb. 28, 1992, BOHP, npn; Dorothy Hill, interviewed by Tesha Hollis, Mar. 7, 1992, BOHP, npn; Ella Gibson, interviewed by Lakecia Denson, Nov. 2, 1989, BOHP, npn.

32. William Gordon, interviewed by Joe Steele, Mar. 4, 1990, BOHP, p. 5; Geneva Mack, interviewed by Connie Franklin, Mar. 1, 1992, BOHP, npn; Viola Elder, interviewed by Jojuana Davis, Mar. 6, 1992, BOHP, npn; Beula Youngblood, interviewed by Bryant Ellington, May 22, 1990, BOHP, p. 8.

33. Ronald Grele, *Envelopes of Sound: The Art of Oral History* (New York: Praeger, 1991, 2nd ed.), 127–54.

34. Clifford Oxford, interviewed by Brad Yearta, May 11, 1992, BOHP, pp. 5–6; Ella Gibson, interviewed by Lakecia Denson, Nov. 2, 1989, BOHP, p. 2.

Chapter 2. "I thought he was God's half-brother"

1. Bessie Fowler, interviewed by Christy Gresham, Mar. 9, 1992, BOHP, npn; James Shope, unknown interviewer, no date, BOHP, npn; Delmas Easterwood, interviewed by Terry Wilkerson, Feb. 26, 1991, BOHP, npn; Irene Bolding, interviewed by Robin Johns, May 25, 1991, BOHP, npn.

2. Roosevelt's inaugural address as quoted in T. H. Watkins, *The Great Depression: America in the 1930s* (Boston: Little, Brown, 1993), 141; William Perreyclear, interviewed by Jerri Webb, Nov. 12, 1991, BOHP, npn; Norma Brumback, interviewed by Kathy Deegan, Apr. 10, 1990, BOHP, npn; Brewer Hoyt Douglas, interviewed by Phillip Hines, May 15, 1991, BOHP, p. 12; Lela Knight, interviewed by Shannon Lott, Oct. 12, 1990, BOHP, npn; M. Oxford, interviewed by Brad Yearta, May 11, 1992, BOHP, p. 3.

3. Paul Conkin, *The New Deal* (New York: Crowell, 1967), 85; Joe Johnson, interviewed by John Womack, May 30, 1990, BOHP, npn; Urban Farnsworth, interviewed by Nathan Gaunt, May 13, 1992, BOHP, pp. 2–3; Geraldine Beck, interviewed by Matt Jobe, May 17, 1992, BOHP, p. 1; Frances Clements, interviewed by Angie Clements, Feb. 29, 1992, BOHP, npn.

4. Gilbert C. Fite, *Cotton Fields No More: Southern Agriculture, 1865–1980* (Lexington: University of Kentucky Press, 1984), 120–40; Roger Biles, *The South and the New Deal* (Lexington: University Press of Kentucky, 1994), 18–39; Paul E. Mertz, *New Deal Policy and Southern Rural Poverty* (Baton Rouge: Louisiana State University Press, 1978), 2–10, 51; Pete Daniel, *Breaking the Land: The Transformation of Cotton, Tobacco, and Rice Cultures since 1880* (Chicago: University of Chicago Press, 1985), 3–22, 65–75.

5. George B. Tindall, *The Emergence of the New South* (Baton Rouge: Louisiana State University Press, 1967), 478–81; Wayne Flynt, *Poor but Proud: Alabama's Poor Whites* (Tuscaloosa: University of Alabama Press, 1989), 23–26; Michael Holmes, *The New Deal in Georgia: An Administrative History* (Westport, Conn.: Greenwood Press, 1975), 9–13; Numan V. Bartley, "The Era of the New Deal as a Turning Point in Southern History," in *The New Deal and the South: Essays by Frank Friedel*, ed. James C. Cobb and Michael V. Namorato (Jackson: University Press of Mississippi, 1984), 135–43.

6. Henri Herron, interviewed by Meacy Gess, May 31, 1990, BOHP, npn; Wyolene Warren, interviewed by Kimberly DeVane, Nov. 4, 1990, BOHP, npn; Viola Elder, interviewed by JoJuana Davis, Mar. 6, 1992, BOHP, npn; Warren Brockway, interviewed by Kim Thomson, May 25, 1991, BOHP, npn.

7. Martha Bailey, interviewed by Michelle Bailey, Feb. 16, 1991, BOHP, p. 5; Joseph Foster, interviewed by Jacqueline Cheek, May 9, 1992, BOHP, npn; Anne

Pierce, interviewed by Taylor St. Clair, May 26, 1991, BOHP, npn; *FDR's Fireside Chats*, ed. Russell D. Buhite and David Levy (New York: Penguin Books, 1993), xv. When FDR entered the White House in 1933, he understood that the key to his administration's ability to deal with the ravages of the Depression lay in his ability to communicate with the people. His Democratic administration worked hard to project an image of being the people's government and wanted to create a town-meeting type of atmosphere by keeping the people as informed about the issues as possible. Within this philosophy, Roosevelt and his staff had to find a way to use the media to get the message out to the people. Under the leadership of press secretary Stephen Early, the administration created a variety of departments and offices that helped to disseminate information to the print media and gave them unprecedented opportunity to question the president's policies. He held 337 press conferences during the first administration alone. The administration wanted something about what the executive branch was trying to accomplish in the papers or magazines as often as possible, and given FDR's affinity for newspaper folk, he went out of his way to make himself and his cabinet available. By 1936, however, the print media had come to be seen by those in the Democratic party and within the administration as anti-Roosevelt. This "85 percent" of the press, as Roosevelt labeled them, often lampooned the New Deal and FDR's plan for recovery, which the administration interpreted as being in cahoots with the opposition. While FDR wanted to get his message out to the people, his staff came to understand that this goal was not going to be achieved via the print media. See Richard W. Steele, *Propaganda in an Open Society: The Roosevelt Administration and the Media, 1933–1941* (Westport, Conn.: Greenwood Press, 1985), 43–54; Betty Houchin Winfield, *FDR and the News Media* (New York: Columbia University Press, 1994 [orig. 1990]), 6, 79–94 (see also pp. xi–xvi for an excellent bibliography of FDR and the media); Graham J. White, *FDR and the Press* (Chicago: University of Chicago Press, 1979), 69–92; Buhite and Levy, *FDR's Fireside Chats*, xiii. For an interesting appraisal of the differing styles between Hoover and Roosevelt, see Davis W. Houck, *Rhetoric as Currency: Hoover, Roosevelt, and the Great Depression* (College Station: Texas A&M University Press, 2001).

8. Roosevelt quote from Winfield, *FDR and the News Media*, 104; Steele, *Propaganda in an Open Society*, 21; J. Fred MacDonald, *Don't Touch That Dial: Radio Programming in American Life from 1920–1960* (Chicago: Nelson-Hall, 1974), 25–62; Susan Smulyan, *Selling Radio: The Commercialization of American Broadcasting, 1920–1934* (Washington, D.C.: Smithsonian Institution Press, 1994), 93–153; Warren Susman, "The Thirties," in *The Development of an American Culture*, ed. Stanley Coben and Lormar Ratner (Englewood Cliffs, N.J.: Prentice Hall, 1970), 225–31; Kathy M. Newman, "Poisons, Potions, and Profits: Radio Rebels and the Origins of the Consumer Movement," in *Radio Reader: Essays in the Cultural History of Radio*, ed. Michele Hilmes and Jason Loviglio (New York: Routledge, 2002), 157–81; Bruce Lenthall, "Critical Reception: Public Intellectuals Decry Depression-era Radio, Mass Culture, and Modern America," in *Radio Reader*, 41–62.

In *Swing, That Modern Sound* (Jackson: University Press of Mississippi, 2001), I argue that the impact of radio on emerging jazz and swing musicians led to a conformity of style and helped to popularize and disseminate swing music to a national audience.

9. Steele, *Propaganda in an Open Society*, 17–25; Kenneth J. Bindas, *All This Music Belongs to the Nation: The WPA's Federal Music Project and American Society, 1935–1939* (Knoxville: University of Tennessee Press, 1995), 19–35, 47–59; Smulyan, *Selling Radio*, 148–53.

10. Buhite and Levy, *FDR's Fireside Chats*, iv–vii; *Ah That Voice: The Fireside Chats of Franklin Delano Roosevelt*, comp. Kenneth D. Yeilding and Paul H. Carlson (Odessa, Tex.: John Ben Shepperd Jr. Library of the Presidents, 1974), ix–xxi; Winfield, *FDR and the News Media*, 104–6; Roosevelt quote from Smulyan, *Selling Radio*, 149–50.

11. Paul Morgan, interviewed by Greg McElwee, Nov. 17, 1991, BOHP, npn; Maria Jett, interviewed by Catherine Jett, Mar. 3, 1990, BOHP, npn; Ed Isakson, interviewed by Alison Gaissert, Oct. 13, 1991, BOHP, p. 6; Elenora Hunt, interviewed by Nicholas Mulcare, Nov. 15 and 21, 1991, BOHP, npn; Geneva Davenport, interviewed by Kelly Sanford, Oct. 28, 1990, BOHP, npn; Dorothy Bartley, interviewed by Christa Buffalow, May 3, 1991, BOHP, p. 6.

12. Bertha Hicks, interviewed by Cindy Clifton, May 18, 1992, BOHP, npn; Irene Bolding, interviewed by Robin Johns, May 25, 1991, BOHP, npn; James Thompson, interviewed by Andrea Davis, Mar. 3, 1992, BOHP, npn; Laura Lambert, interviewed by Christy Baker, May 21, 1991, BOHP, npn; William D. Smith, interviewed by Jennifer Riley, Apr. 28, 1991, BOHP, p. 8; Charles Ricks, interviewed by Lori McDugald, May 8, 1992, BOHP, p. 5.

13. David Michael Ryfe, "Franklin Roosevelt and the Fireside Chats," *Journal of Communication* 49 (1999), 80–103, argues that FDR's speeches were crafted intentionally to coincide with the emerging culture industries and were deliberate in their attempt to break the boundary between listener and speaker. Melvin G. Holli, *The Wizard of Washington: Emil Hurja, Franklin Roosevelt, and the Birth of Public Opinion Polling* (New York: Pelgrave, 2002) details the lengths to which the administration went to ensure that the message was getting across as desired. Joe Johnson, interviewed by John Womack, May 30, 1990, BOHP, npn; Norma Brumback, interviewed by Kathy Deegan, Apr. 10, 1990, BOHP, npn.

14. Sherman Shockley, interviewed by Robert Jennings, June 1, 1990, BOHP, p. 6; Jennie Kilburn, interviewed by Lea Kilburn, Mar. 1, 1990, BOHP, p. 4; Brewer Hoyt Douglas, interviewed by Phillip Hines, May 15, 1991, BOHP, p. 9; Joe Johnson, interviewed by John Womack, May 30, 1990, BOHP, npn.

15. Verna Bland, interviewed by Michael Bland, Nov. 3, 1991, BOHP, p. 5; George Pope, interviewed by Craig Davis, Feb. 2, 1989, BOHP, npn; Mildred Curtis, interviewed by Michael Curtis, Apr. 19, 1992, BOHP, p. 6; Antonio Maniaci, interviewed by Shannon Tillman, May 27, 1990, BOHP, p. 5.

16. William D. Smith, interviewed by Jennifer Riley, Apr. 28, 1991, BOHP, p. 5; William Perreyclear, interviewed by Jeri Webb, Nov. 12, 1991, BOHP, npn; Maurice Sponcler, interviewed by Dan Umbach, Sept. 14, 1990, BOHP, p. 8; R. D. Simpson, interviewed by Angellique Shaw, Mar. 9, 1992, BOHP, npn; E. B. Cane, interviewed by Paul Noble, Mar. 4, 1990, BOHP, npn; Genevieve Meredith, interviewed by Julie Jennings, Nov. 13, 1991, BOHP, p. 11.

17. Ernest Porter, interviewed by Noel Turner, Feb. 25, 1992, BOHP, npn; Mary Slack, interviewed by Merrill Cheatham, Nov. 16, 1991, BOHP, npn; Sadie Wright, interviewed by Steven Wright, Mar. 20, 1991, BOHP, p. 10; Lucille Campbell, interviewed by John Campbell, Oct. 20, 1990, BOHP, p. 6; Travis Dorrough, interviewed by Kathy Bullock, Oct. 26, 1990, BOHP, p. 8; Thomas Lipford, interviewed by Chantrice Truitt, May 23, 1992, BOHP, npn; Paul Maddox, interviewed by Shelia Yearta, Feb. 22, 1990, BOHP, p. 9.

18. Jennie Kilburn, interviewed by Lea Kilburn, Feb. 27, 1990, BOHP, p. 2; Merrill Cheatham, interviewed by Mary Slack, Nov. 16, 1991, BOHP, npn; William D. Smith, unknown interviewer, no date, BOHP, p. 2; Katherine Melton, interviewed by Candi Chester, Feb. 23, 1991, BOHP, p. 4; A. Young Lester, interviewed by Ken Hammon, May 8, 1992, BOHP, npn; Ruth Rhymer, interviewed by Laura Sutton, Nov. 5, 1989, BOHP, p. 5.

19. Doc Harris, interviewed by Stephanie Miles, May 28, 1991, BOHP, npn; Marguritte Lilly, interviewed by Don Lindsey, Nov. 17, 1991, BOHP, p. 2; John Redden, interviewed by Beverly Redden, Mar. 8, 1992, BOHP, p. 4; Leonard Crenshaw, interviewed by Lisa Williams, May 16, 1990, BOHP, npn; Sadie Wright, interviewed by Steven Wright, Mar. 20, 1991, BOHP, p. 7.

20. Edna Mann, interviewed by Leslie Ann Connell, Apr. 18, 1992, BOHP, p. 3; Harry B. Johnson, interviewed by Erik Monroe, Oct. 18, 1991, BOHP, p. 2; Mary McClain, interviewed by LeAnn Shippey, Oct. 27, 1990, BOHP, p. 3; Ruby Painter, interviewed by Michelle Saren, Nov. 16, 1991, BOHP, npn; Ruby Barlow, unknown interviewer, no date, BOHP, npn; B. D. Stephens, interviewed by Richard Berkowitz, Nov. 20, 1989, BOHP, npn.

21. Tindall, *Emergence of the New South*, 473–95; Biles, *The South and the New Deal*, 53–69; Douglas L. Fleming, "The New Deal in Atlanta: A Review of the Major Programs," in *Hope Restored: How the New Deal Worked in Town and Country*, ed. Bernard Sternsher (Chicago: Ivan Dee, 1999), 7–31; Jane Walker Herndon, "Ed Rivers and Georgia's Little New Deal," *Atlanta Historical Journal* 30 (Spring 1986) <http://www.cviog.uga.edu/Projects/gainfo/FDRarticle5.htm>, pp. 1–11; "The Great Depression, the New Deal, and Alabama's Political Leadership," <www.alabama-moments.state.al.us/sec48det>; Carroll Van West, *Tennessee's New Deal Landscape: A Guidebook* (Knoxville: University of Tennessee Press, 2001).

22. David L. Carlton and Peter Coclanis, eds., *Confronting Southern Poverty in the Great Depression: The Report on Economic Conditions in the South with Related*

Documents (New York: Bedford Books, 1996); Tindall, *Emergence of the New South*, 625–28; Bruce Clayton and John Salmond, *Debating Southern History* (New York: Rowman and Littlefield, 1999), 120–23; Biles, *The South and the New Deal*, 146.

23. Biles, *The South and the New Deal*, 70–71; Billy G. Hinson, "The Civilian Conservation Corps in Mobile County, Alabama," *Alabama Review* 45 (Oct. 1992), 32–40.

24. Sam Davis, interviewed by Ruth Davis, Mar. 2, 1992, BOHP, p. 5; Roy Patterson, interviewed by Paul Cannon, Mar. 8, 1992, BOHP, p. 3; Henry Clark, interviewed by Leigh Wilhite, Feb. 24, 1990, BOHP, p. 3; Henry Felton, unknown interviewer, no date, BOHP, npn; Anne Pierce, interviewed by Jeff Estes, Nov. 10, 1990, BOHP, npn; Lena Stimpson, interviewed by Amy Wilkes, Nov. 11, 1990, BOHP, npn.

25. John R. Beach, interviewed by Tisha Avrett, Mar. 1, 1990, BOHP, pp. 1–2; Sam Davis, interviewed by Ruth Davis, Mar. 2, 1992, BOHP, p. 5; Roy Patterson, interviewed by Paul Cannon, Mar. 8, 1992, BOHP, p. 3.

26. Willie Clackum, unknown interviewer, no date, BOHP, p. 5; Ptleene Chapman, interviewed by Catherine Chapman, Nov. 11, 1990, BOHP, p. 7; Ernest Porter, interviewed by Noel Turner, Feb. 25, 1992, BOHP, npn; Charles Clayton, interviewed by Diane Streetkerk, May 25, 1992, BOHP, p. 13; Lowell Bean, interviewed by Chad Bean, Nov. 13, 1993, BOHP, p. 7; Albert Cicero, interviewed by Cheryl McCain, May 25, 1990, BOHP, npn.

27. Delmas Easterwood, interviewed by Terry Wilkerson, Feb. 26, 1991, BOHP, npn; Lois Scroggins, interviewed by Amie Barber, May 17, 1990, BOHP, npn; Gladys Partridge, interviewed by Chris Otwell, Nov. 10, 1990, BOHP, npn; Genevieve Meredith, interviewed by Julie Jennings, Nov. 13, 1991, BOHP, pp. 3–4.

28. Geneva Ariail, interviewed by Amanda Ariail, Mar. 5, 1992, BOHP, p. 7; Miriam Merrell, interviewed by Kimberly DeVane, Nov. 4, 1990, BOHP, p. 7; M. B. Guy, interviewed by Anthony Clifton, Nov. 22, 1991, BOHP, npn; Lita Vance, unknown interviewer, BOHP, p. 4; Hub Waters, interviewed by David Feeney, Feb. 17, 1990, BOHP, p. 3.

29. *Final Report on the WPA Program, 1935–1943* (Westport, Conn.: Greenwood Press, 1976 [orig., GPA, 1947]); Holmes, *New Deal in Georgia*, 95–166; Biles, *The South and the New Deal*, 74–76; Geneva Ariail, interviewed by Amanda Ariail, Mar. 5, 1992, BOHP, p. 8.

30. Merrill Horton, interviewed by Kimberly DeVane, Nov. 4, 1990, BOHP, p. 3; Clifford Oxford, interviewed by Brad Yearta, May 11, 1992, BOHP, p. 3; Clare Doherty, unknown interviewer, no date, BOHP, npn.

31. Gladys H. Burroughs, interviewed by Amy Bridges, May 26, 1990, BOHP, npn; Sarah Riddle, interviewed by Lori McDonald, May 8, 1992, BOHP, npn; Allan Furline, interviewed by Jeff Denney, Mar. 2, 1991, BOHP, npn; Delmas Easterwood, interviewed by Terry Wilkerson, Feb. 26, 1991, BOHP, npn; Josephine Taff, inter-

viewed by Don Lindsey, Nov. 20, 1990, BOHP, p. 9; Madie Myers, interviewed by Horace Senior, May 24, 1991, BOHP, p. 3; E. LeRoy Jordan, interviewed by Kelli Allen, May 24, 1992, BOHP, p. 3.

32. Geneva Stewart, interviewed by Stephanie Marlow, May 28, 1990, BOHP, npn; Naomi Jean Bowden, interviewed by Melissa Holloway, May 20, 1990, BOHP, p. 232; Sylvia Selman, interviewed by Karen VanNest, Nov. 12, 1991, BOHP, npn.

33. Lillian Wrinkle, interviewed by Aaron Killebrew, May 19, 1990, BOHP, pp. 3–4; William Gordon, interviewed by Joe Steele, Mar. 4, 1990, BOHP, pp. 1–3.

34. Stella Bowie, interviewed by Stacy Murray, May 1, 1990, BOHP, p. 2; A. Young Lester, interviewed by Ken Hammon, May 8, 1992, BOHP, npn; Paul Maddox, interviewed by Sheila Yearta, Feb. 22, 1990, BOHP, p. 6; James Harper, interviewed by Angie Maddox, May 22, 1990, BOHP, p. 4.

35. Lizzie Johnson, interviewed by Yvette Hester, May 17, 1991, BOHP, npn; Lois Scroggins, interviewed by Amie Barber, May 17, 1990, BOHP, npn; Tom Skelton, interviewed by Lisa Simmons, Nov. 2, 1990, BOHP, npn.

36. Maurice Sponcler, interviewed by Dan Umbach, Sept. 14, 1990, BOHP, p. 7; George Potts, interviewed by Rebecca Hoffman, May 16, 1992, BOHP, p. 6; Lillian Chambers, interviewed by Kelly Chambers, Feb. 2, 1991, BOHP, p. 5; Bessie Fowler, interviewed by Cristy Gresham, Mar. 9, 1992, BOHP, p. 7; Lynna Vaugh, interviewed by Brenda Baker, Nov. 12, 1990, BOHP, npn.

37. Wayne Flynt, "The New Deal and Southern Labor," in *The New Deal and the South*, ed. James C. Cobb and Michael V. Namorato, (Jackson: University Press of Mississippi, 1984), 63–96; Biles, *The South and the New Deal*, 84–87; Joseph P. Foster, interviewed by Jacqueline Cheek, May 9, 1992, BOHP, npn.

38. Ada Kane, interviewed by Steve Starnes, May 26, 1991, BOHP, npn; Lucy Wagner, interviewed by Missy Powell, Nov. 8, 1991, BOHP, npn; George Weaver, interviewed by Mark MacAllaster, Feb. 24, 1990, BOHP, p. 4; Wyolene Warren, interviewed by Kimberly DeVane, Nov. 4, BOHP, pp. 14–15; Margaret Askew, interviewed by Michael Stratton, Feb. 27, 1992, BOHP, npn; Delmas Easterwood, interviewed by Terry Wilkerson, Feb. 26, 1991, BOHP, npn; Dora Holcombe, interviewed by Amanda Tuggle, Nov. 23, 1991, BOHP, npn.

39. Winnie Murphee, interviewed by Benjamin Paredes, May 16, 1992, BOHP, npn; Maggie Jones, interviewed by Jennifer Crumpton, May 25, 1990, BOHP, p. 2; Flynt, *Poor but Proud*, 302–3.

40. Viola Elder, interviewed by JoJuana Davis, Mar. 6, 1992, BOHP, npn; Audrey Willingham, interviewed by Jill Phillips, Oct. 12, 1991, BOHP, p. 3.

41. Norma Brumback, interviewed by Kathy Deegan, Apr. 10, 1990, BOHP, npn; Dorothy Askin, interviewed by Denise Askin, Oct. 26, 1990, BOHP, p. 21; F. C. Dougherty, interviewed by John Cox, Mar. 8, 1992, BOHP, p. 1; Oscar Heimerich, interviewed by Jennifer Kelly, Oct. 20, 1990, BOHP, pp. 2–3; Odus Duffey, interviewed by Donna Smith, Nov. 12, 1990, BOHP, npn; Edgar Rhodes, interviewed by Eric McDonald, Nov. 22, 1991, BOHP, p. 3.

42. Biles, *The South and the New Deal*, 36–57; Holmes, *New Deal in Georgia*, 209–68.

43. Raymond Giles, interviewed by Christy Calhoun, Oct. 31, 1990, BOHP, p. 3; Dolly Hancock, unknown interviewer, no date, BOHP, p. 2; E. LeRoy Jordan, interviewed by Kelli Allen, May 24, 1992, BOHP, p. 8; Allan Furline, interviewed by Jeff Denney, Mar. 2, 1991, BOHP, npn; Leonard Crenshaw, interviewed by Lisa Williams, May 16, 1990, BOHP, npn; Helen Rakeshaw, interviewed by Jennifer Rakeshaw, May 29, 1990, BOHP, npn.

44. Maggie Robinson, interviewed by Macari Woods, Mar. 2, 1990, BOHP, npn; Lizzie Johnson, interviewed by Lucia Bush, Feb. 20, 1991, BOHP, npn; Geneva Stuart, interviewed by Stephanie Marlow, May 28, 1990, BOHP, npn; Lillian Chambers, interviewed by Kelley Chambers, Feb. 10, 1991, BOHP, p. 7; Woodrow and Frances Maffet, interviewed by Brad Batchelor, Oct. 23, 1990, BOHP, p. 2.

45. Henry Clark, interviewed by Leigh Wilhite, Feb. 24, 1990, BOHP, p. 2; Lee Weaver, interviewed by John Weaver, Nov. 5, 1989, BOHP, npn; Almedia Wray, interviewed by Queecha Blackum, May 3, 1993, BOHP, npn; Bessie Birdsong, interviewed by Gail Smith, Nov. 1, 1990, BOHP, pp. 8–12, quote from p. 12.

46. Jennie Kilburn, interviewed by Lea Kilburn, Feb. 27, 1990, BOHP, p. 3; Nell Everett, interviewed by Jena Freeman, Nov. 3, 1991, BOHP, npn; Anne Pierce, interviewed by Taylor St. Clair, May 26, 1991, BOHP, p. 2; Stewart Hull, interviewed by Lisa Weeks, Nov. 9, 1991, BOHP, p. 3; Charles Ricks, interviewed by Lori McDonald, May 8, 1992, BOHP, p. 3; Lucy Wagner, interviewed by Missy Powell, Nov. 8, 1991, BOHP, npn; Annie Mae Cook, interviewed by Scott Marlowe, Nov. 9, 1990, BOHP, p. 2; Braudis Barrett, interviewed by Molly Painter, May 2, 1992, BOHP, npn; Geneva Ariail, interviewed by Amanda Ariail, Mar. 5, 1992, BOHP, p. 13.

47. Magolalene Martin, interviewed by Pamela West, Nov. 22, 1991, BOHP, p. 8; Ann Curry, interviewed by Quen Curry, May 20, 1992, BOHP, npn; Sewell Barron, interviewed by Kevin Hunt, Mar. 3, 1992, BOHP, npn.

48. George Stoval, interviewed by Christopher Well, May 27, 1991, BOHP, npn; Isabel Hester, interviewed by Michael Brock, May 29, 1991, BOHP, npn.

49. Norma Brumback, interviewed by Kathy Deegan, Apr. 10, 1990, BOHP, npn; Frank Hudson, interviewed by Dan Umbach, Sept. 12, 1990, BOHP, p. 9; Bill Curtis, interviewed by Michael Curtis, Apr. 19, 1992, BOHP, p. 7; Charles Ricks, interviewed by Lori McDonald, May 8, 1992, BOHP, p. 4; Miriam Merrell, interviewed by Kimberly DeVane, Nov. 4, 1990, BOHP, p. 9.

50. Urban Farnsworth, interviewed by Nathan Gaunt, May 13, 1992, BOHP, p. 12; Earnest Pierce, interviewed by Taylor St. Clair, May 26, 1991, BOHP, npn; Louis Dickey, interviewed by DeAnda Davis, Jan. 6, 1990, BOHP, p. 12; Paul Morgan, interviewed by Greg McElwee, Nov. 17, 1991, BOHP, npn; Paul Maddox, interviewed by Sheila Yearta, Feb. 22, 1990, BOHP, p. 8.

51. Ed Isakson, interviewed by Alison Gaissert, Oct. 13, 1991, BOHP, npn.

Chapter 3. "The finer things of life were a little bit scarce"

1. Ann Rehberg, interviewed by Robert Rehberg, Nov. 11, 1990, BOHP, p. 1; Mary McClain, interviewed by LeAnne Shippey, Oct. 27, 1990, BOHP, p. 8; Helen Vasant, interviewed by Heather Prichard, no date, BOHP, npn.

2. Gary Cross, *An All-Consuming Century: Why Commercialism Won in Modern America* (New York: Columbia University Press, 2000), quotes from pp. 2 and 14; see also pp. 17–80.

3. Lela Knight, interviewed by Shannon Lott, Oct. 26, 1990, BOHP, npn. For an excellent overview of the scholarship and how the shift from production to consumption has changed our understanding of the past, see Tom Pendergast, "Consuming Questions: Scholarship on Consumerism in America to 1940," *American Studies International* 36 (June 1998), 23–43; see also Kathleen G. Donohue, *Freedom from Want: American Liberalism and the Idea of the Consumer* (Baltimore: Johns Hopkins University Press, 2004).

4. Mary McClain, interviewed by LeAnn Shippey, Oct. 27, 1990, BOHP, p. 6.

5. Charles McGovern, "Consumption and Citizenship in the United States, 1900–1940," in *Getting and Spending: European and American Consumer Societies in the Twentieth Century*, ed. Susan Strasser, Charles McGovern, and Matthias Judt (New York: Cambridge University Press, 1998), 37–58. Quotes from pp. 37, 43, 46. The scholarship and debate regarding the role consumption played in the creation of the economic collapse and its ramifications during the Depression era have been lively. For a good overview from many perspectives, see Christina D. Romer, "The Great Crash and the Onset of the Great Depression," *Quarterly Journal of Economics* 105 (1990), 597–624; Martha L. Olney, "Consumer Durables in the Interwar Years: New Estimates, New Patterns," *Research in Economic History* 12 (1989), 119–50; David Greasly, Jakob B. Madsen, and Les Oxley, "Income Uncertainty and Consumer Spending during the Great Depression," *Explorations in Economic History* 38 (2001), 225–51; Paul Craig Roberts and Lawrence M. Stratton, "The Fed's Depression and the Birth of the New Deal," *Policy Review* (Aug.–Sept. 2001), 19–32; Roland Marchand, "Where Lie the Boundaries of the Corporation? Explorations in 'Corporate Responsibility' in the 1930s," *Business and Economic History* 26 (1997), 80–100; and Meg Jacobs, "'Democracy's Third Estate': New Deal Politics and the Construction of a 'Consuming Public,'" *International Labor and Working Class History* 55 (Spring 1999), 27–51.

6. Lawrence Glickman, *A Living Wage: American Workers and the Making of Consumer Society* (Ithaca, N.Y.: Cornell University Press, 1997), 11. This monograph is perhaps the best source by which to understand Glickman's thesis and place it in context.

7. David L. Carlton and Peter A. Coclanis, eds., *Confronting Southern Poverty in the Great Depression: The Report on Economic Conditions of the South with Related Documents* (New York: Bedford Books, 1996), 63–80.

8. Harvey Bray, interviewed by Bryan Bray, Oct. 7, 1990, BOHP, npn; Walt Wilson, interviewed by J. W. Cobb, Nov. 13, 1990, BOHP, npn; Larry Carroll, interviewed by Chris Stahler, Mar. 6, 1992, BOHP, p. 2; Jennie Kilburn, interviewed by Lea Kilburn, Feb. 22, 1990, BOHP, p. 3; Annie Priest, interviewed by Taylor St. Clair, May 26, 1991, BOHP, npn.

9. Ada Hardin, interviewed by David Scott Wyatt, Apr. 12, 1992, BOHP, npn; Horace Maynard, interviewed by Eric Maynard, Nov. 9, 1991, BOHP, npn; Ruby Henry, interviewed by Brian Reeves, Oct. 30, 1990, BOHP, p. 10; Nellie Blackwelder, interviewed by Thomas Vaughan, May 29, 1990, BOHP, npn; A. B. Baughtman, interviewed by Michael Baughtman, Nov. 11, 1990, BOHP, p. 4; Josephine Taff, interviewed by Don Lindsey, Nov. 20, 1991, BOHP, p. 3; Henry Clark, interviewed by Leigh Wilhite, Feb. 24, 1990, BOHP, npn.

10. Sewell Barron, interviewed by Kevin Hunt, Mar. 3, 1992, BOHP, p. 17.

11. Melissa Walker, *All We Knew Was to Farm: Rural Women in the Upcountry South, 1919–1941* (Baltimore: Johns Hopkins University Press, 2000), 239–41, quotes from pp. 240–41; Thelma Moncus, interviewed by Matt Moncus, Nov. 4, 1990, BOHP, npn; Jean Baudrillard, "Consumer Society," in *Consumer Society in American History: A Reader*, ed. Lawrence Glickman (Ithaca, N.Y.: Cornell University Press, 1999), 49. See also Lawrence Glickman, "Inventing the 'American Standard of Living': Gender, Race, and Working-Class Identity, 1880–1925," *Labor History* 34 (Spring–Summer 1993), 221–35; Michael Denning, *The Cultural Front: The Laboring of American Culture in the Twentieth Century* (New York: Verso, 1996), 1–114.

12. Lena Stimpson, interviewed by Amy Wilkes, Nov. 11, 1990, BOHP, npn; Grover Hardin, interviewed by David Scott Wyatt, Apr. 19, 1992, BOHP, npn; Catherine Bohn, interviewed by Linda Bohn, Oct. 25, 1991, BOHP, pp. 10–11; Ruth Rhymer, interviewed by Todd Hadaway, May 26, 1991, BOHP, p. 6; Ann Rehberg, interviewed by Robert Rehberg, Nov. 11, 1990, BOHP, p. 4; Bessie Birdsong, interviewed by Gail Smith, Nov. 1, 1990, BOHP, p. 16; Ed Isakson, interviewed by Alison Gaissert, Oct. 13, 1991, BOHP, npn.

13. Dolly Hancock, interviewed by Stan Lepard, Feb. 11, 1990, BOHP, p. 5; Travis Dorrough, interviewed by Kathy Bullock, Oct. 26, 1991, BOHP, p. 5.

14. Mary Jackson, interviewed by Brad Jackson, Nov. 12, 1990, BOHP, npn; Ethel Shockley, interviewed by Robert Jennings, June 1, 1990, BOHP, npn; Henry Green, interviewed by Cynthia Brackett, Nov. 17, 1991, BOHP, npn; Gene Autry, interviewed by Shannon Howard, Mar. 2, 1991, BOHP, p. 9; George Weaver, interviewed by Mark MacAllaster, Feb. 24, 1990, BOHP, p. 1; Lee Weaver, interviewed by John Weaver, Nov. 5, 1989, BOHP, npn; A. Young Lester, interviewed by Ken Hammon, May 8, 1992, BOHP, npn; Annie Priest, interviewed by Taylor St. Clair, May 25, 1991, BOHP, npn; Lanier Weathers, interviewed by Wendy Weathers, Nov. 14, 1993, BOHP, npn.

15. Carlton and Coclanis, *Confronting Southern Poverty*, 40–78. Quote from p. 59.

16. Lawrence Glickman, "Born to Shop? Consumer History and American History," in *Consumer Society in American History: A Reader*, ed. Lawrence Glickman (Ithaca, N.Y.: Cornell University Press, 1999), 1–16. See also Colin Campbell, "Consuming Goods and the Good of Consuming," in *Consumer Society in American History*, 19–32; Glickman, *A Living Wage*, 1–92.

17. Ernest Porter, interviewed by Noel Turner, Feb. 25, 1992, BOHP, npn; Robert S. Lynd and Helen Merrell Lynd, *Middletown in Transition: A Study of Cultural Conflicts* (New York: Harcourt Brace, 1937), 10–75; Daniel Horowitz, *The Morality of Spending: Attitudes toward the Consumer Society in America, 1875–1940* (Baltimore: Johns Hopkins University Press, 1985), 155–58.

18. Opal Hunter, interviewed by Donna Smith, Nov. 10, 1990, BOHP, npn; Cornelia Presley, interviewed by Larry Irwin, Feb. 24, 1991, BOHP, npn; Vivian Zelizer, *The Social Meaning of Money* (New York: Basic Books, 1994).

19. Jean Baudrillard, "Consumer Society," 33–56, quote from p. 47. Terry Smith, *Making the Modern: Industry, Art, and Design in America* (Chicago: University of Chicago Press, 1993) explores the varieties and impact of modernity in 1930s America.

20. Davis quote from Glickman, *A Living Wage*, 149. See also pp. 133–56; Lawrence B. Glickman, "The Strike in the Temple of Consumption: Consumer Activism and Twentieth-Century American Political Culture," *Journal of American History* (online version) 88 (June 2001), 1–30, particularly pp. 1–6; Horowitz, *Morality of Spending*, 134–54.

21. Lena Stimpson, interviewed by Amy Wilkes, Nov. 11, 1990, BOHP, npn; Clare Doherty, interviewed by Kathleen Romo, Mar. 5, 1992, BOHP, npn; Ruby Henry, interviewed by Brian Reeves, Oct. 30, 1990, BOHP, p. 7; John Gillespie, interviewed by Kristi Harp, May 18, 1991, BOHP, p. 11; Mildred Williams, interviewed by Chad Golden, Nov. 20, 1993, BOHP, npn.

22. Ray Carter, unknown interviewer, no date, BOHP, p. 5: Meg Jacobs, "'Democracy's Third Estate': New Deal Politics and the Construction of a 'Consuming Public,'" *International Labor and Working-Class History* 55 (Spring 1999), 27–51, quotes from pp. 28–29; McGovern, "Consumption and Citizenship," 38.

23. Ted Ownsby, *American Dreams in Mississippi: Consumers, Poverty, and Culture* (Chapel Hill: University of North Carolina Press, 1999), 1–6, 82–109; Mildred Williams, interviewed by Chad Golden, Nov. 20, 1993, BOHP, npn; X. Rogers, unknown interviewer, no date, BOHP, npn; Stewart Hull, interviewed by Lisa Weeks, Nov. 9, 1991, BOHP, p. 6; Emma Wallace, interviewed by Laura Rodriguez, Nov. 10, 1989, BOHP, pp. 5–6; Margaret Askew, interviewed by Michael Stratton, Feb. 27, 1992, BOHP, npn.

24. Era Dennis, interviewed by Lisa Dennis, May 28, 1990, BOHP, p. 7; Charles

Clayton, interviewed by Diane Streefkerk, May 25, 1992, BOHP, p. 13; Ray Carter, unknown interviewer, no date, BOHP, p. 7.

25. Lizabeth Cohen, *Making a New Deal: Industrial Workers in Chicago, 1931–1939* (New York: Cambridge University Press, 1990), 1–25, 100–158; Lizabeth Cohen, "The Class Experience of Mass Consumption: Workers as Consumers in Interwar America," in *The Power of Culture: Critical Essays in American History*, ed. Richard Wrightman Fox and T. J. Jackson Lears (Chicago: University of Chicago Press, 1993), 135–62, quote from p. 138; Lee Weaver, interviewed by John Weaver, Nov. 5, 1989, BOHP, npn; George Maddox, interviewed by Jennifer Alonso, Mar. 11, 1992, BOHP, p. 3; Nell Everett, interviewed by Jena Freeman, Nov. 3, 1991, BOHP, npn; Francis Maffet, interviewed by Brad Batchelor, Oct. 23, 1990, BOHP, p. 4.

26. Brenita Reid, interviewed by Laura Melson, Mar. 6, 1990, BOHP, npn; on the division and uses of money within the household in a social context, see Zelizer, *The Social Meaning of Money* (New York: Basic Books, 1994), particularly pp. 36–70.

27. John Gillespie, interviewed by Kristi Harp, May 18, 1991, BOHP, p. 2; Clara Knowlton, interviewed by Casmen Knowlton, Oct. 28, 1989, BOHP, npn; Velma Morgan, interviewed by Ben Avansky, Mar. 3, 1990, BOHP, npn; Martelle Payne, interviewed by Brad Yearta, May 11, 1992, BOHP, p. 4; Ploma Morrow, interviewed by Bridgette Morrow, BOHP, npn; James Beavers, interviewed by Stephen Ward, Nov. 10, 1990, BOHP, p. 2.

28. Clara Knowlton, interviewed by Casmen Knowlton, Oct. 28, 1989, BOHP, npn; Charity Thomas, interviewed by Kippi Riddle, Feb. 23, 1991, BOHP, npn; Ruth Pickett, interviewed by Tanya Simmons, Oct. 6, 1991, BOHP, p. 5.

29. Guy Knight, interviewed by Sherry Holloway, Nov. 22, 1991, BOHP, npn; Mildred Hammond, interviewed by Greg Hammond, Nov. 11, 1990, BOHP, p. 4; Inez Parkerson, interviewed by Kevin Parkerson, Nov. 16, 1991, BOHP, npn.

30. Ralph McCain, interviewed by Rebecca Reeves, Feb. 23, 1991, BOHP, p. 20; Horowitz, *Morality of Spending*, 134–65.

31. Delmas Easterwood, interviewed by Terry Wilkerson, Feb. 26, 1991, BOHP, pp. 2–3; Dot Robinson, interviewed by Shelley Townsend, May 9, 1992, BOHP, p. 2; Sidney Clotfelter, interviewed by Laurence Montier, Oct. 21, 1990, BOHP, p. 2; Mildred Garlich, interviewed by Jackie Garlich, Oct. 18, 1991, BOHP, p. 1; Henry Arnold, interviewed by Tony Arnold, May 23, 1992, BOHP, p. 3; Gladys Burroughs, interviewed by Amy Bridges, May 26, 1990, BOHP, npn.

32. Cecil Tate, interviewed by Chad Rogers, Nov. 17, 1991, BOHP, p. 3; Violet Lowe, interviewed by Dawn Shirey, Oct. 28, 1989, BOHP, npn; Guy Knight, interviewed by Sherry Holloway, Nov. 22, 1991, BOHP, npn.

33. Edwin Harman, interviewed by Amber Holland, May 9, 1992, BOHP, p. 5; Mabel LeFeure, interviewed by Rick Forepaugh, Apr. 6, 1989, BOHP, npn; Mary Jackson, unknown interviewer, no date, BOHP, npn.

34. Sarah Riddle, interviewed by Lori McDougal, May 8, 1992, BOHP, npn; Guy Knight, interviewed by Sherry Holloway, Nov. 22, 1991, BOHP, npn; William Worley, interviewed by John Dehman, Nov. 11, 1990, BOHP, npn.

35. Jessie Pierce, interviewed by Taylor St. Clair, May 26, 1991, BOHP, npn; Myrtle Hall, interviewed by Ginger Walker, Dec. 3, 1989, BOHP, p. 5.

36. Nell Everett, interviewed by Jena Freeman, Nov. 3, 1991, BOHP, npn; Guy Gordon, interviewed by Lallemand Christophe, Mar. 8, 1992, BOHP, npn; Nell Lovelady, interviewed by Karen Todd, May 19, 1990, BOHP, p. 7; Mary McClain, interviewed by LeAnne Shippey, Oct. 27, 1990, BOHP, npn; Whitley Morris, interviewed by Shea Jackson, Feb. 28, 1992, BOHP, p. 2; Violet Scott, interviewed by Susan Dodd, May 2, 1992, BOHP, p. 7.

37. James Thompson, interviewed by Andrea Hines, Mar. 3, 1992, BOHP, p. 1; Violet Lowe, interviewed by Susan Dodd, May 2, 1992, BOHP, npn.

38. Viola Bass, interviewed by Scarlett Gaddy, Mar. 20, 1990, BOHP, npn; Henri P. Herron, interviewed by Meacy Gess, May 31, 1990, BOHP, npn; Opal Jackson, interviewed by Donald Shock, Nov. 14, 1990, BOHP, npn; Louise Smith, interviewed by Kelly Bedford, Apr. 17, 1992, BOHP, p. 4; Ruby Henry, interviewed by Brian Reeves, Oct. 30, 1990, BOHP, p. 8; Ernest Porter, interviewed by Noel Turner, Feb. 25, 1992, BOHP, npn; Bessie Birdsong, interviewed by Gail Smith, Nov. 1, 1990, BOHP, p. 9.

Chapter 4. "I was just fixin' to tell her about the washin'!"

1. Paul Thompson, *The Voice of the Past: Oral History* (New York: Oxford University Press, 1988, 2nd ed.), 1–23, 220–45, 309–23.

2. Bernell and Zead Sullivan, interviewed by Patricia Kelly Sullivan, Nov. 24, 1991, BOHP, pp. 1–14.

3. Numerous studies have informed this section, including Warren J. Belasco, *Appetite for Change: How the Counterculture Took on the Food Industry, 1966–1988* (New York: Pantheon Books, 1989); Mary Douglas, "Standard Social Uses of Food: Introduction," in *Food in the Social Order: Studies of Food and Festivities in Three American Communities*, ed. Mary Douglas (New York: Russell Sage Foundation, 1984), 1–39; Donna R. Gabaccia, *We Are What We Eat: Ethnic Food and the Making of Americans* (Cambridge, Mass.: Harvard University Press, 1998); Sidney W. Mintz, *Tasting Food and Tasting Freedom: Excursions into Eating, Culture, and the Past* (Boston: Beacon Press, 1996); Sherrie A. Inness, "Introduction," in *Kitchen Culture in America: Popular Representations of Food, Gender, and Race*, ed. Sherrie A. Inness (Philadelphia: University of Pennsylvania Press, 2001); Warren Belasco and Philip Scranton, eds., *Food Nations: Selling Taste in Consumer Societies* (New York: Routledge, 2002); Mark Weiner, "Consumer Culture and Participatory Democracy: The Story of Coca-Cola during World War II," *Food and Folkways* 2 (1996), 109–29.

4. Roxie Etheridge, interviewed by Andy Mills, May 16, 1992, BOHP, npn.

5. Gene Autry, interviewed by Shannon Howard, Mar. 2, 1991, BOHP, p. 2.

6. Ruby Henry, interviewed by Brian Reeves, Oct. 30, 1990, BOHP, pp. 7–8.

7. For a good overview of how women faced the changes in the Depression, see Susan Ware, *Holding Their Own: American Women in the 1930s* (Boston: Twayne, 1982), 1–20; see also Scott Holzer, "The Modernization of Southern Foodways: Rural Immigration to the Urban South during World War II," *Food and Folkways* 2 (1996), 93–107.

8. Wayne W. Copeland, interviewed by Alison King, May 21, 1992, BOHP, npn.

9. Myrtle McCormick, unknown interviewer, no date, BOHP, npn.

10. Jewel Cheek, interviewed by Jennifer Cheek, May 23, 1992, BOHP, npn.

11. Jim Teague, interviewed by Scott Gregory, Nov. 8, 1990, BOHP, p. 21.

12. Robert C. Johnson, interviewed by Diane Bennefild, Nov. 7, 1989, BOHP, p. 6.

13. Marguritte Lilly, interviewed by Don Lindsey, Nov. 17, 1991, BOHP, p. 2.

14. Steve Dearing, interviewed by Tappie Musgrove, May 27, 1990, BOHP, npn.

15. Violet Scott, interviewed by Susan Dodd, May 2, 1992, BOHP, p. 8.

16. John M. Gillespie, interviewed by Kristi Harp, May 18, 1991, BOHP, p. 10.

17. Edna Mann, interviewed by Leslie Ann Connell, Apr. 18, 1992, BOHP, p. 4.

18. Erma Dennis, interviewed by Lisa Dennis, May 28, 1990, BOHP, p. 7.

19. Lanier and Rozelle Weathers, interviewed by Wendy Weathers, Nov. 14, 1993, BOHP, npn.

20. Brenita Reid, interviewed by Laura Melson, Mar. 6, 1990, BOHP, npn.

21. Sarah Riddle, interviewed by Steanie Marlow, May 28, 1990, BOHP, npn.

22. John M. Gillespie, interviewed by Kristi Harp, May 18, 1991, BOHP, p. 13.

23. Frank Winn, interviewed by Tricia Eastman, Feb. 22, 1992, BOHP, npn.

24. Ima Burns, interviewed by Anita Cook, Nov. 18, 1989, BOHP, npn.

25. Mrs. Ralph McCain, interviewed by Rebecca Reeves, Feb. 23, 1991, BOHP, p. 10.

26. Dorothy Hill, interviewed by Tesha Hollis, Mar. 7, 1992, BOHP, npn.

27. Geneva Mack, interviewed by Connie Franklin, Mar. 1, 1992, BOHP, npn.

28. Thelma Hughes, interviewed by Cheryl Anthony, Oct. 20, 1989, BOHP, npn.

29. Virginia Thelan, interviewed by Kelly Thelan, Feb. 25, 1992, BOHP, p. 2.

30. Myrtle McCormick, unknown interviewer, no date, BOHP, npn.

31. Ophelia Dearing, interviewed by Tappie Musgrove, May 27, 1990, BOHP, npn.

32. Katherine Melton, interviewed by Candi Chester, Feb. 23, 1991, BOHP, p. 5.

33. Jim Teague, interviewed by Scott Gregory, Nov. 8, 1990, BOHP, pp. 19–20.

34. Henry Clark, interviewed by Leah Wilhite, Feb. 20, 1990, BOHP, npn.

35. Kathryn Anderson and Dana C. Jacks, "Learning to Listen: Interview Techniques and Analyses," in *Women's Words: The Feminist Practice of Oral History*, ed. Sherna Berger Gluck and Daphne Patai (New York: Routledge, Chapman, and Hall, 1991), 11–26; Emily Honig, "Striking Lives: Oral History and the Politics

of Memory," *Journal of Women's History* 9 (Spring 1997), 139–57; Marie-Françoise Chanfrault-Duchet, "Narrative Structures, Social Models, and Symbolic Representation in the Life Story," in *Women's Words*, 77–92.

36. Louis Swint, interviewed by Vette Swint, May 12, 1991, BOHP, p. 7.

37. Mary Will McClain, interviewed by LeAnne Shippey, Oct. 27, 1990, BOHP, pp. 12–13.

38. John G. Baggett Sr., interviewed by Len Queen, Mar. 11, 1992, BOHP, p. 9; Marie Sanderlin, interviewed by Amelia Salman, Nov. 6, 1991, BOHP, npn.

39. Isabel Hester, interviewed by Michael Brock, May 29, 1991, BOHP, npn.

40. Mildred Garlich, interviewed by Jackie Garlich, Oct. 18, 1991, BOHP, npn.

41. Jim Teague, interviewed by Scott Gregory, Nov. 8, 1990, BOHP, pp. 12–14.

42. Ellen Litwicki, *America's Public Holidays, 1865–1920* (Washington, D.C.: Smithsonian Institution Press, 2000), 1–8.

43. Allen Furline, interviewed by Jeff Denney, Mar. 2, 1991, BOHP, npn.

44. William Gordon, interviewed by Joe Steele, Mar. 4, 1990, BOHP, npn.

45. Imogene Florence, interviewed by Bryan Blount, Feb. 17, 1991.

46. Raymond Giles, interviewed by Christy Calhoun, Oct. 31, 1990, BOHP, npn.

47. Isabel Hester, interviewed by Rachele Sisco, Oct. 31, 1991, BOHP, npn.

48. Louise Smith, interviewed by Kelly Bedford, May 26, 1992, BOHP, npn.

49. J. B. Campbell, interviewed by John Campbell, Oct. 20, 1990, BOHP, npn.

50. Joe Salituro, interviewed by Ralph Salituro, Feb. 15, 1992, BOHP, npn.

51. Al Leiker, interviewed by Rhett Lyons, Nov. 26, 1989, BOHP, npn.

52. Nell Everett, interviewed by Jena Freeman, Nov. 3, 1991, BOHP, npn.

53. Frank Favors, interviewed by Wanda Thompson, May 10, 1992, BOHP, npn.

54. Mildred Williams, interviewed by Chad Golden, Nov. 20, 1993, BOHP, npn; Guy Knight, interviewed by Sherry Holloway, Nov. 22, 1991, BOHP, npn.

55. Frances Clements, interviewed by Angie Clements, Feb. 29, 1992, BOHP, npn; Ruby Henry, interviewed by Brian Reeves, Oct. 30, 1990, BOHP, npn.

56. Guy Knight, interviewed by Sherry Holloway, Nov. 22, 1991, BOHP, npn.

57. Isabel Hester, interviewed by Rachel Sisco, Oct. 31, 1991, BOHP, npn.

58. Frances Clements, interviewed by Angie Clements, Feb. 29, 1992, BOHP, npn.

59. Brenita Reid, interviewed by Laura Melson, Mar. 6, 1990, BOHP, npn.

60. Linda Shopes, "What Is Oral History?" from the Making Sense of Evidence series on *History Matters: The US Survey on the Web*, located at <http://historymatters.gmu.com>, quote from p. 5; Lorraine T. Dorfman, Susan A. Murray, Ronnie J. Evans, Jerry G. Ingram, and James R. Power, "History and Identity in the Narratives of Rural Elders," *Journal of Aging Studies* 18 (2004), 187–203.

Chapter 5. "We thought they was good ol' days back then"

1. Fred Lockaby, interviewed by Susan Lockaby, Nov. 9, 1991, BOHP, npn. Sev-

eral oral history sources discuss the meaning and validity of this subjective analysis, including Alessandro Portelli, *The Death of Luigi Trastulli and Other Stories: Form and Meaning in Oral History* (Albany: State University Press of New York, 1991); Samuel Schrager, "What Is Social in Oral History?" in *The Oral History Reader*, ed. Robert Perks and Alistair Thomson (New York: Routledge, 1998), 284–99; Penny Summerfield, *Reconstructing Women's Wartime Lives: Discourse and Subjectivity in Oral Histories of the Second World War* (New York: St. Martin's, 1998).

2. Roy Patterson, interviewed by Paul Cannon, Mar. 8, 1992, BOHP, npn.

3. Louis Dickey, interviewed by DeAnda Davis, Oct. 10, 1999, BOHP, p. 3; Pat Inpecoven, interviewed by Chuck Durbin, Mar. 7, 1992, BOHP, npn.

4. Shirley Spruill, interviewed by Jonathan Samples, Nov. 10, 1991, BOHP, npn.

5. George Pope, interviewed by Craig Davis, Feb. 25, 1989, BOHP, p. 4.

6. Don Lawler, interviewed by John Lawler, Feb. 25, 1990, BOHP, npn.

7. Jefferson C. Brock, interviewed by Barry Blalock, Nov. 20, 1989, BOHP, pp. 3–4.

8. Horace Bright, interviewed by Hayes Findley, Nov. 26, 1993, BOHP, npn.

9. Bertha Hicks, interviewed by Cindy Clifton, May 18, 1992, BOHP, npn.

10. Cecil Tate, interviewed by Chad Rogers, Nov. 17, 1991, BOHP, p. 3.

11. Laurel Haskins, interviewed by Virginia Carol Kelley, May 15, 1991, BOHP, p. 5.

12. Billy Stephenson, interviewed by Cindy Hughie, May 15, 1992, BOHP, npn.

13. The literature on tall tales and allegory is vast, but among those who focus on their theoretical meaning are Carolyn S. Brown, *The Tall Tale in American Folklore and Literature* (Knoxville: University of Tennessee Press, 1987), especially ch. 1 and 2; Ralph Flores, *A Study of Allegory in Its Historical Context and Relationship to Contemporary Theory* (Lewiston, Maine: Edwin Mellon, 1996), particularly pp. 1–25; and Rei Terada, *Feeling in Theory: Emotion after the "Death of the Subject"* (Cambridge, Mass.: Harvard University Press, 2001), 1–15, 48–80.

14. James Peterson, interviewed by Kristen Taylor, Nov. 13, 1990, BOHP, pp. 1–2.

15. Essi Whitley, interviewed by Jonathan Samples, Nov. 10, 1991, BOHP, npn.

16. Rose Conerly, interviewed by Kim Marlow, June 2, 1990, BOHP, npn.

17. Z. A. Sullivan, interviewed by Patricia Kelly Sullivan, Nov. 24, 1991, BOHP, npn.

18. Inez Parkerson, interviewed by Kevin Parkerson, Nov. 16, 1991, BOHP, npn.

19. Magdolene Martin, interviewed by Pamela West, Nov. 22, 1991, BOHP, npn.

20. Lema Mason, interviewed by Molly Mason, Dec. 10, 1991, BOHP, npn.

21. Geneva Stewart, interviewed by Tracy Rolfe, June 1, 1990, BOHP, npn.

22. Thelma Hughes, interviewed by Cheryl Anthony, Oct. 20, 1989, BOHP, npn.

23. Ima Burns, interviewed by Anita Cook, Nov. 18, 1989, BOHP, npn.

24. Janice Skelton, interviewed by Lisa Simmons, Nov. 2, 1990, BOHP, npn.

25. Cecil Tate, interviewed by Chad Rogers, Nov. 17, 1991, BOHP, npn.

26. Norma Brumback, interviewed by Kathy Deegan, Apr. 10, 1990, BOHP, npn.

27. Clara Mae Knowlton, interviewed by Cosmen Knowlton, Nov. 3, 1989, BOHP, npn.

28. Edgar Rhodes, interviewed by Eric McDonald, November 11, 1991, BOHP, npn.

29. Maggie Tiller, interviewed by Becky Herndon, June 1, 1990, BOHP, pp. 3–4.

30. Claude Davis, interviewed by Jill Pendley, Apr. 22, 1990, BOHP, pp. 1–2.

31. Mrs. Charles Trimby, interviewed by Catherine McKenzie, Apr. 21, 1990, BOHP, npn.

32. Jan Whitt, *Allegory and the Modern Southern Novel* (Macon, Ga.: Mercer University Press, 1991), vii, 3; Sallie McFague, *Speaking in Parable: A Study in Metaphor and Theology* (London: SCM Press, 2002 [orig. 1975]), xi–xvii, quote from p. 6; see also chapter 3.

33. Rita Beine, interviewed by Matt Beine, Apr. 6, 1990, BOHP, pp. 3–4.

34. Sam Davis, interviewed by Ruth Davis, Mar. 2, 1992, BOHP, pp. 5–6.

35. Josephine Taff, interviewed by Don Lindsey, Nov. 20, 1991, BOHP, npn.

36. Norma Brumback, interviewed by Kathy Deegan, Apr. 10, 1990, BOHP, p. 2.

37. Stella Bowie, interviewed by Stacey Murray, May 1, 1990, BOHP, npn.

38. John R. Beach, interviewed by Tisha Avrett, Mar. 1, 1990, BOHP, p. 1.

39. Preacher Cain, interviewed by Cindy Beck, no date, BOHP, npn.

40. Bessie Mae Chandler Birdsong, interviewed by Gail Smith, Nov. 1, 1990, BOHP, p. 2.

41. Viola Elder, interviewed by JoJuana Davis, Mar. 6, 1992, BOHP, p. 2.

42. Mrs. Wasdin, interviewed by Michel Adriaens, Jan. 18, 1992, BOHP, npn.

43. E. B. Cane, interviewed by Paul Noble, Mar. 4, 1990, BOHP, npn.

44. Maurice Sponcler, interviewed by Dan Umbach, Sept. 14, 1990, BOHP, pp. 6–7.

45. Annie Louise Curry, interviewed by Quen Curry, May 20, 1992, BOHP, npn.

46. Marjorie Batson, interviewed by Holly Harris, Feb. 14, 1992, BOHP, npn.

47. Virginia Thelan, interviewed by Kelly Thelan, Feb. 25, 1992, BOHP, p. 5.

48. Laurel Haskins, interviewed by Virginia Carol Kelley, May 15, 1991, BOHP, p. 6.

49. Georgia Mae Calloway, interviewed by Celena Sims, Feb. 28, 1992, BOHP, npn.

50. Tom Skelton, interviewed by Lisa Simmons, Nov. 2, 1990, BOHP, p. 4.

51. Ruth Rhymer, interviewed by Todd Hadaway, May 26, 1991, BOHP, p. 3.

52. Bessie Pendergrass, interviewed by Chris Lewandowski, Oct. 29, 1990, BOHP, npn.

53. Earnest Pierce, interviewed by Jeff Estes, Nov. 11, 1990, BOHP, pp. 5–6.

54. Jim Teague, interviewed by Scott Gregory, Nov. 8, 1990, BOHP, p. 6.

55. Dorothy Hill, interviewed by Tesha Hollis, Mar. 7, 1992, BOHP, npn.

56. Lynna Vaughn, interviewed by Brenda Baker, Nov. 12, 1990, BOHP, npn.

57. Faye Ivey, interviewed by Josie Strange, Apr. 23, 1991, BOHP, npn.

58. Lizzie Johnson, interviewed by Yvette Hester, May 17, 1991, BOHP, npn.

59. Steve Dearing, interviewed by Tappie Musgrove, May 27, 1990, BOHP, npn.

60. Geneva Stewart, interviewed by Tracy Rolfe, June 1, 1990, BOHP, npn.

61. Augustus Jackson Sharpe, interviewed by Phillip LeFevre, Mar. 11, 1992, BOHP, p. 3.

62. Carter Ray, interviewed by Mickie Ezell, May 19, 1990, BOHP, npn.

63. Larry P. Carroll, interviewed by Chris Stahler, Mar. 6, 1992, BOHP, p. 6.

64. Joe Johnson, interviewed by John Womack, May 30, 1990, BOHP, p. 4.

65. Laura Kolb, interviewed by Jennifer Medlock, Mar. 13, 1992, BOHP, npn.

66. Al Leiker, interviewed by Rhett Lyons, Nov. 26, 1989, BOHP, npn.

67. Martha Loren Scott, interviewed by Alan Weldon, May 1, 1992, BOHP, p. 7.

68. Claudia Ward, interviewed by Michelle Mize, May 27, 1990, BOHP, npn.

69. Wyolene Warren, interviewed by Kimberly DeVane, Nov. 4, 1990, BOHP, p. 9.

70. Kathleen Bartlett, interviewed by Stephanie Marlow, May 28, 1990, BOHP, npn.

71. Geraldine Chadwick, interviewed by Dania Macias, Feb. 25, 1991, BOHP, npn.

72. Ruby Henry, interviewed by Brian Reeves, Oct. 30, 1990, BOHP, npn.

73. Paul Johnson, interviewed by Jacqueline Austin-Trucks, Mar. 3, 1991, BOHP, p. 6.

Conclusion. "It's been wonderful talkin' to ya"

1. Ethel Carraway, interviewed by Chris Carraway, no date, BOHP, p. 5.

2. Joe Salituro, interviewed by Ralph Salituro, Feb. 15, 1992, BOHP, p. 2. I choose to label their recollections collective consciousness intead of collective memory as I have focused more on how their recollections portray the past and identify its social meaning more so than define memory as history.

3. Gene Autry, interviewed by Shannon Howard, Mar. 2, 1991, BOHP, p. 1.

4. Alessandro Portelli, "What Makes Oral History Different," in *The Oral History Reader*, ed. Robert Perks and Alistair Thomson (London: Routledge, 1998), 63–74, quote from p. 67; Michael Frisch, *A Shared Authority: Essays on the Craft and Meaning of Oral and Public History* (Albany: State University of New York Press, 1990).

INDEX

Abercrombie, Mac, 2, 152n12
Adams, June, 17, 151–52n10
Adriaens, Michel, 170n42
African Americans: education, 32; population density, 2; urban employment, 32; women's work, 27
Agan, Jerry, 153n22
Agriculture Adjustment Act, 58
Alabama, 13, 15, 16, 24, 37, 38, 47, 68, 153–54n24; Alexander City, 13; Athens, 19; Birmingham, 18, 27, 143; Decatur, 82; Gadsden, 58; Heflin, 23, 57; Lake Martin, 51; Leeds, 45; Malore, 51; Mobile, 18; Ranburne, 136; Randolph County, 75, 76; Redbag, 69; Rockmills, 72
Alexander, W. W., 150–51n2, 151–52n10, 153–54n24
Allen, Barbara, 149n10
Allen, Kelli, 159–60n31, 161n43
Alonso, Jennifer, 165n25
Anderson, Kathryn, 149n11, 167–68n35
Anthony, Cheryl, 153n21, 167n25, 169n22
Ariail, Amanda, 154n28, 159nn28,29, 161n46
Ariail, Geneva, 29, 51, 52, 60, 154n28, 159nn28,29, 161n46
Armitage, Susan H., 149–50n12
Armstrong, Louis, 110
Arnold, Henry, 165n31
Arnold, Lillian, 31, 154n30
Arnold, Tony, 165n31
Askew, Margaret, 57, 76, 160n38, 164n23
Askin, Dorothy, 58, 160n41
Austin-Trucks, Jacqueline, 171n73
Autry, Gene, 20, 70, 93, 144, 152nn12,13, 163n14, 166n5, 171n3
Avansky, Ben, 165n27
Avrett, Tisha, 159n25, 170n38

Baggett, John, 105, 168n38
Bailey, Martha, 40, 155–56n7
Bailey, Michelle, 155–56n7
Baker, Brenda, 160n36, 171n56
Baker, Christy, 157n12
Banks, Ann, 148n3
Barber, Amie, 153n20, 159n27, 160n35
Barlow, Ossie, 154n30
Barlow, Ruby, 46, 158n20
Barrett, Braudis, 60, 161n46
Barron, Sewell, 61, 68, 161n47, 163n10
Barter. *See* Consumption
Barthel, Diane, 147n1
Bartlett, Kathleen, 140, 171n70
Bartley, Dorothy, 42, 157n11
Bartley, Numan V., 155n5
Bass, Viola, 166n38
Batchelor, Brad, 154n29, 161n44, 165n25
Batson, Marjorie, 132, 170n46
Baudrillard, Jean, 163n11, 164n19
Baughtman, A. B., 12, 68, 150n1, 163n9
Baughtman, Michael, 150n1, 163n9
Baynard, Addie, 32, 154n30
Beach, John R., 50, 129, 159n25, 170n38
Bean, Chad, 159n26
Bean, Lowell, 51, 159n26
Beavers, James, 78, 165n27
Beck, Cindy, 170n39
Beck, Geraldine, 38, 155n3
Bedford, Kelly, 151n8, 166n38, 168n48
Beine, Matt, 170n33
Beine, Rita, 127, 170n33
Belasco, Warren J., 166n3
Berkowitz, Richard, 158n20
Biggart, Mae, 7, 24, 149n9, 153n20
Biles, Roger, 148n3, 151n9, 153–54n24, 154n25, 155n4, 158–59n22, 159nn23,29, 161n42
Bindas, Kenneth J., 157n9

Bingham, Alfred M., 79

Birdsong, Bessie, 23, 60, 70, 84, 130,
    152–53n18, 161n45, 163n12, 166n38, 170n40

Birdsong, Lester, 23

Blackum, Queecha, 161n45

Blackwelder, Julia, 21, 152n16

Blackwelder, Nellie, 163n9

Blalock, Barry, 169n7

Bland, Michael, 157n15

Bland, Verna, 43, 157n15

Bleser, Carol, 153n21

Blight, David, 147n1

Blount, Bryan, 154n28, 168n45

Bohn, Linda, 151–52n10, 163n12

Bohne, Catherine Hoyt, 18, 69, 151–52n10,
    163n12

Bolding, Irene, 13, 26, 37, 42, 151n3, 153n23,
    155n1, 157n12

Bornat, Joanna, 147–48n2

Bowden, Naomi Jean, 53, 160n32

Bowie, Stella, 54, 128, 160n34, 170n37

Bowman, Clarence, 18, 152n11

Brackett, Cynthia, 153n23, 163n14

Bray, Bryan, 163n8

Bray, Harvey, 67, 163n8

Bridges, Amy, 159–60n31, 165n31

Bright, Horace, 117, 169n8

Brock, Jefferson, 117, 169n7

Brock, Michael, 154n27, 161n48, 168n39

Brockway, Warren, 40, 155n6

Brown, Carolyn S., 169n13

Brown, James Seay, Jr., 148n3

Brown, Stephanie, 153n21

Brumbeck, Norma, 38, 43, 58, 61, 124,
    127, 155n2, 157n13, 160n41, 161n49,
    170nn26, 36

Buehler, Doug, 152n17

Buffalow, Christa, 157n11

Buhite, Russell, 155–56n7, 157n10

Buidrillard, Jean, 69

Bullock, Kathy, 158n17, 163n13

Burns, Ima, 100, 123, 167n24, 169n23

Burroughs, Gladys, 52, 80, 159–60n31,
    165n31

Bush, Lucia, 161n44

Butcher, Harry, 41

Bynum, Mildred, 57

Cairns, Thomas, 13, 151n3

Calhoun, Christy, 152n12, 161n43, 168n46

Calloway, Cab, 110

Calloway, Georgia Mae, 31, 133, 154nn30, 31,
    170n49

Camp, Mamie, 151n4

Campbell, Colin, 164n16

Campbell, Lucille, 24, 45, 153n20, 158n17

Campbell, J. B., 109, 168n49

Campbell, John, 153n20, 158n17, 168n49

Candy: as social event, 96–99; making,
    95–96

Cane, E. B. (Preacher), 44, 130, 158n16,
    170nn39,43

Cannon, Paul, 159nn24,25, 169n2

Carlson, Paul, 157n10

Carlton, David L., 158–59n22, 162n7, 163n15

Carraway, Chris, 171n1

Carraway, Ethel, 143, 171n1

Carroll, Larry, 67, 138, 163n8, 171n63

Carroll, Mary, 24, 153n20

Carter, Ray, 75, 76, 138, 164n22, 164–65n24,
    171n62

Cawthon, Jay, 151n8

Columbia Broadcasting System (CBS), 40

Chadwick, Geraldine, 140, 171n71

Chambers, Kelley, 152–53n18, 153n20, 160n36,
    161n44

Chambers, Lillian, 23, 24, 55, 59, 152–53n18,
    153n20, 160n36, 161n44

Chanfrault-Duchet, Marie-Françoise,
    149–50n12, 167–68n35

Chapman, Catherine, 159n26

Chapman, Ptleene, 50, 159n26

Chase, Stuart, 79

Cheatum, Merrill, 45, 158nn17,18

Cheek, Jacqueline, 155–56n7, 160n37

Cheek, Jennifer, 167n10

Cheek, Jewel, 94, 167n10

Chester, Candi, 152n15, 158n18, 167n32

Christophe, Lallemand, 166n36

Cicero, Albert, 159n26

Index

Kenneth J. Bindas is a professor of history at Kent State University. He is the author of *Swing, That Modern Sound* (2001) and *All of This Music Belongs to the Nation* (1995), and editor of *America's Musical Pulse* (1992).